OECD Development Pathways

# Social Protection System Review of Kyrgyzstan

OECD DEVELOPMENT CENTRE

**Please cite this publication as:**
OECD (2018), *Social Protection System Review of Kyrgyzstan*, OECD Development Pathways, OECD Publishing, Paris.
*http://dx.doi.org/10.1787/9789264302273-en*

ISBN 978-92-64-30226-6 (print)
ISBN 978-92-64-30227-3 (PDF)

Series: OECD Development Pathways
ISSN 2308-734X (print)
ISSN 2308-7358 (online)



**Photo credits:** Cover © Design by the OECD Development Centre

Corrigenda to OECD publications may be found on line at: *www.oecd.org/about/publishing/corrigenda.htm*.

# *Foreword*

Kyrgyzstan has taken huge strides since gaining independence in 1991. Having embarked upon a rapid transition to a market economy, it has been equally bold in developing the political and social institutions of a modern democratic state. Although progress has not always been smooth, recent elections have demonstrated the growing stability of Kygyzstan's political system, while its economy has shown great resilience in recent years.

Social protection has played a key role in Kyrgyzstan's transition. The Government of Kyrgyzstan (GoK) has not only maintained the sizeable social insurance system that existed prior to independence but has also introduced several new social assistance and labour market policies. Social protection is the largest component of public spending, accounting for more than expenditure on health and education combined.

However, social protection provision must continue to adapt to meet a number of emerging challenges, including pervasive informality, high rates of labour migration and unemployment and the prospect of rapid growth in the elderly population. Income poverty and broader measures of deprivation have fallen dramatically since the early 2000s but remain high. The pension system achieves near-universal coverage among the elderly population but at great cost; its long-term sustainability is in doubt.

This Social Protection System Review explores ways by which social protection in Kyrgystan can be enhanced through a systemic approach. The GoK has committed to systematising social protection in recent social protection strategies; this Review intends to support the GoK in realising its new vision by presenting a broad vision of the sector and improving the evidence base needed for reforms to establish a coherent, sustainable and effective set of programmes.

The Review is the result of a collaboration between the OECD and senior government officials, researchers and civil society representatives in Kyrgyzstan. It has also received considerable support from development partners in the country. The recommendations it includes were jointly produced by the OECD and its many collaborators in this initiative. The Review is supported by the EU Social Protection Systems Programme, co-financed by the European Union, the OECD and the Government of Finland.

Mario Pezzini
Director of the Development
Centre and Special Advisor
to the Secretary-General on Development
OECD

Isakunova Taalaikul Bazarkulovna
Minister of Labour and
Social Development
Government of Kyrgyzstan

# Acknowledgements

"The Social Protection System Review of Kyrgyzstan" was prepared by the Social Cohesion Unit of the OECD Development Centre as part of the European Union Social Protection Systems Programme.

The team was led by Alexandre Kolev, Head of the Social Cohesion Unit, under the guidance of Mario Pezzini, Director of the OECD Development Centre and Special Advisor to the OECD Secretary-General on Development and Naoko Ueda, Deputy-Director of the OECD Development Centre. The report was drafted by Riku Elovainio, Alexander Pick and Caroline Tassot, drawing from a background paper prepared by the Economic Policy Research Institute in collaboration with CASE Kyrgyzstan. Justina La provided assistance at every stage.

The report was reviewed by Bert Brys (OECD) and Jürgen Hohmann from the European Commission. It also benefited from valuable inputs and comments from Robert Brudzynski (European Union Delegation, Kyrgyzstan), Zhypara Rysbekova (Ministry of Labour and Social Development), Gulsana Turusbekova (UNICEF Kyrgyzstan), Volodymyr Kuzminskyi, Roza Rayapova (both from the European Union programme in Kyrgyzstan), Irina Lushakova and Roman Mogilevsky (CASE Kyrgyzstan); and Sharifbek Sohibnazar (World Food Programme Kyrgyzstan).

The review and the recommendations it contains benefited considerably from comments received in a Recommendations Workshop held in Bishkek on 14 March 2018. Participants included Gulzina Boobekova, Cholpon Egeshova, Yulia Kalinichenko, Cholpon Kalmyrzaeva, N Kenenbaeva, Aina Koshmolova, Almagul Mamasaipova, Aina Mambetova, Gulmira Mamyrkanova, Roman Mogilevskyi, Roza Rayapova, Samat Sartbaev, Elmira Shishkaraeva, Sharifbek Sohibnazarov, Elmira Suyumbaeva, Aikol Turganbaeva and Gulsana Turusbekova.

The OECD Development Centre's publication team, led by Delphine Grandrieux, produced the publication. The cover was designed by Aida Buendía.

The European Union Social Protection Systems Programme is co-financed by the European Union, the OECD and the Government of Finland.

*This publication has been produced with the assistance of the European Union and Finland. The contents of this publication are the sole responsibility of the OECD and can in no way be taken to reflect the views of the European Union or the Government of Finland.*

# *Table of contents*

## Tables



## Figures

## Boxes

# *Abbreviations and acronyms*

| | |
|---|---|
| ADB | Asian Development Bank |
| ADP | Additional drug package |
| ART | Antiretroviral therapy |
| DALY | Disability-Adjusted Life Years |
| DBR | Disability boards of review |
| DHS | Demographic and Health Survey |
| DTP3 | Diphtheria-tetanus-pertussis |
| EEU | Eurasian Economic Union |
| EPL | Extreme poverty line |
| FAP | Feldsher-Obstetrical Ambulatory point |
| FFDC | Fully funded defined contribution |
| FGP | Family group practice |
| FHIWP | Fund for Health Improvement of the Working People |
| FMC | Family medicine centres |
| GDP | Gross domestic product |
| GIZ | German Development Organisation - Deutsche Gesellschaft für Internationale Zusammenarbeit |
| GMI | Guaranteed Minimum Income, Kyrgyzstan |
| GoK | Government of Kyrgyzstan |
| HDI | Human Development Index |
| ILO | International Labour Organization |
| IZA | Institute of Labor Economics |
| KGS | Kyrgyz som |
| KIHS | Kyrgyz Integrated Household Survey |
| LCA | Latent Class Analysis |
| M&E | Monitoring and Evaluation |
| MBPF | Monthly Benefit for Poor Families with children |
| MCV | Meningococcal vaccine |
| MHIF | Mandatory Health Insurance Fund |

| | |
|---|---|
| MICS | Multiple Indicator Cluster Surveys |
| MoES | Ministry of Education and Science, Kyrgyzstan |
| MoF | Ministry of Finance, Kyrgyzstan |
| MoH | Ministry of Health, Kyrgyzstan |
| MoLMY | Ministry of Labour, Migration and Youth, Kyrgyzstan |
| MoLSD | Ministry of Labour and Social Development, Kyrgyzstan |
| MSB | Monthly Social Benefit |
| MSMEs | Micro, small and medium-sized enterprises |
| MTBF | Medium-term budgetary framework for 2017-2019, Kyrgyzstan |
| NEET | Not in Education, Employment, or Training |
| NGO | Non-Governmental Organisation |
| NSC | National Statistics Committee, Kyrgyzstan |
| ODA | Official Development Assistance |
| OECD | Organisation for Economic Co-operation and Development |
| OOP | Out of pocket |
| OPL | Overall poverty line |
| PAYGO | Pay-as-you-go |
| PES | Public Employment Services |
| SF | Social Fund |
| SGBP | State Guaranteed Benefits Package |
| SMSB | Supplementary Monthly Social Benefit |
| SP1 | Solidarity Pillar 1 |
| SP2 | Solidarity Pillar 2 |
| SPDS | Social Protection Development Strategy 2012-14, Kyrgyzstan |
| SPSD | Social Protection System Development Programme 2015-17, Kyrgyz Republic |
| TVET | Technical Vocational Education and Training |
| UMB | Unified Monthly Benefit |
| UN | United Nations |
| UN DESA | United Nations Department of Economic and Social Affairs |
| UNDP | United Nations Development Programme |
| UNESCO | United Nations Educational, Scientific and Cultural Organization |
| USD | United States dollar |
| USSR | Union of Soviet Socialist Republics |
| VAT | Value-added tax |

# *Executive summary*

Social protection in Kyrgyzstan covers a broad range of risks, receives a significant proportion of government funding and plays a critical role in alleviating poverty. However, provision is unevenly distributed; expenditure on social insurance is approximately five times higher than spending on social assistance, while social services and labour market policies for vulnerable workers are extremely small. Moreover, important gaps in social protection coverage exist, particularly for the urban poor, young people and the significant numbers of workers employed abroad.

Social protection in Kyrgyzstan has only partially transitioned from the cradle-to-grave system established under the Union of Soviet Socialist Republics (USSR). The Soviet labour market was predicated on full employment, with the result that social protection was almost entirely based on contributory social insurance arrangements, with additional in-kind benefits provided for deserving groups. When the Soviet Union collapsed (and with it Kyrgyzstan's economy), the social protection system lacked both the resources and the programmes required to protect the population amid a surge in unemployment and poverty in the early 1990s.

Following Kyrgyzstan's rapid transition to a market economy, targeted social assistance and labour-market programmes were introduced in the late 1990s. However, the resources available to the Government of Kyrgyzstan (GoK) were extremely limited, meaning the new programmes were necessarily very small in terms of both coverage and expenditure. Over the same period, reforms to the pension system were introduced that safeguarded entitlements acquired previously while protecting its future sustainability. The health sector also embarked on a series of major reforms. While these reforms expanded the range of risks covered by social protection, they were not implemented in a coherence fashion, leading to a fragmentation of coverage.

The structure of social protection established by these reforms remains largely in place today. Pension coverage among retired workers is close to universal and pensioners exceed the number of individuals with access to social assistance or labour market policies. Meanwhile, the small scale of social assistance limits its impact in reducing poverty. Although extreme poverty has almost been eliminated, the national poverty rate remained steady at above 30% between 2008 and 2015 then dropped sharply in 2016 to 25%. Poverty rates are highest among young children, which makes the Monthly Benefit for Poor Families with children (MBPF) critically important. The MBPF is the largest social assistance programme by expenditure and coverage, although the number of beneficiaries has fallen over the past decade while benefit levels have increased.

Broader measures of deprivation remain high, especially in rural areas. Where services exist, they are often under-resourced, leading to inadequate outcomes in health and education, for example. Moreover, a large portion of the non-poor population can be classified as vulnerable, meaning a minor income shock can send them into poverty. Upward and downward income mobility has become more pronounced in recent years despite a stabilisation of the political and economic environment since unrest in 2010.

It will not be possible to sustain the current structure of social protection long into the future. The sustainability of the pension system is being eroded as increases in the number of beneficiaries outpace growth in the contributor base. This reflects rapid growth in the rate of informal employment in recent years, as well as high levels of emigration and declining female labour force participation. As a result, the Social Fund (the institution responsible for social insurance) is increasingly reliant on transfers from the Republican Budget to meet its obligations.

Looking ahead, an ever-smaller proportion of today's workforce can expect to receive a pension in retirement. Although Kyrgyzstan's demographics are favourable for now, the country is on the cusp of rapid growth in the elderly population; failure to fix structural problems within the pension system will lead to severe problems in the longer term.

The cost of sustaining the contributory system is also making it very challenging to sustain the non-contributory arrangements required to protect and promote the most vulnerable individuals. Analysis shows that social assistance is reaching very few poor households, with those in urban areas almost completely excluded from the MBPF. A process is currently underway to reform state benefits for households with children by combining universal and poverty-targeted support. The likely benefits in terms of poverty reduction have to be balanced against the cost of these reforms.

At the same time, social services for children and other vulnerable groups are under-resourced and under-developed; residential institutions remain the primary form of social service. Local governments bear significant responsibility for providing social services but lack the resources and capacity to do so. Labour market policies suffer from similar resource constraints and do not have a significant impact.

Fiscal space to expand social protection is scarce. Moreover, social protection already receives the largest allocation of any function of government – more than health and education combined – due to the level of pension spending. For social protection to respond to changes in the needs of the population, it will require a rebalancing between social assistance (including social services), social insurance and labour market policies.

These reforms should take place within the GoK's broader objective of systematising social protection. The process of establishing such a system will be driven by the Ministry of Labour and Social Development (MoLSD), which is responsible for co-ordination of social protection policy. However, the MoLSD's internal structure is not well aligned to a systemic approach and its collaboration with local government in the delivery of social assistance is undermined by the latter's lack of capacity and low levels of resources. It is also unable to exert influence over social insurance policy, which remains under the control of the Social Fund.

New information and administrative systems for social protection are under development, most notably the Corporate Information System for Social Assistance (CISSA), which could provide the ideal foundation for a coherent social protection system. Ensuring the functionality and sustainability of CISSA is a priority in the short term, as is linking it to other social protection information systems and registries for the broader population.

# *Assessment and recommendations*

Kyrgyzstan made a rapid transition to a market economy following independence from the Soviet Union. However, social protection provision has been much slower to adapt to the post-Communist context, due in part to the social insurance system that it inherited. Although pension receipt is almost universal among the elderly and thus serves as a critical buffer against poverty for them and their families, the cost of maintaining this system has imposed severe constraints on the development of social assistance, social services and labour market policies in place.

A rebalancing of social protection provision is essential for enhancing its impact and ensuring its political and financial sustainability. This report explains how this rebalancing should be carried out within a broader process of systematisation that seeks to increase coherence and co-ordination across the sector, thereby optimising resources, expanding coverage and maximising the impact of social protection at an individual, household and national level. The breadth of social protection coverage, which combines the USSR's cradle-to-grave system with relatively young programmes, provides considerable potential for such efficiencies and synergies.

This report is intended for a broad audience, including social protection stakeholders both within Kyrgyzstan and abroad. Although Kyrgyzstan's trajectory since independence has in various ways been unique, the challenges it confronts in transitioning from a Soviet-era social protection system to one that is appropriate for a market-based economy are common to many former Soviet Republics. Meanwhile, it faces many of the same difficulties as other developing countries in ensuring that poverty-targeted benefits reach intended recipients and in promoting social insurance in a context of high informality.

## Social protection must align to changing needs in Kyrgyzstan

The national poverty rate remains high. It soared post-independence, declined rapidly in the early 2000s, stabilised at around 30% between 2008 and 2015 and then dipped to 25.4% in 2016. A large proportion of the population remains vulnerable: in 2015, 35% of the population had income between the national poverty line and 1.5 times that level. Broader measures of deprivation have shown signs of improvement after provision of basic services deteriorated dramatically following independence. Financial constraints limit the quality of services, especially in rural areas. Income inequality rose sharply in the years following independence but has since fallen.

The aggregate shift in the income distribution masks important dynamics among groups at different income levels. Upward and downward income mobility has intensified in recent years, and there was greater downward mobility than upward mobility between 2010 and 2015, suggesting that social protection is not able to maintain individuals' incomes in times of difficulty. Moreover, analysis of the poor population indicates that only a small proportion of poor individuals receive social assistance, although many poor households contain one or more pensioner benefiting from the contributory system.

Lifecycle risks are concentrated among Kyrgyzstan's large young population. The prevalence of poverty among children is striking: the poverty rate among those aged 6 and under was 43.1% in 2015, more than ten percentage points higher than the overall poverty rate. Stunting is a concern across income groups. Although child mortality has declined significantly since 2000, the maternal mortality rate rose over this period and is highest in the region. Vaccination rates have increased for children in rural areas but declined for those in urban areas.

Pre-school enrolment has risen significantly in recent years, to around 25%, but this level is far below Soviet-era enrolment rates and is concentrated in urban areas. While enrolment in primary and lower secondary education is close to universal, it is substantially lower for upper secondary school, at around 53%. In urban areas, upper secondary enrolment rose from 47% in 2009/10 to 59% in 2013/14 while enrolment in rural areas declined over the same period. Enrolment in upper secondary is higher for girls than for boys. Attendance rates for primary and secondary education are higher in rural areas than urban areas but urban children tend to perform much better than their rural counterparts. In general, education outcomes are very low and many school-leavers lack basic skills when they enter the labour market.

The transition from school to work is very challenging, especially for girls. Some 15.4% of the entire youth population (aged 15-29) was not in education, employment or training in 2013. This rate was much higher among females than among males. The unemployment rate among youth classified as economically active was 12% in 2014, down from 14% in 2009 but higher than the overall unemployment rate in 2014 (8.2%). Meanwhile, childbirth among underage women has increased steadily since 2000, with the increase particularly pronounced in urban areas.

Working-age individuals in Kyrgyzstan confront three major risks: unemployment, informality and emigration. For female workers, withdrawal from the labour market represents a fourth risk: less than 50% of the female population over age 15 was economically active in 2015. The unemployment rate has averaged around 8.5% over the past decade, while 20% of employed workers are working fewer hours than they would like, 26% earn low pay and over 40% are working excessive hours.

Informality is rising fast, accounting for 71.8% of total employment in 2014, up from 60.2% in 2002. The rate is higher among men than among women and higher in rural areas than in urban areas. The high rate of social insurance contributions is a key driver of informality.

Between 15% and 20% of the population is estimated to be working abroad (almost all in Russia), where wages are considerably higher than in Kyrgyzstan. Younger workers from the south of the country are the most likely to emigrate. Migration has major benefits to the economy: remittances equated to 34.5% of gross domestic product (GDP) in 2016, one of the highest levels in the world. The unemployment rate would probably be higher (or wages much lower) were it not for high levels of emigration. However, migrants (and the families they support) are highly vulnerable, and emigration is associated with various social problems within Kyrgyzstan.

Kyrgyzstan suffers from a double burden of disease. Infectious diseases, such as tuberculosis (TB) and (increasingly) HIV/AIDS, are a persistent problem but the burden of non-communicable diseases has become an even greater challenge. Inequalities in health outcomes exist, with health care not equally accessible to all segments of the population. Among the 2.3 million individuals who required medical assistance in 2015, 31.8% did not access any health services. Financial hardship related to the cost of health services is common; 39% of total health expenditure was out-of-pocket in 2014.

According to the 2015 Kyrgyz Integrated Household Survey, 0.9% of the total population lives with some kind of disability. Poverty is more prevalent among households that include people with disabilities, which reflects partly the additional associated cost and partly low levels of labour-force participation among people with disabilities. The disability rate among young people has risen rapidly in recent years, which could reflect either a deterioration of health outcomes among children or better reporting. The latter might have been driven by recent increases in the value of social assistance benefits for children with disabilities.

The contributory pension system acts as a crucial buffer against poverty among people with disabilities and the elderly, provided they spent a significant amount of time in formal employment. Although pension coverage among the current elderly population is nearly universal – a legacy of the near-full employment prior to independence – the value of pension payments tends not to be high.

Different surveys provide different evidence on the subjective wellbeing of Kyrgyz people. Gallup data indicate that Kyrgyz people are among the least positive in the region but domestic surveys paint a more positive picture, showing that around half the population expects their situation to improve in the future.

Looking ahead, changing demographics will have a major bearing on the economy and on demand for social protection. Although the age structure of the population is currently favourable, the population is ageing. An increased number of elderly will put significant pressure on pension spending, already one of the largest public expenditures. Kyrgyzstan's population will remain predominantly rural until around 2050 and thus particularly vulnerable to climate change, which poses both short- and long-term threats.

The overall macroeconomic context in Kyrgyzstan is improving. Recent elections occurred without incident and the economy has shown great resilience in recent years. However, Kyrgyzstan's openness to trade and its reliance on its neighbours – Russia in particular – leave it vulnerable to events outside its borders. Domestically, the energy sector is a major concern; costly electricity subsidies for residential consumers are a major burden on the state's resources and will be very difficult politically to eliminate.

## Social assistance and labour market policies have less impact than social insurance

Amid the economic and fiscal crises that followed independence, the Government of Kyrgyzstan (GoK) managed to maintain Soviet-era arrangements despite severe fiscal constraints and surging demand for benefits. Once the economic situation stabilised (briefly) in the middle of the 1990s, the GoK embarked on a series of measures to address massive deficits in the pension and health systems and introduced a poverty-targeted social assistance programme – the Unified Monthly Benefit – to reduce poverty among households with young children.

Further reforms to the structure of social protection provision were undertaken towards the end of the first decade of the 2000s. A new, fully funded individual account component was added to the pension system and in-kind benefits for privileged groups of the population were replaced with monetary benefits. However, the reforms of the past two decades have not been enough to guarantee the sustainability of social insurance arrangements or ensure the effectiveness of social assistance and labour market policies for vulnerable groups. They have also led to a fragmentation of social protection provision.

The social insurance system (which is managed by the Social Fund, a Ministry-level institution) provides benefits in the event of old age, disability or death of a contributor. For individuals who were employed for a significant proportion of their careers under the Soviet system, social insurance is functioning relatively well. However, coverage among today's workforce is much lower.

The number of Social Fund beneficiaries is increasing much faster than the number of contributors, partly due to high levels of informality and emigration. Moreover, the proportion of contributors who pay the full contribution rate is declining, which is putting strain on the pay-as-you-go component of the system. Transfers by the Republican Budget to the Social Fund finance the basic pension component, on which workers with low levels of contributions rely for the majority of pension benefits. They also finance non-contributory pensions for the military, which is a rapidly growing burden on public finances.

The pension system is caught in a vicious circle. To ensure sustainability, it must reduce benefits, increase the number of contributors or raise the contribution rate. Reducing benefit levels or increasing the contribution rate is likely to further deter individuals from contributing, while growth of the informal sector will make it very difficult to expand the contribution base. Meanwhile, the growing burden of financing the basic pension component is crowding out non-contributory programmes.

Social assistance, which is managed by the Ministry of Labour and Social Development (MoLSD), is implemented on a much lower scale than social insurance. In 2017, the MBPF was the largest programme by both coverage and expenditure, providing a monthly cash transfer to households with children under age 16 (or under 18, if they are still in education) and whose per capita income does not exceed the value of the guaranteed minimum income.

Coverage of the MBPF has declined significantly in recent years. Only 4.9% of the population lived in households eligible for the MBPF in 2015. This is much lower than the overall poverty rate, reflecting the fact that the MBPF was established to eradicate *extreme* poverty, which today affects a very small proportion of the population. However, the MBPF has been shown to exclude a large proportion of the poorest of the poor, due in large part to the programme's administrative challenges. Households that are deemed ineligible for the MBPF might also be excluded from co-payment exemptions for health services.

Overall, the MBPF does not have a large impact on the incidence or depth of poverty. This is due partly to its low coverage and partly to low benefit levels, which, although they have risen significantly in recent years, remain far below the extreme poverty line. As a consequence, the GoK is considering reforming state benefits from 2018; the new dispensation is likely to combine categorical targeting with means-testing and is expected to have a greater impact on poverty than the current MBPF but at a higher cost.

The other main social assistance programme – the Monthly Social Benefit (MSB) – is the umbrella term for cash benefits payable to different vulnerable groups regardless of income. These groups include people with disabilities (including children), orphans, mothers who have had seven or more children (known as heroine mothers), and elderly individuals who are not eligible for pensions from the contributory system. Benefit levels vary between these groups but tend to be higher than the value of the MBPF. Coverage of the MSB has risen much faster than the population as a whole in recent years, while the value of benefits has increased for some groups and not for others. Maternity and funeral benefits also exist but are only payable to workers who worked in the formal sector.

Cash payments (compensations for privileges) are paid monthly to some 25 groups. Some categories receive these benefits based on merit rather than vulnerability and should not necessarily be considered social protection recipients. However, other recipients are from vulnerable groups, indicating potential overlap with the MSB. The number of individuals receiving these compensations has declined for most categories and the value of the benefits has been frozen in real terms in recent years. As a result, expenditure has declined significantly both in real terms and as a proportion of total spending.

The provision of social services is dominated by residential institutions; other services are very scarce due to resource and capacity constraints at a local government level, as well as a lack of legislation to clarify the state's obligations in this area. The GoK has made important advances in improving oversight of residential institutions, which are managed by a range of different institutions, but is making slow progress in reducing the number of children enrolled therein.

The MoLSD also oversees active labour market policies for vulnerable groups, although these exist on a very small scale. Public Employment Services act as a gatekeeper for labour market policies, assisting with job searches and connecting the unemployed with micro-credit, but are constrained by a lack of information on the labour market. The largest active labour market policy is public works programmes, which are implemented in a highly decentralised manner and overwhelmingly employ men rather than women. An unemployment benefit exists but the value is extremely low and strict eligibility criteria mean it is paid to a very small number of the unemployed.

Overall, social protection provision covers a wide range of risks but the allocation of resources across the sector is very unbalanced. The proportion of elderly receiving pensions is close to 100%, while less than 10% of the population access social assistance and labour market policies. The most notable gaps in coverage are instruments for the urban poor, unemployed youth (especially women) and migrant workers. These gaps will often result in pensioners living with younger generations, stretching their (often low) pension benefits across large households.

## Fiscal space for expanding social protection is limited

Imbalances in provision of social protection are reflected in the structure of expenditure, which is growing in real terms and was equal to 10.7% of GDP in 2015, making it the largest component of government expenditure – higher than spending on health and education combined. Old age pensions (including the military) accounted for 72% of this expenditure, while the MBPF, MSB and compensations combined were worth around 15%. Assuming the overall resource envelope for social protection remains unchanged, pensions will absorb an ever greater proportion of expenditure, not only due to financial imbalances in the Social Fund (currently covered by the Republican Budget) but also rapid growth in spending on military pensions.

Economic growth and increased tax revenues have accommodated growth in social protection spending in recent years but Kyrgyzstan relies on external support to finance its spending and recently breached its maximum debt threshold. Over the long-term, reprioritisation within the social protection sector is a more promising source of fiscal space for expanding social protection spending than additional allocations to the sector.

Fiscal incidence analysis shows the fiscal system is progressive, although the size of the pension system means there is likely to be significantly more horizontal redistribution (between individuals of similar income) than vertical redistribution (between individuals at different level of income).The impact of high taxes (of which indirect taxes account for the lion's share) and high social protection spending on poverty is approximately neutral. The incidence of public services – particularly health and education – is thus an important determinant of the overall impact of the fiscal framework on poverty.

## Rebalance social protection through a systemic approach

The GoK should rebalance social protection provision to align it to the needs of Kyrgyzstan today and to ensure its future sustainability. This rebalancing should occur in the context of a broader reform to establish a social protection system in Kyrgyzstan, as envisaged by recent social protection strategies.

Kyrgyzstan's broad range of social protection programmes, high level of expenditure, the concentration of social protection policy at central level and the acceptance of social protection as a basic right all pave the way for promoting coherence and co-ordination across the social protection sector. However, the structure of the MoLSD is not well aligned to a systemic approach and the provision of social assistance and social services is undermined by low capacity and a lack of clear roles and responsibilities at local level. At the same time, the MoLSD has so far been unable to influence social insurance policy.

There has been important progress in establishing an effective information infrastructure for social assistance beneficiaries through the Corporate Information System for Social Assistance (CISSA). This database will significantly improve the efficiency and transparency of all business processes related to social assistance. However, steps are needed to improve its functionality, ensure its sustainability and link it to other databases being developed for social protection and for the population as a whole.

Systematisation of social protection would also require a reallocation of expenditure across social protection pillars and major changes to the structure of key programmes. Merging the MBPF with a categorical benefit for children would be a major step towards enhancing the impact of social assistance. Strengthening the mandate of the MoLSD to provide social services at a local level might improve the operation of social protection at a local level but would require a significant reform to the inter-governmental system. A similarly bold decision is required for social insurance to protect the sustainability of the system and ensure adequate protection for future generations of retirees, possibly including the introduction of a universal old-age grant as the basis for retirement provision.

## Recommendations

### *Introduce a universal infant benefit as part of state benefit reform*

- Establish a three-component state benefit for families with children, incorporating universal grants for newborns and infants and a poverty-targeted grant for older children.
- Provide the infant benefit to children up to their second birthday initially but increase the eligibility age to three within five years.

- Ensure that vulnerable children are linked to social services, health and education (in particular pre-school facilities), creating a subsystem of social protection specifically for children and vulnerable families.
- Eliminate the guaranteed minimum income from the calculations for eligibility and benefit value for the poverty-targeted component.
- Simplify the eligibility assessment for the poverty-targeted component.

### *Reform and scale up social services*

- Create a legislative framework for the provision of social services according to a guaranteed minimum level of services for specified vulnerable groups.
- Identify clear roles and responsibilities between social protection experts employed by aiyl okmotu (local government) and the staff of the MoLSD for the provision of social services at a local level.
- Expand the capacity of the social workforce by ensuring social workers possess the required skills and training as well as adequate resources.
- Ensure that children at residential institutions (and their families) are linked to other social protection arrangements, especially after they leave institutions.

### *Scale up public works programmes to revive labour market policies*

- Catalogue and analyse existing implementation of public works programmes.
- Design a national strategy and policy framework for public works programmes at the same time as enhancing MoLSD's capacity in this area.
- Establish participation quotas for women, the youth and people with disabilities and ensure skills acquisition is mainstreamed into projects.
- Ensure the involvement of local communities and administrations in identifying participants and designing activities to ensure that projects are useful.
- Set up stringent monitoring and evaluation systems to assess their impact.

### *Establish a universal social pension based on the basic contributory pension and the MSB*

- Introduce contributions and increase the retirement age for military pensions.
- Align retirement ages and indexation policy for old-age and adult disability MSB benefits with basic pension component.
- Over time, consider merging the old-age and adult disability MSB and basic pension component to create a social pension.
- Use social pension as the basis for a broader reform of retirement provision to safeguard the long-term sustainability of the Social Fund while maintaining universal coverage of public retirement benefits.
- Establish an inter-governmental task team chaired by the Vice Prime Minister on social affairs to guide retirement reform.

### *Restructure MoLSD to enhance systematisation of non-contributory programmes and co-ordination across social protection sector*

- Move the unit responsible for co-ordinating social protection policy to report directly to the Minister of Labour and Social Development.
- Align units with a labour/employment portfolio to specific labour market programmes.
- Establish specific capacity for social insurance and social services to reflect other proposed changes.

### *Ensure functionality and sustainability of CISSA*

- Accelerate the implementation of CISSA as the principal information tool for non-contributory benefits, ensuring its functionality for users outside Bishkek.
- Link CISSA to other databases currently being developed for the social protection sector as well as to population registries.
- Capacitate the MoLSD to manage CISSA at a central level and in the regions.

### *Close equity gaps in access to health services*

- Close avenues for opting out of the Mandatory Health Insurance Fund.
  - Gather data regarding different individuals' capacity to pay in order to increase contributions from informal sector workers.
  - Enforce the enrolment mandate and establish appropriate incentive mechanisms such as matching contributions from budgetary funds.
- Use funds from increased contributions to retain physicians in rural areas and incentivise improved quality of care, for instance by developing indicators for output- and quality-based performance payments.
- Further strengthen health service integration, using the integration of TB drugs in the Additional Drug Package as a model.
- Better target user-fee exemptions and increase coverage of exemptions for pharmaceuticals.

# Chapter 1. A forward-looking assessment of social protection needs

*Following the shock of the collapse of the Soviet Union and the disruption caused by the rapid transition to a market economy, Kyrgyzstan is enjoying a period of economic and political stability. However, the decline in income poverty has slowed over the past decade and certain measures of broader deprivation are alarmingly high, reflecting the challenge of improving services in a context of severe fiscal constraints. Tight labour market conditions are resulting in high levels of international migration, which is a boon for the Kyrgyz economy but socially disruptive. Major long-term threats related to demographics and climate change are on the horizon.*

Since the collapse of the Union of Soviet Socialist Republics (USSR) in 1991, Kyrgyzstan has undergone fundamental political, economic and social changes. Its rapid transition to a market economy initially compounded the economic shock caused by the fall of the USSR, on which Kyrgyzstan had relied heavily both as trade partner and provider of fiscal subsidies. Further shocks in the 1990s and 2000s – internal and external, political and economic – disrupted Kyrgyzstan's emergence as an independent state. However, since 2010, the country has enjoyed a prolonged period of political and economic stability, attaining middle-income status in 2014.

Social protection has been at the centre of government policy before and since independence. It is the single-largest component of public spending – exceeding expenditure on health and education expenditure combined – and comprises a large range programmes to cover a wide array of risks. However, social protection is still transitioning from a Soviet-era system, premised on full employment, to one appropriate for Kyrgyzstan's current population.

This Chapter discusses the current context of social protection policy in Kyrgyzstan and assesses how it might evolve in the future. It examines the dynamics and determinants of poverty and inequality, explores how basic services have responded to dramatic reductions in resources since the collapse of the USSR and conducts a forward-looking analysis of the risks confronting different groups at different stages of the lifecycle and the economy as a whole.

## Decline in poverty stalled after 2008 but resumed in 2016

Poverty is a long-standing challenge for Kyrgyzstan, though its position on major international trade routes has allowed it to benefit from the economic might of its neighbours throughout its history. Natural resources, particularly gold and water, make important contributions to the economy but are either not as abundant as in some neighbouring countries or are far harder to access due to Kyrgyzstan's mountainous terrain.

Kyrgyzstan was among the poorest republics when the Soviet Union collapsed. Although Soviet authorities were not transparent regarding poverty levels in the USSR, Goskomstat (the state statistical agency) calculated that 33% of the Kyrgyz population was "underprovisioned" in 1989 – roughly the same rate as in 2015 (Pomfret, 1999[1]).

The collapse of the Soviet Union led to successive and dramatic contractions in Kyrgyzstan's economy in the early 1990s. A rapid increase in poverty was compounded by the shock liberalisation of the economy, which exacerbated the collapse in employment, and by the abrupt termination of transfers from the Soviet Union.

Having undergone the most rapid transition of any former republic (Hoen, 2010[2]), the economy stabilised towards the middle of the decade, with foreign lenders providing substantial support. The situation worsened dramatically with the 1998 Russian financial crisis. The economy was more stable in the 2000s, although growth rates still fluctuated.

**Box 1.1. National and international poverty measures and terms used in this report**

**Monetary or income poverty**: Poverty status based on either household consumption or income as household welfare metrics.

- **Overall poverty line (OPL)**: This poverty line is monetary and calculated using data from the Kyrgyz Integrated Household Survey, drawing upon expenditures for food, non-food items, services, and durable goods. For 2015, the value of a bundle of food and non-food goods and services that ensure a certain minimum level of consumption yielding the general national per capita monthly poverty line was KGS 2 631, equivalent to USD 40.80 per capita (current USD).
- **Vulnerability line**: The vulnerability line is equal to 1.5 times the national poverty line.
- **Extreme poverty line (EPL)**: The monetary equivalent of food needed to ensure 2100 kcal per person per day as per the World Health Organization's minimum caloric intake requirements for transitional economies. In general, the value of the extreme poverty line is set at approximately two times less than that of the OPL.
- **Subsistence minimum (SM)**: The value of a minimum bundle of food and non-food goods and services necessary for livelihood and for maintaining health, including mandatory taxes and duties. The subsistence minimum is estimated quarterly on per capita basis for the following population groups: total population; able-bodied population (female, male, altogether); population of retirement age; and children (0-7, 7-14, 14-17 years old, and altogether). Each of these thresholds is calculated at the national level and separately for its seven oblasts and Bishkek.
- **Global poverty lines**: Poverty lines defined by the World Bank based on the 15 poorest countries in 2005. Until 2015, the poverty line was set at USD 1.25/day; in 2005 Purchasing Power Parity (PPP, computed on the basis of price data across the world), with an upper poverty line set at USD 2/day. Following an update of 2011 prices, the poverty line is now set at USD 1.90/day in 2011 PPP, with an upper poverty line set at USD 3.20/day.

**Multi-dimensional or non-income poverty**: Poverty status based on deprivations of a household in areas beyond monetary poverty.

- The Oxford Poverty and Human Development Initiative (OPHI) **multi-dimensional Poverty Index (MPI)** covers three areas: education, health and standard of living through 10 indicators. The indicators are weighted to create a deprivation score: a deprivation score of 33.3% indicates multi-dimensional poverty, a score of 50% or more indicates severe multi-dimensional poverty, and a score between 20-33.3% indicates near multi-dimensional poverty.
- The United Nations Development Programme (UNDP) **Human Development Index (HDI)** covers three areas: health, education and standard of living. It is a summary measure based on the geometric mean of normalised indices for each dimension (life expectancy at birth, average and expected years of schooling, gross national income per capita).

**Poverty rate**: The proportion of the population that lives below the national poverty line. For 2016, the overall monetary poverty rate was 25.4%.

**Poverty gap**: How far (on average) poor households are below the poverty line, expressed as a percentage of the level at which the poverty line is set.

Between 2000 and 2008, the proportion of individuals with incomes below the overall poverty line (as defined in Box 1.1) halved, from 62.6% to 31.7% (Figure 1.1). Over the same period, extreme poverty was almost eliminated. According to the World Bank (2015[3]), this reduction in poverty was largely driven by favourable demographic trends: the working age population grew relative to other age groups at the same time as high levels of emigration drove up domestic wages.

However, the decline in poverty stalled after 2008; the poverty rate remained above 30% until 2016, when it dropped to 25.4%. The poverty gap has followed a similar trajectory, declining sharply between 2000 and 2007 (from 17.7% to 6.6%) before fluctuating within a range of 5.0% to 8.0%.

**Figure 1.1. National poverty is far below 2000 levels**

Poverty headcount ratios (2000-16)

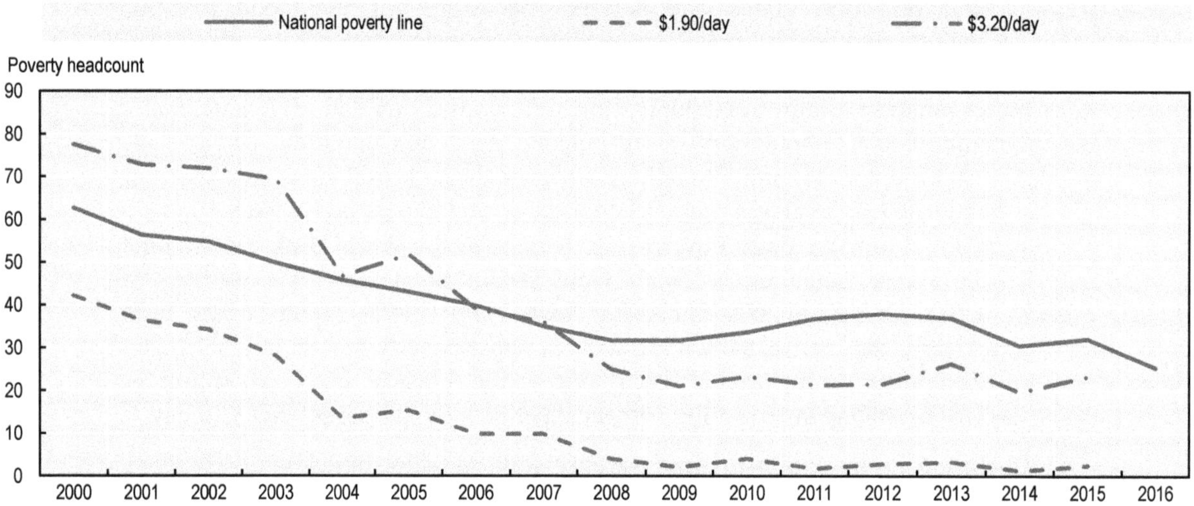


*Source*: NSC (2017[4]), "Poverty rate", stat.kg/en/statistics/uroven-zhizni-naseleniya.

The disparity between rural and urban poverty has decreased significantly over the past decade (Figure 1.2) but widened again in 2016. Although poverty in rural areas remains higher than in urban areas, the gap closed to just four percentage points in 2015, before widening to 10 percentage points in 2016. As this chapter will discuss, the urban poor population has very little access to social assistance.

**Figure 1.2. Rural poverty is converging with urban poverty**

Poverty rates in rural and urban areas (1996-2016)

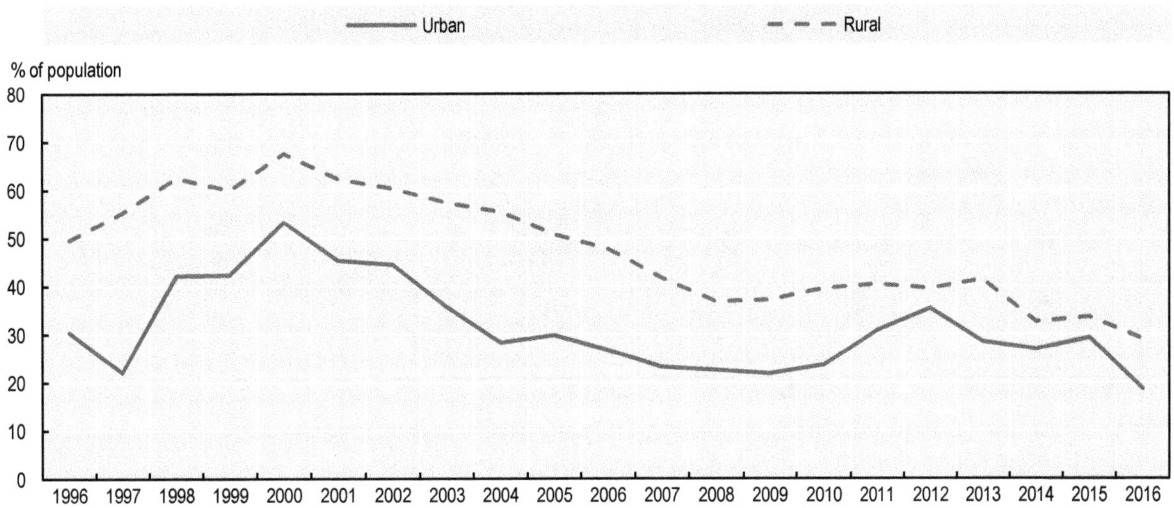


*Source*: NSC (2017[5]), "Number of households with incomes below subsistence level", available at stat.kg/en/statistics/uroven-zhizni-naseleniya.

The stalling (in some years reversal) of the decline in poverty coincided with political and economic instability at home and abroad. The 2008 global financial crisis was followed by a violent uprising in 2010 that had significant negative effects on livelihoods. The trajectory of Kyrgyzstan's gross domestic product (GDP) shows how economic volatility has continued since these two events (Figure 1.3), contracting in 2012 then growing by 10.9% in 2013.

Growth rates from 2011 onwards demonstrate both the underlying resilience of the Kyrgyz economy and the impact of global gold prices on the economy owing to the Kumtor gold mine's contribution to GDP. Excluding the output from Kumtor, the economy maintained a relatively steady growth rate between 2011 and 2015; including Kumtor, growth was more volatile and lower, on average.

**Figure 1.3. Fluctuations in gold prices of have heightened the volatility of GDP growth**

GDP growth with and without Kumtor gold mine (2005-22)

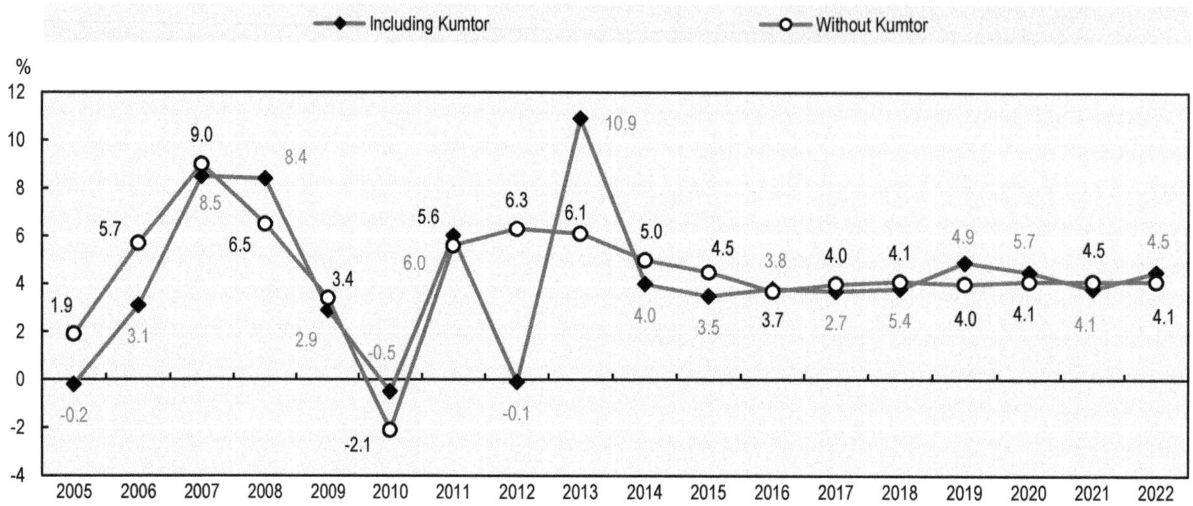


*Source*: IMF (2017[6]), *World Economic Outlook (October 2017)*, imf.org/external/datamapper/datasets/WEO.

The structure of the economy has changed significantly since the collapse of the Soviet Union. In 1990, the composition of value added was divided equally between agriculture, industry and services (Figure 1.4A). However, industrial output collapsed when demand from elsewhere in the USSR for many manufactured products disappeared. The contribution of agriculture increased between 1990 and 1995 as individuals moved to rural areas in search of work, but it has since declined steadily. In 2014, it accounted for only 17% of value added, despite employing 32% of the workforce the previous year (Figure 1.4B).

Services are the mainstay of the economy and employment. The tertiary sector has grown continually since 1990, to account for 56% of value added (up from 31% in 1990) in 2014 and 48% of the workforce in 2013. The size of the industrial contribution varies in line with the performance of Kumtor but is far from its level in 1990.

**Figure 1.4. Services dominate output and employment**

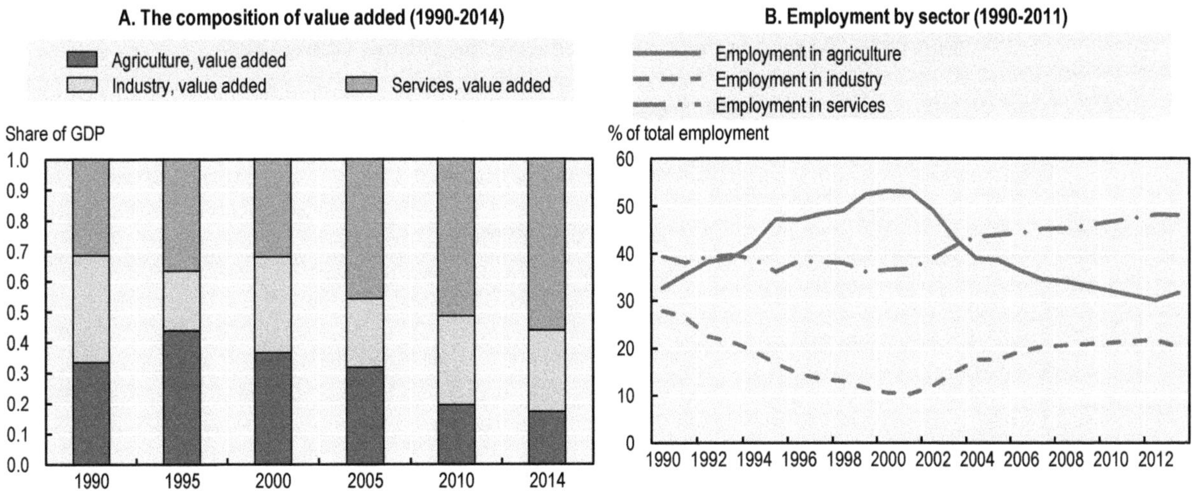


*Source*: World Bank (2017[7]), *World Development Indicators* (database), available at data.worldbank.org/products/wdi.

Inflation has fluctuated since 2005. Years of high inflation (around 20% per annum) in 2007-08 and 2010 were followed by low inflation in 2009 and after 2011 (Figure 1.5). The average annual inflation rate between 2005 and 2015 was 8.9% measured by the consumer price index. In 2016, the inflation rate was -0.5% but rose to 3.7% in 2017.

**Figure 1.5. Inflation has fluctuated since 2005**

Consumer price inflation (2005-2016)

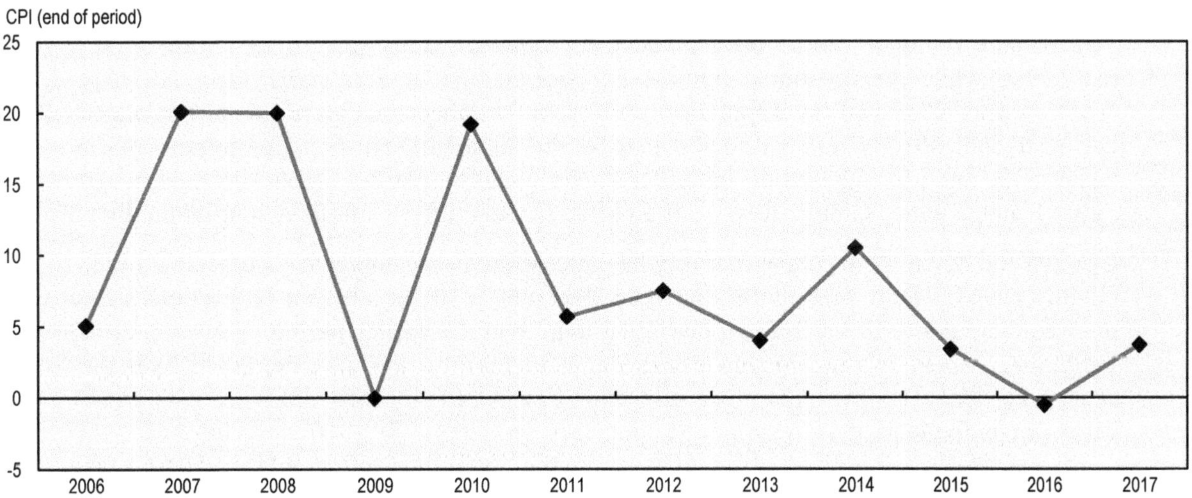


*Source*: NSC (2017[8]), "Basic consumer price index in the Kyrgyz Republic (core inflation)", available at stat.kg/en/statistics/uroven-zhizni-naseleniya.

In spite of the reduction in poverty since 2000, a large proportion of the population remains vulnerable. Figure 1.6 shows the change in the income distribution between 2004 and 2014; the proportion of the population with incomes below the poverty line fell over this period but the majority of the population was only just above the poverty line. In 2015, 77% of the population was poor or vulnerable.

**Figure 1.6. Many people have left poverty but remain vulnerable**

Kyrgyzstan income distribution (2004, 2014)

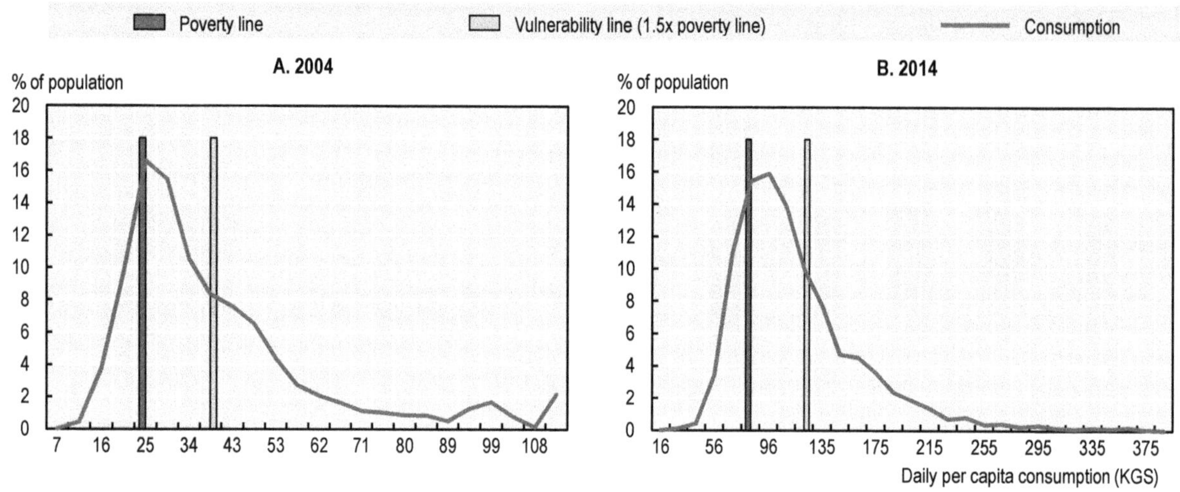


*Source*: NSC (2004[9]; 2014[10]), *Kyrgyz Integrated Household Survey* (database).

The aggregate shift in the income distribution masks important dynamics among groups at different income levels. Transitions analysis based on the KIHS for 2004, 2010 and 2015 (Figure 1.7) shows how the proportion of households classified as vulnerable increased over time, both as households emerged from poverty and as incomes in households initially neither poor nor vulnerable fell below the vulnerability threshold.

The Sankey diagram shows poverty declined between 2004 and 2015 (from 52.5% to 32.7%), while the combined number of poor and vulnerable individuals fell only slightly (from 77.6% of the population to 74.5%). Numbers in Figure 1.7 do not match the headcount poverty numbers calculated by the National Statistics Committee (NSC) because the analysis is based on individuals who could be tracked across all three waves rather than the entire sample. It was not possible to weight these numbers longitudinally.

Upward and downward income mobility has intensified in recent years. The decline in the poverty rate was more pronounced between 2004 and 2010 but a higher proportion of the poor exited poverty between 2010 and 2015 than over the earlier period. The number of individuals whose income moved above the vulnerability line also increased over the same timeframe. However, there was also more downward mobility in this second period: 21.7% of individuals who were neither poor nor vulnerable in 2010 were in poverty in 2015 and 36.3% of individuals who were neither poor nor vulnerable in 2010 were vulnerable in 2015.

This downward income mobility suggests that the current social protection system – and in particular social insurance arrangements (the largest component of this system) – achieves limited success in protecting people from income shocks. Given that the majority of social insurance expenditure is in the form of old-age pensions, it is likely that working age individuals are most vulnerable to income shocks.

**Figure 1.7. Income mobility has intensified since 2010**

Transitions in and out of poverty (2004, 2010, 2015)

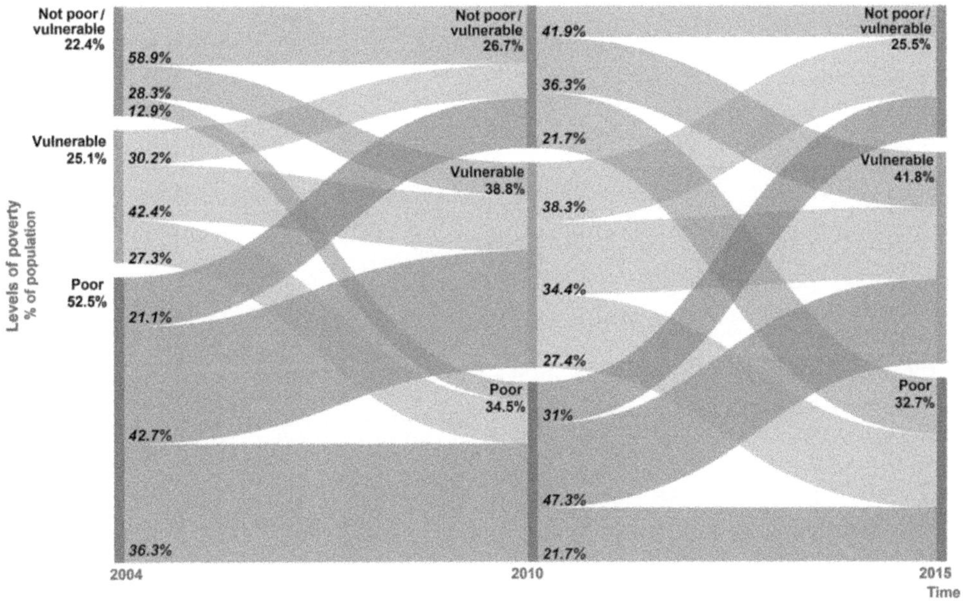


*Note:* The numbers do not match the headcount poverty numbers calculated by the National Statistics Committee (NSC) because the sample includes only individuals surveyed consistently across all three waves, rather than the cross-sectional sample upon which the NSC calculates the headcount poverty ratio.
*Source*: NSC (2015[11]), *Kyrgyz Integrated Household Survey* (database).

## Most poor individuals lack access to social assistance

OECD experts conducted Latent Class Analysis[1] on the 2015 KIHS to better understand the profile of poor households in Kyrgyzstan (Figure 1.8). This technique clusters poor households based on their characteristics, such that households are the most homogenous within a group and as distant as possible from those in another group.

**Figure 1.8. Few poor households receive social assistance**

Latent Class Analysis clusters (2015)

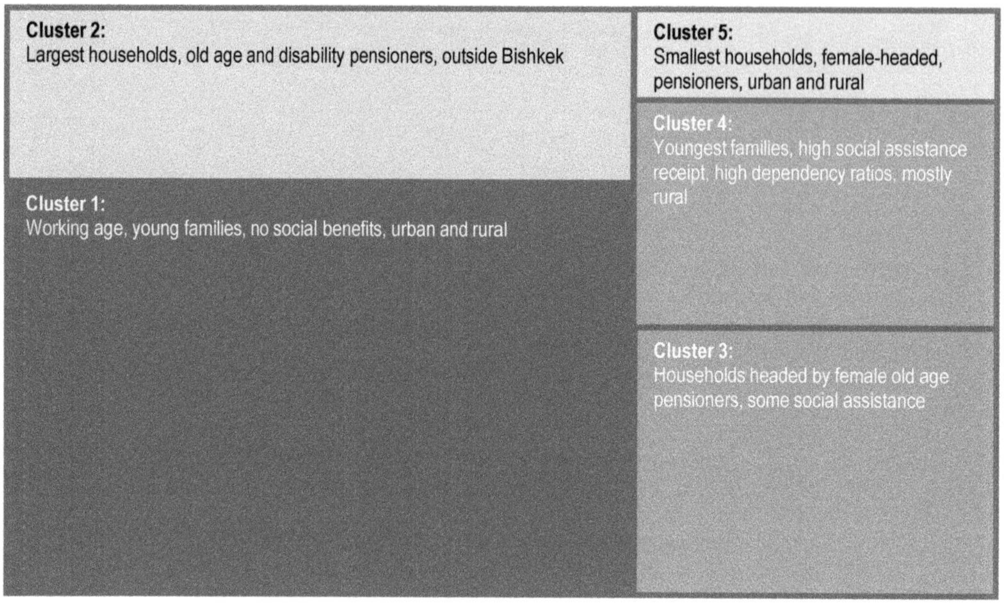


*Source*: Author's calculations based on NSC (2015[11]), *Kyrgyz Integrated Household Survey* (database).

LCA creates clusters of poor individuals based on a large number of variables, including economic activity of the head of the household in which they reside (employed, disabled pensioner, old-age pensioner, unemployed or inactive), presence of elderly dependants or children in the household, marital status of the household head, place of residence (rural, urban or Bishkek) and receipt of social protection benefits or private remittances. The social protection category distinguishes between recipients of pensions, social assistance or compensations for privileges.

The model identifies five household clusters:

- The largest cluster of households (representing 45% of the poor) is predominantly headed by young employed men who attended secondary school. Among this cluster, 27% of household heads are aged 38 and under. The average household size is 5.4 members. Upwards of 95% contain children under age 16, 41% contain children under age 3 and just 2% contain elderly people. This group of households is almost as likely to live in urban areas as in rural areas, with 24% in Bishkek alone.
- The second-largest cluster (representing 19% of the poor) is predominantly headed by men receiving old age pensions (44%) or disability pensions (20%). The average household size of this cluster (6.1 members) is the largest of the five groups; 88% of these households contain children under the age of 16. Household heads are not young: some 69% of them are aged 54 and above. Some 75% are in rural areas, with the rest in urban areas outside Bishkek.
- Among the third-largest cluster, representing 17% of the poor, 66% are headed by women, and two-thirds of household heads are widows. Some 91% of household heads are aged 54 and above, 75% receive old-age pensions, and 32% have low

education levels (primary or less). These households are second largest in size (5.9 members) and are mostly in rural areas (67%).

- Among households in the fourth-largest cluster, representing 14% of the poor, 97% are headed by men. This is the youngest cohort, with 32% of household heads aged 38 and under. Although 80% of household heads are employed, this cluster is by far the most likely to receive state benefits (64% receive some form of social assistance). These households have the highest dependency ratios and are the most likely to contain children under age 3 (46%). Some 87% are in rural areas.
- The fifth-largest cluster, representing 5% of the poor, is the oldest: 72% of household heads are aged 64 and above. Household heads are overwhelmingly women (85%), pensioners (100%) and widowed (85%). Education levels are the lowest: 35% of household heads attained primary or less. Although 56% of households have 5 members or more, this cluster has the smallest household size on average (4.9 members) and is the least likely to contain children. This cluster is the most urban, with 57% in cities (mostly Bishkek).

LCA demonstrates a major gap in the social protection system. Over 95% of households in cluster 1, by far the largest cluster of poor households, do not receive either social assistance or social insurance. Although they have young children, only a small proportion is deemed eligible for the MBPF – the only poverty-targeted state benefit. On the other hand, cluster 4, which is much smaller, is well covered by social assistance. This disparity in coverage rates indicates a rural bias in the MBPF (discussed in Chapter 2).

Another key result related to social protection is a preponderance of poor households receiving pensions. Pension coverage is universal in the three clusters where the household head is elderly, equating to 40% of the poor population. While this might raise questions about the adequacy of pension levels, the analysis also suggests the poverty-alleviating impact of pensions is diminished by the number of individuals within a household relying on this income.

Pensions appear, therefore, to be a vital source of income for both the elderly and for other clusters with low income potential. Given the age of household heads, children under age 16 are surprisingly numerous in households in the elderly clusters. LCA does not identify three-generation or skip-generation (children living with grandparents) households receiving pensions, but it does demonstrate pensions are a key source of income for children as well as retirees.

Unemployment rates among household heads in the two younger clusters are 13.2% and 14.8%, respectively – above the average for the population as a whole but not by a wide margin. In both cases, informality is the norm: 73% and 74% of household heads are in informal employment in clusters 1 and 2, respectively. These household heads are typically well educated: 79% of the more urban cluster attended secondary school, and 14% received some tertiary education, while 92% of the more rural cluster attended secondary school. Nevertheless, it appears that the employment income of household heads is not high enough to keep these households out of poverty.

Importantly, very few poor households receive remittances: less than 10% of households, on average, across the five clusters. This finding should mitigate concerns that public transfers crowd out private transfers. Remittances can also be seen be a crucial means of keeping households out of poverty. The prevalence of working poverty and the low coverage by remittances make a strong push case for emigration, incentivising poor rural and urban households alike to send workers abroad to alleviate household poverty.

## Inequality indicators are mixed

Inequality rose sharply in the years following the collapse of the Soviet Union. However, by most standard measures, inequality has since fallen. The Gini coefficient was 0.23 in 2015, versus 0.54 in 1993, when it was the highest among the sample of countries used to benchmark Kyrgyzstan in this review (Georgia, Mongolia, Russian Federation, Tajikistan and Uzbekistan). According to the World Development Indicators (WDIs), Kyrgyzstan's Gini is among the lowest in this sample (Figure 1.9A). Calculations based on the 2015 KIHS indicate that inequality is marginally higher in urban areas (Gini of 0.24) than in rural areas (Gini of 0.22).

The WDIs also show the distribution of income remained relatively steady between 2000 and 2012, aside from a spike in inequality in 2005 and 2006 (Figure 1.9B). On average over this period, the lowest quintile received 8.5% of total income, while the highest received 40.5%.

**Figure 1.9. Kyrgyzstan's level of income inequality is the lowest among its peer group**

Income inequality in the benchmark countries and income distribution

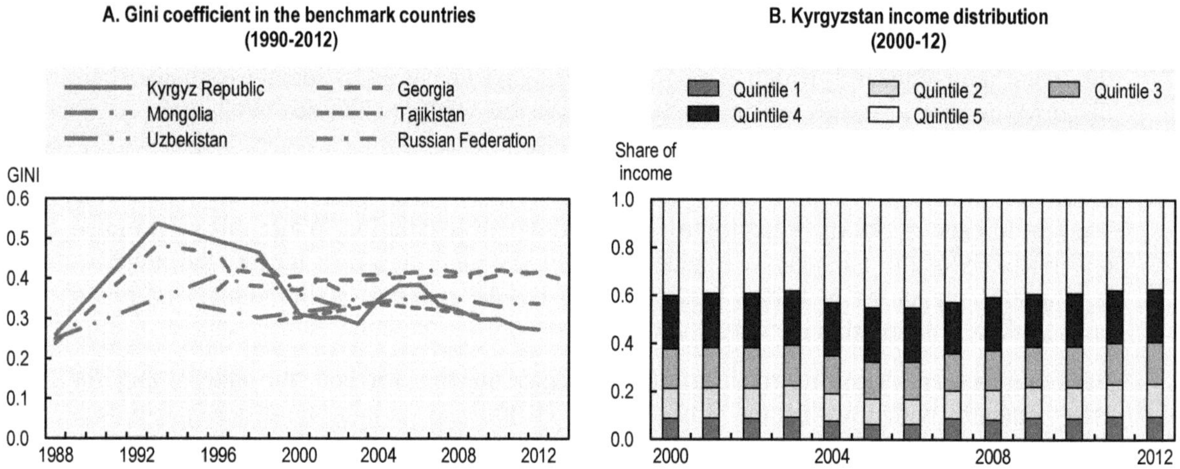


*Source*: NSC (2015[11]), *Kyrgyz Integrated Household Survey* (database).

There is evidence the income of the wealthiest households might be increasing much faster than that of other income groups. The Palma ratio, which measures the income of the top 10% of the income distribution as a proportion of the income of the bottom 40%, has increased since 2008 (Figure 1.10). Figure 1.10 also shows that the Palma is very close to the ratio of income for the top and bottom deciles, which suggests that there is little income inequality at the bottom end of the distribution but significant movement at the very top. The ratio of top and bottom *quintiles* follows a much flatter trajectory, further suggesting inequality is being driven by increased incomes at the very top of the distribution.

**Figure 1.10. Income growth amongst the top decile is fuelling inequality**

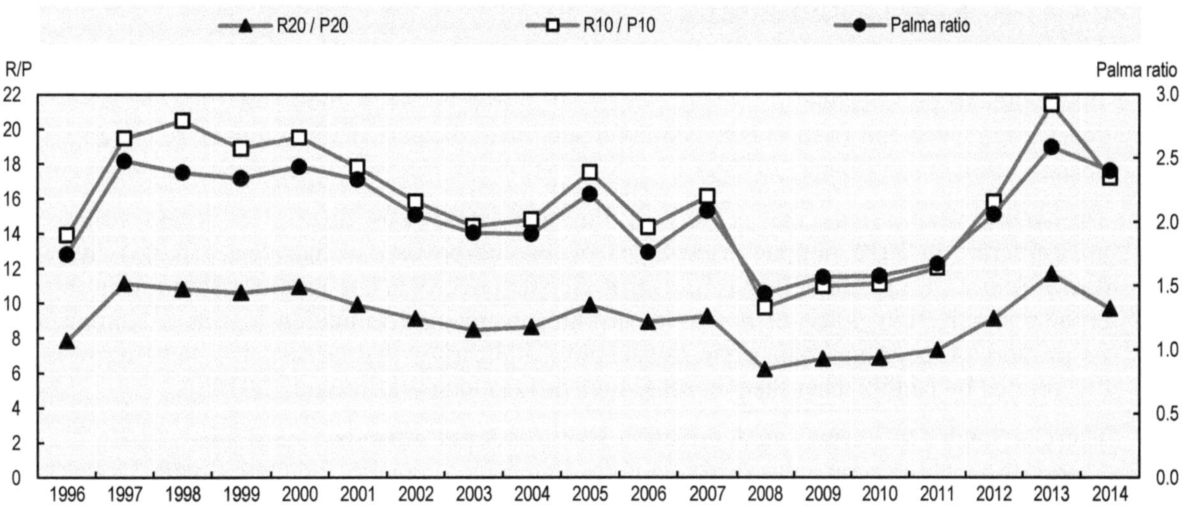


*Source*: Author's calculations based on NSC (2014[10]), *Kyrgyz Integrated Household Survey* (database).

## Multi-dimensional poverty has fallen at different rates across Kyrgyzstan

Broader measures of deprivation have recovered after declining sharply upon the collapse of the USSR, although per capita incomes remain below their level of 25 years ago. Kyrgyzstan is ranked 120th in the UNDP HDI, with a score of 0.664. This is the second-lowest among the benchmark countries, ahead of only Tajikistan (0.627), but 8% above the level in 1990 (Figure 1.11).

**Figure 1.11. Kyrgyzstan's human development indicators have recovered post-independence**

Human Development Index – score in the benchmark countries (1990-2015)

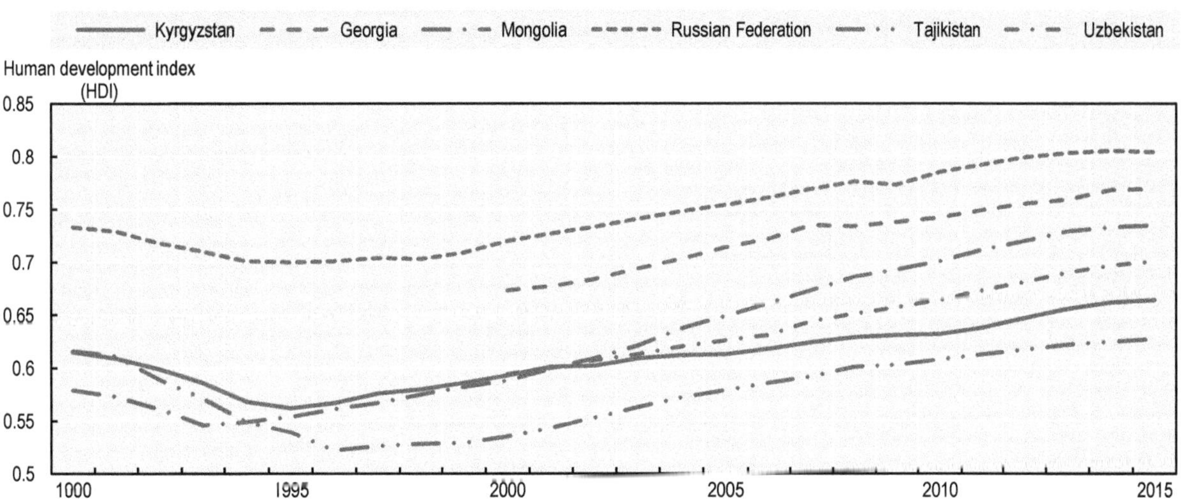


*Source*: UNDP (2016[12]), *Human Development Index* (database), hdr.undp.org/en/data.

The improvement in Kyrgyzstan's score between 1990 and 2015 was driven by increases in life expectancy by 4.5 years, mean years of schooling by 2.2 years and expected duration of schooling by 1.2 years. However, gross national income per capita in 2015 was 9.1% below the 1990 level, which reflects the impact on the size of the economy inflicted by the collapse of the USSR and the abrupt end of economic support to Kyrgyzstan it entailed (UNDP, 2016[12]).

The dynamics of income poverty and multi-dimensional poverty differ (Figure 1.12). While the steepest decline in income poverty occurred between 2000 and 2008, broader deprivation levels fell furthest between 2008 and 2012, the period when monetary poverty began to stall (World Bank, 2015[3]).

The World Bank finds that 37.4% of the population was unable to access basic infrastructure in 2012, similar to the level of income poverty in that year (38.0%) and down from 77.4% in 2008. It also finds that income poverty is not a major determinant of broader deprivation. Lack of access to drinking water and sanitation affects a similar proportion of poor and non-poor households, indicating that access is likely to be determined by factors other than income, such as location (World Bank, 2015[3]).

There are major differences in deprivation levels between urban and rural areas. In 2012, 51.9% of people in rural areas suffered multi-dimensional poverty, compared with 12.4% of people in urban areas. This is reflected in inter-regional variation: in Talas, a small, remote region in the north-east, the multi-dimensional poverty rate was 70.9% in 2012 down from 97.7% in 2008, while only 3.5% of the Bishkek population faced multidimensional deprivation in 2012, down from 24.5% in 2008.

**Figure 1.12. Monetary and multi-dimensional poverty rates differ by region**

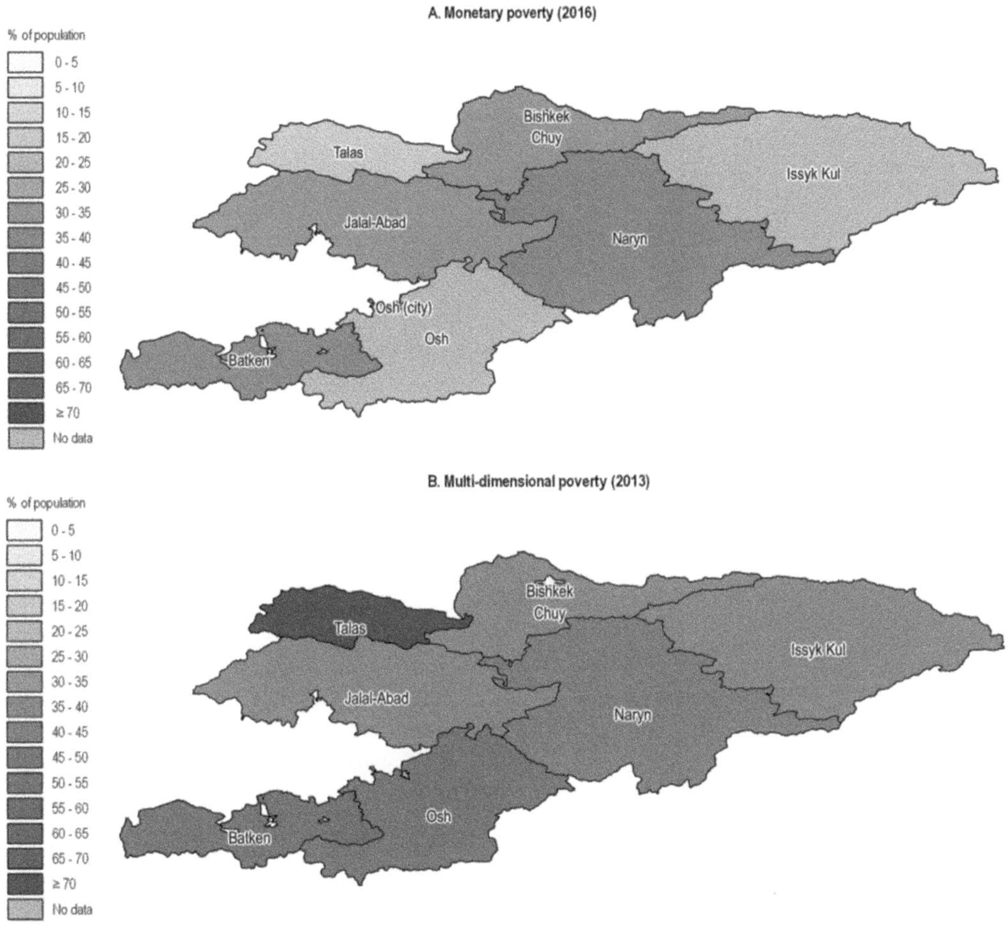


*Note*: 2016 monetary poverty figures in Figure 1.12A calculated by the NSC (2016[13]); 2013 multi-dimensional poverty figures in Figure 1.12B calculated by the World Bank (2015[14]).
*Sources*: NSC (2016[13]), "Poverty rate", stat.kg/en; World Bank (2015[14]), "Kyrgyz Republic: Poverty profile for 2013", openknowledge.worldbank.org/handle/10986/22958.

These heat maps showing the level of poverty and multi-dimensional poverty in different regions demonstrate the regional disparities in both. Monetary poverty levels do not necessarily mirror measures of broader deprivation in different regions but aggregating multi-dimensional poverty masks the high disparity between urban and rural deprivation within each province and across the country. A north-south divide is apparent in both heat maps.

The OPHI MPI analyses a broader range of potential areas of deprivation and gives a much lower level of multi-dimensional poverty than the World Bank due to differences in methodology. Figure 1.13 shows the evolution of different components of multi-dimensional poverty in Kyrgyzstan in 2006, 2012 and 2014 based on the OPHI analysis.

**Figure 1.13. Mortality and malnutrition are the largest drivers of multi-dimensional poverty**

Multi-dimensional poverty contributions

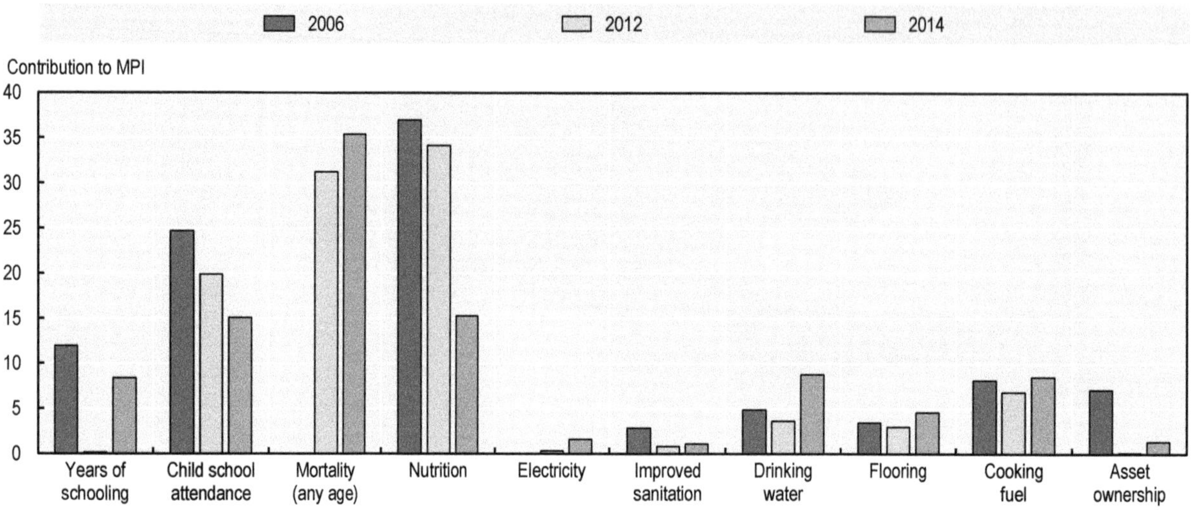


*Source*: OPHI (2016[15]), "Country briefing: Kyrgyz Republic", *Global Multidimensional Poverty Index (MPI) At a Glance*, ophi.org.uk/policy/multidimensional-poverty-index.

Mortality was the largest contributor to multi-dimensional poverty in 2014, overtaking nutrition, which declined significantly between 2012 and 2014. Education deprivations, captured by years of schooling and child school attendance, declined over this timeframe but were the next largest contributors. Lack of access to electricity and drinking water became larger contributors between 2006 and 2014.

Only the populations of Bishkek and Chui Oblast have access to sewage systems. Access to sewage in Osh Oblast decreased in 2014 as Osh City was disaggregated from the Osh Oblast in national statistics. Data from Multiple Indicator Cluster Surveys (MICS) in 2014 showed that only 1.6% of rural households were connected to a sewer system, compared with 43.4% of urban ones.

Overall, broader measures of deprivation improved at a time when the decline in income poverty had stalled. In the case of Bishkek, levels of deprivation are far lower than income poverty, although in many other regions the two measures were closer as of 2012. However, improved access to basic services is not the same as improved quality of these services. Where the quality of assets or services is of a low standard, the outcomes associated with high levels of deprivation might not improve with improved access.

## Maternal mortality and child poverty pose major risks early in the life cycle

A consequence of Kyrgyzstan's high fertility rate and large young population is high demand for services for pregnant women, babies and children. The provision of these services is mixed; although improvements have been made in reducing infant mortality and vaccinating children in rural areas, maternal mortality rates remain very high and vaccinations in urban areas have declined. This variable performance is equally likely to reflect the quantity or the quality of the services in question. Another major concern is that children bear a disproportionately high burden of income poverty.

### *Pre-natal and birth*

Kyrgyzstan's maternal mortality ratio in 2015 was higher than in 2000 (76 and 74 deaths per 100 000 live births respectively) and was the highest in Eastern Europe and Central Asia. The maternal mortality rate is approximately twice the average among the benchmark countries, though it is not the only country within the sample where the rate has stagnated: the rates in 2015 for Georgia and Uzbekistan show little change from 2000 (Figure 1.14).

**Figure 1.14. Maternal mortality is high by regional standards**

Maternal deaths per 100 000 live births in the benchmark countries (2000-15)

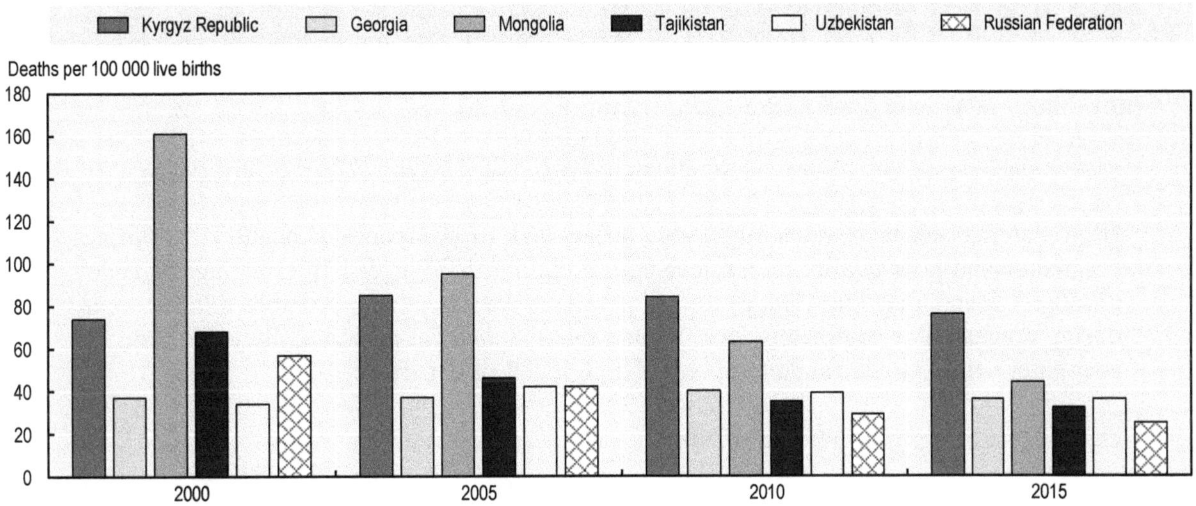


*Source*: WHO/UNICEF/UNFPA/World Bank/United Nations Population Division (2015[16]), "Trends in maternal mortality: 1990 to 2015", available at who.int/reproductivehealth/publications/monitoring/maternal-mortality-2015/en.

The high rate of maternal mortality likely reflects a disparity between access to services and quality of services. This is consistent with Kyrgyzstan's broader inability to maintain the high standards of health provision (in terms of infrastructure, services and personnel) that existed during Soviet times due to a significant reduction in resources.

Supply-side indicators for maternal health services are largely positive. A majority of pregnant women have access to skilled personnel at childbirth (Figure 1.15A). This indicator is above 90% at all income levels, which reflects that births ordinarily happen in maternity wards of district hospitals (Wiegers, Boerma and de Haan, 2010[17]). Moreover, access to ante-natal care has historically been high and has recently improved, especially among low-income groups (Figure 1.15B). However, there is a shortage of staff, even in hospitals, which is partly due to large numbers of doctors leaving public hospitals to join the private sector or to find work abroad. This problem is especially acute for medical facilities in rural areas (Ibraimova A., Akkazieva and Ibraimov, 2011[18]).

**Figure 1.15. Almost all pregnant women have access to maternal health service**

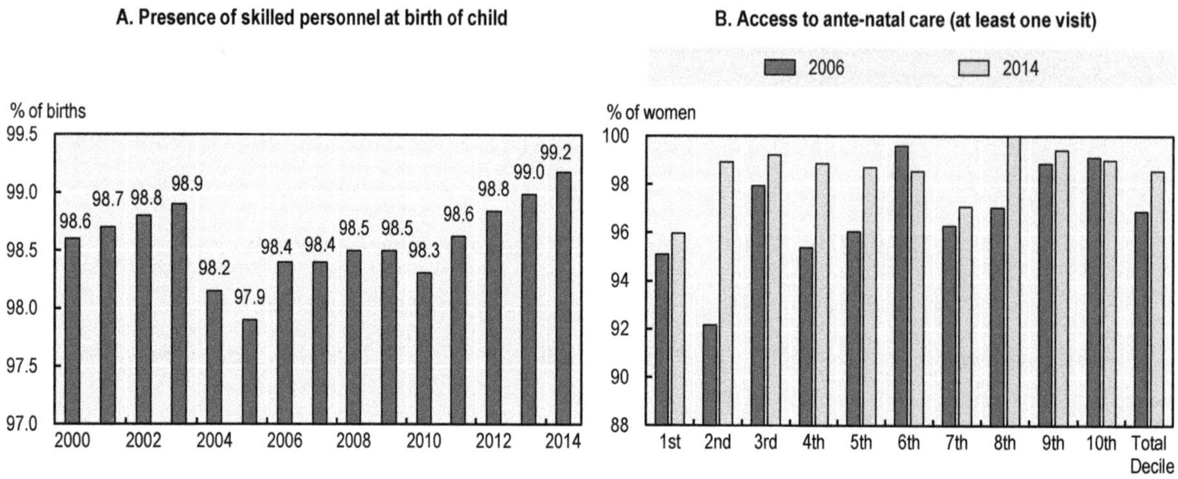


*Source*: Authors' calculations based on NSC (2014[10]), *Kyrgyz Integrated Household Survey* (database).

High maternal mortality rates might also reflect lack of awareness of health risks during pregnancy and poor quality of services before childbirth. Wiegers, Boerma and de Haan (2010[17]) found that knowledge among pregnant women about possible danger signs during pregnancy is completely lacking, and that the medical personnel they are likely to encounter before childbirth do not possess high levels of expertise.

### *Infant mortality and immunisation*

Kyrgyzstan has made good progress in reducing infant and child mortality. The rate of infant mortality more than halved between 2000 and 2015, from 42 to 19 deaths per 1 000 live births (IMHE, 2016[19]). This decline also drove a reduction in the mortality of children under age 5. While total deaths have decreased significantly since 1990, nearly 990 children died of communicable, maternal, neonatal and nutritional diseases in 2013 (Figure 1.16). Diarrhoea, lower respiratory and other common infectious diseases were the second-highest cause of death of children aged 28-365 days.

**Figure 1.16. Infant mortality has declined significantly since 1990**

Number of deaths of children aged 28-365 days, by cause (1990-2013)

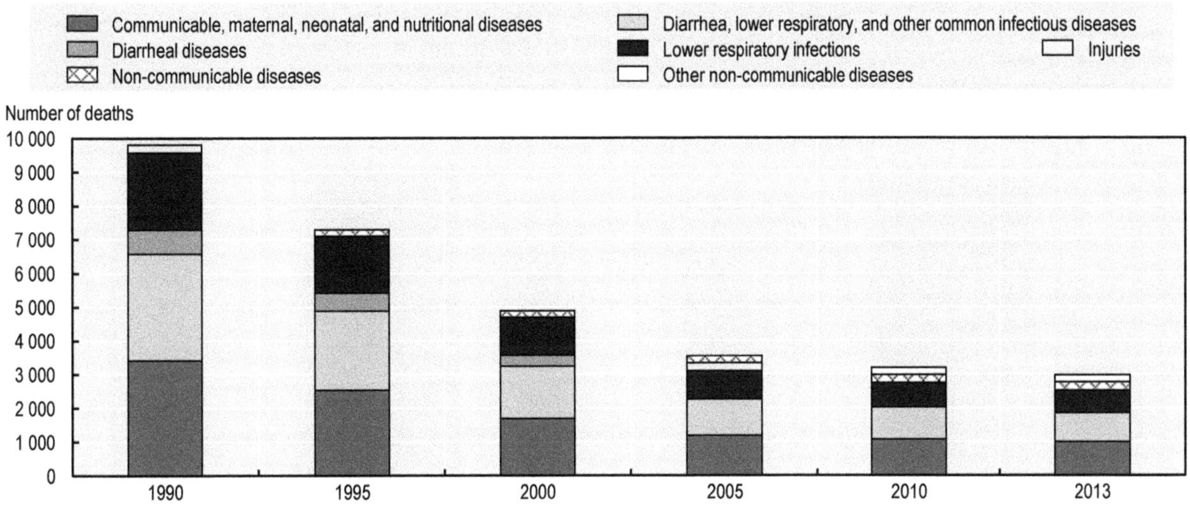


*Source*: IMHE (2016[19]), *Global Burden of Disease 2015* (database).

Official statistics indicate that scheduled immunisation programmes cover 95% of children in Kyrgyzstan.[2] However, independent research indicates that immunisation coverage varies according to the type of vaccine and the region of the country.

Since 1997, urban immunisation rates have declined while the rural immunisation rates have increased for children under age 1. A study found that DTP3 (Diphtheria, Tetanus, and Pertussis) and MCV (Meningococcal Vaccine) vaccinations were more likely to be delayed in Bishkek compared with Issyk-Kul, Jalal-Abad, Talas and Osh (Schweitzer et al., 2015[20]).

The complete immunisation rate for children under age 1 in rural areas increased from 68.5% in 1997 to 86.4% in 2014. This trend appears reversed in urban areas, where only 68.5% had full immunisation coverage in 2013, down from 76.2% in 1997 (Figure 1.17). However, this might partly reflect under-reporting by residents of informal settlements in Bishkek.

**Figure 1.17. Immunisation rates in rural areas have overtaken rates in urban areas**

Full immunisation rate for children under age 1 (1997 & 2014)

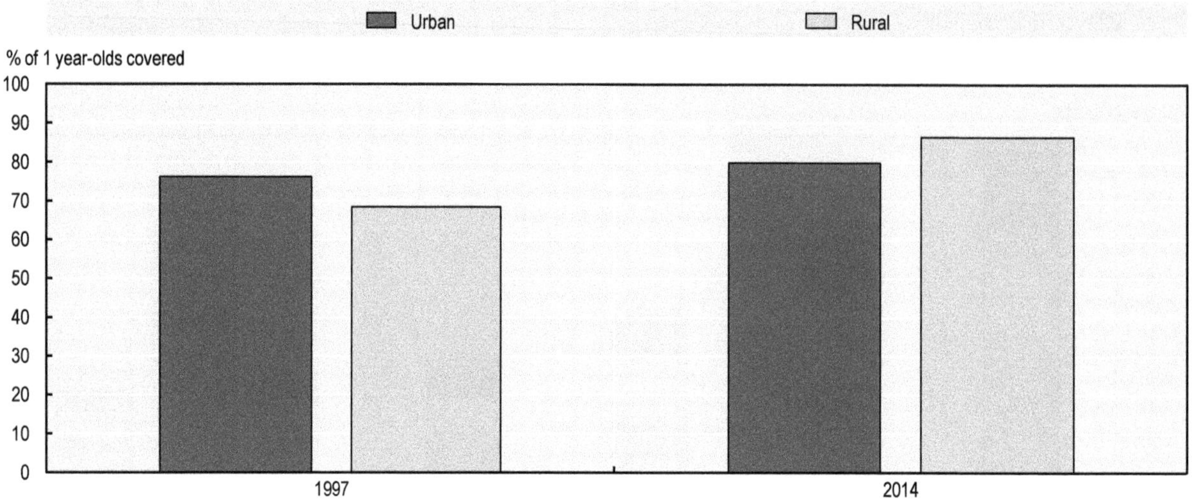


*Note*: The 1997 data are taken from the DHS, while the 2014 data are taken from the MICS.
*Source*: WHO (2016[21]), *Global Health Observatory* (database).

## *Child poverty and nutrition*

The prevalence of child poverty is striking. Disaggregating poverty by age based on data from the 2015 KIHS shows that the poverty rate among those aged six and under was 43.1%, ten percentage points higher than the overall poverty rate. The rate for those aged between six and 15 was 38.2%, also above the overall poverty rate (Figure 1.18). Health and nutrition indicators are also cause for concern.

**Figure 1.18. The burden of poverty is predominantly borne by children**

Poverty by age

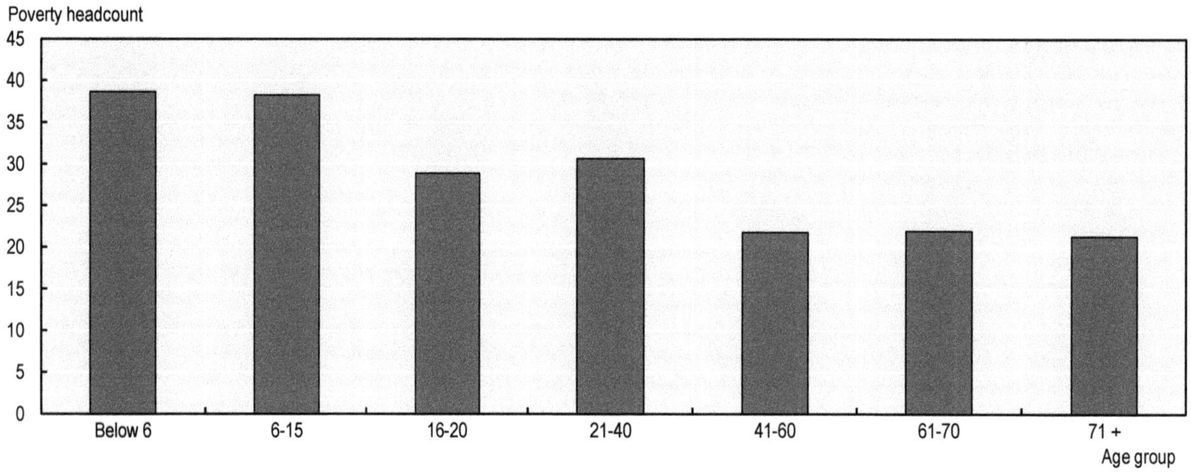


*Source*: NSC (2015[11]), *Kyrgyz Integrated Household Survey* (database).

The rate of stunting, or low height-for-age, is a major concern across the income distribution. According to MICS data, 12.8% of children under age 5 were affected in 2014. Children in the lowest decile were more than twice as likely to be affected, with a stunting rate of 18.9% versus 9.1% in the richest wealth decile but this latter figure is surprisingly high (Figure 1.19A). Although rates decreased nationally between 2006 and 2014, there was a sharp increase in stunting in 2012, possibly as a result of a spike in food prices during that year (Figure 1.19B). The prevalence of stunting, wasting and underweight was higher in rural areas than in urban areas, except in 2012.

**Figure 1.19. Stunting affects children across the income distribution but is more common in rural areas**

Stunting by decile and place of residence (2006, 2012 and 2014)

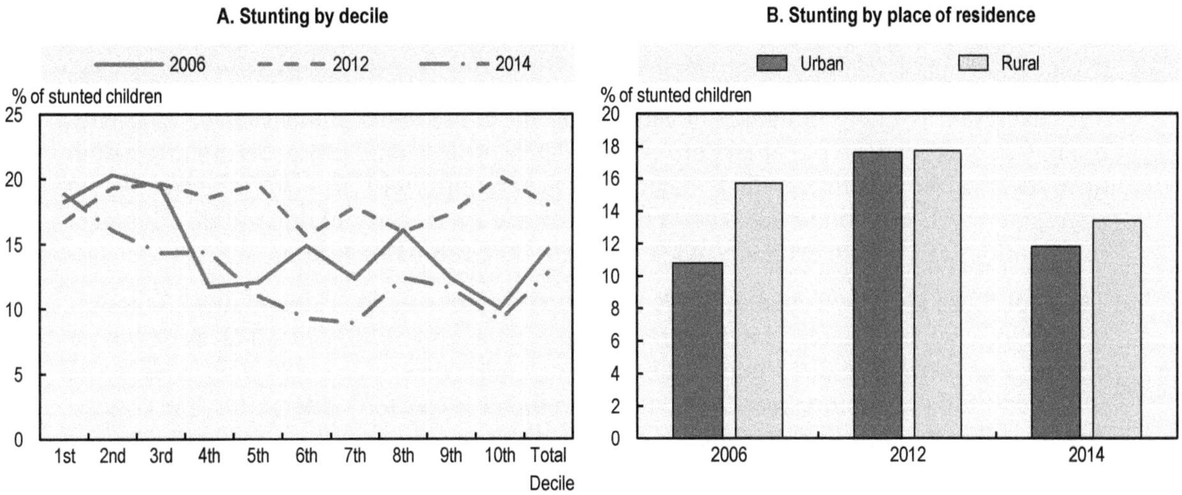


*Source*: Authors' calculations based on NSC (2014[10]), *Kyrgyz Integrated Household Survey* (database).

## Schooling outcomes are uneven

Free access to public primary and secondary school is guaranteed by the Constitution. Compulsory education lasts nine years, from the age of 7 to 15 years old, and enrolment is nearly universal up to age 15. Pre-school and upper secondary enrolment is much lower but increasing for both, although growth varies by region.

High enrolment is not the same as high attendance and high attendance is not the same as good-quality outcomes. As with health services, the education sector has suffered from severe budget cuts since Soviet times, resulting in a deterioration of infrastructure (especially a lack of heating and electricity), as well as a decline in the number of qualified teachers and a lack of learning materials.

### *Pre-school*

Pre-school enrolment fell dramatically with the collapse of the USSR but has partially recovered since the early 2000s. Between 1990 and 1995, the number of pre-school institutions fell from 1 696 to 456 and enrolment dropped from 33.9% to 9.3%. The situation has improved since the early 2000s, particularly since 2010 (Figure 1.20B).

Starting in 2013, the Ministry of Education and Science (MoES) made a major effort to revive preschool education. This involved privatising preschools, simplifying licensing procedures, exempting pre-school education from value-added tax (VAT), providing government buildings to build kindergartens and, most significantly, opening community kindergartens.

These initiatives led to the opening of nearly 500 new kindergartens since 2013. Enrolment has continued to climb as a result, reaching 25.3% in 2014. However, there are significant regional disparities between rural and urban enrolment (Figure 1.20A). In 2014, only 13.5% of children in rural areas had access to pre-school, versus 39.2% in urban areas.

This means that the vast majority of rural children are missing out on the significant benefits in terms of their cognitive development associated with early access to education (Carneiro and Heckman, 2003[22]). It also means that most of the children who receive the poverty-targeted MBPF, more than 90% of whom live in rural areas, are likely to be excluded from pre-school institutions.

This exclusion is likely to impact negatively on these individuals' educational outcomes relative to children who did attend pre-school. Their professional prospects are affected in turn, raising the likelihood that successive generations will live in poverty. At an aggregate level, promoting access to pre-school and other early childhood development interventions can lead to economy-wide productivity gains in the future.

The MoES has also developed multiple catch-up programmes for children aged 3 months to 2 years unable to access kindergarten. These were established in 2013 as 100-hour courses and evolved in 2015 into 240-hour, six-month courses or a 480-hour course that serves as a full preparatory year. Although not a replacement for kindergarten, the courses provide support to nearly all children not enrolled.

**Figure 1.20. Pre-school provision is recovering but remains very low in rural areas**

Gross pre-school enrolment rate, by place of residence, and total enrolment and number of institutions

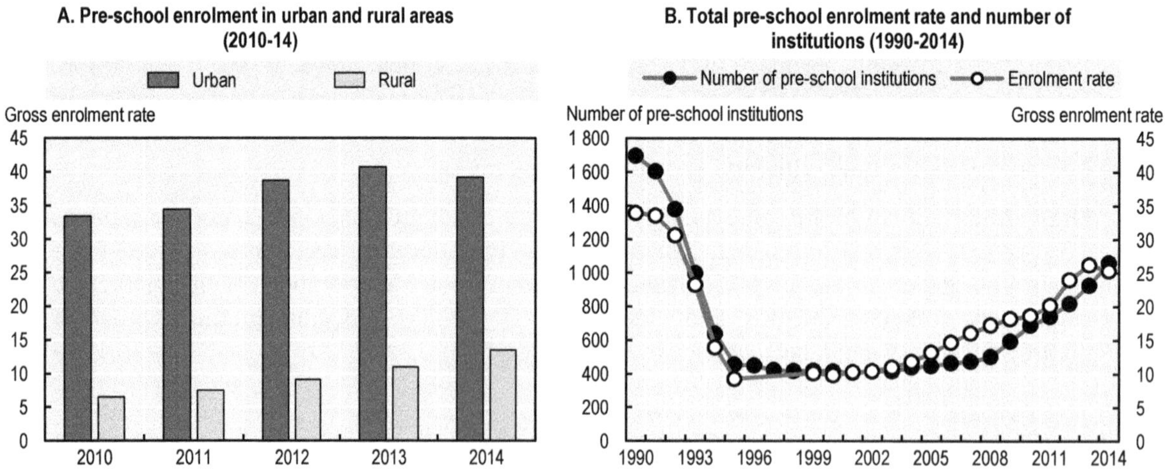


*Note*: Showing rate values for the beginning of the year.

*Source*: Authors' calculations based on NSC (2014[10]), *Kyrgyz Integrated Household Survey* (database), and UNESCO (2016[23]), *UNESCO Institute for Statistics* (database).

### *Primary and secondary school*

Gross enrolment is very high in Kyrgyzstan for the compulsory four years of primary (100%) and five years of lower secondary education (95%) (Figures 1.21A and 1.21B). There is very little difference in enrolment between boys and girls. Urban enrolment exceeds 100% due to the enrolment of children not registered with local authorities (typically because they migrated from elsewhere in the country).

**Figure 1.21. Enrolment in primary and lower secondary school is close to universal**

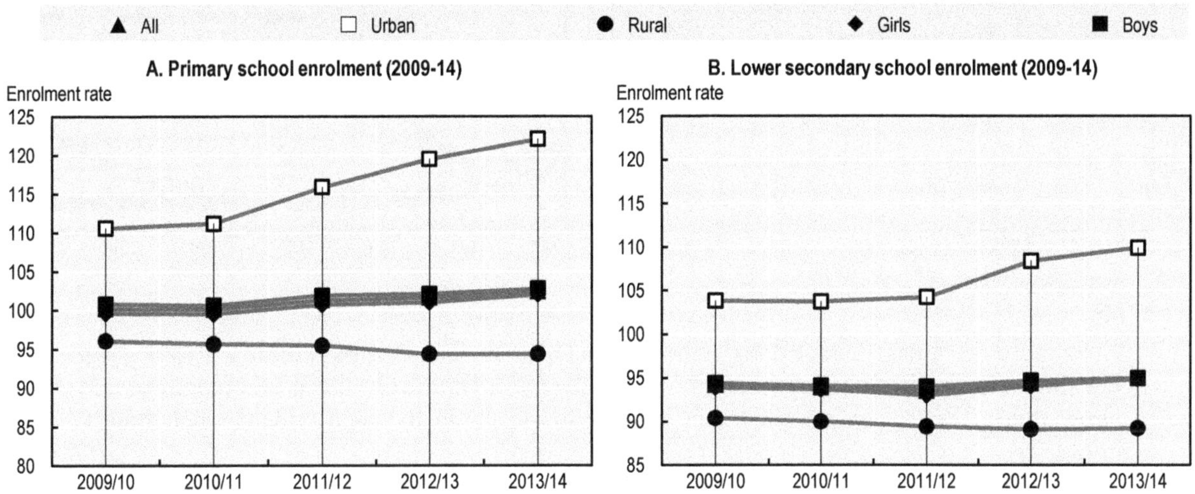


*Source*: Authors' calculations based on NSC (2014[10]), *Kyrgyz Integrated Household Survey* (database), and UNESCO (2016[23]), *UNESCO Institute for Statistics* (database).

Upper secondary school enrolment is substantially lower, at around 53%. In urban areas, enrolment rose from 47% in 2009/10 to 59% in 2013/14 (Figure 1.22A), while in rural areas, it is declining. Girls are more likely to be enrolled than boys. Students who complete lower secondary can continue their studies in initial and intermediate professional education institutions rather than attend upper secondary school. However, most of the growth in enrolment at such institutions has occurred at the higher professional level, which is not an alternative to secondary school (Figure 1.22B).

**Figure 1.22. Upper secondary enrolment is rising among urban youths**

Upper secondary enrolment and professional education

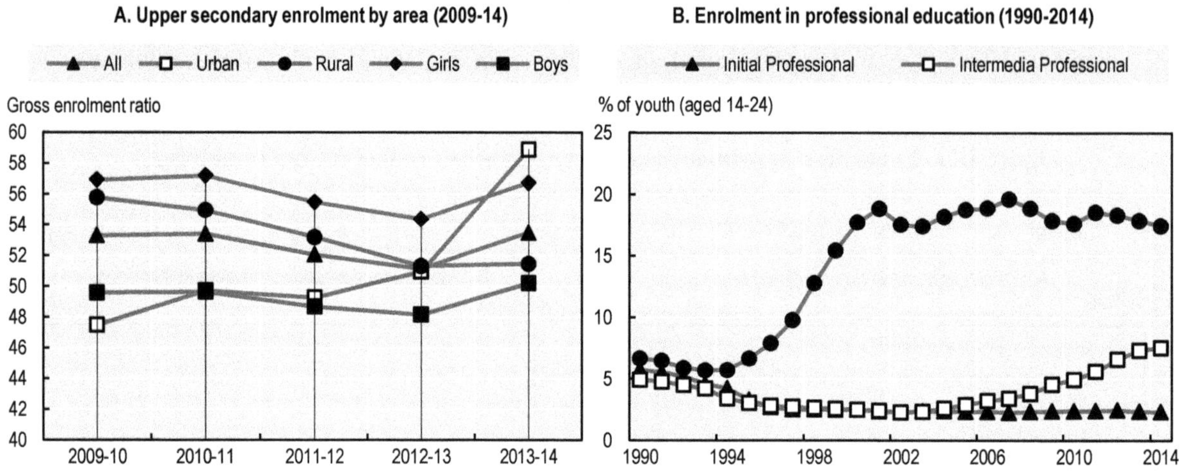


*Source*: NSC (2015[11]), *Kyrgyz Integrated Household Survey* (database).

Enrolment in tertiary education, stood at 51.1% in 2014, only slightly lower than enrolment in upper secondary school (ADB, 2015[24]). Data from the WDIs (Figure 1.23) show that gross tertiary enrolment in Kyrgyzstan ranks in the middle of the benchmark countries.

**Figure 1.23. Enrolment in tertiary education is in line with the regional average**

Gross enrolment in tertiary education in the benchmark countries (2015)

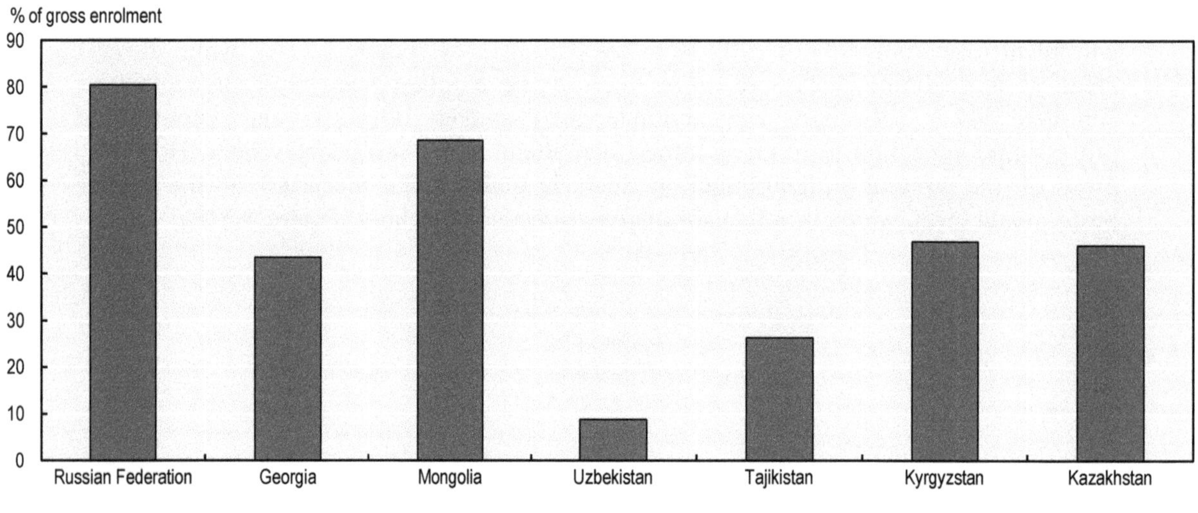


*Source*: World Bank (2017[7]), *World Development Indicators* (database), available at data.worldbank.org/products/wdi, accessed (10 January 2018).

Although school attendance is also high, there are discrepancies between boys and girls and between locations. The overall attendance rate is higher in rural areas than urban areas for primary, lower secondary and upper secondary school. In rural areas, girls are more likely than boys to attend lower secondary and upper secondary school, while in urban areas the opposite is true (UNICEF, 2013[25]).

Attendance is not the same as receiving a quality education. While public spending on education has risen in recent years, there are major systemic problems, including teacher shortages, the low quality of teacher training, outdated curricula and shortages of teaching materials. Learning outcomes are suffering as a consequence: Kyrgyzstan was ranked last in maths, science and reading among nations that participated in the 2006 and 2009 rounds of the Program for International Student Assessment (PISA), (OECD, 2010[26]). The National Sample-Based Achievement Test showed similar results (Hou, 2011[27]).

The result is that many school leavers lack basic skills when they enter the labour market (UNICEF, 2013). This in turn leads to a skills mismatch in the economy that constrains productivity. PISA evaluations also show that urban students tend to perform better at school even after accounting for socio-economic characteristics; the performance gap between rural and urban students is estimated at 80 points, which is equivalent to two years of schooling (OECD, 2010[26]).

### *Child employment*

Child labour is widespread in Kyrgyzstan, although numbers have decreased in recent years. The majority of children in employment also attend school and not all child employment constitutes child labour: forms of employment that pose no physical, mental or developmental harm and that do not deprive children of educational opportunities, are admissible under Kyrgyz labour law.

According to the 2007 Child Labour Force Survey, 672 000 children aged 5-17 were in some form of employment, representing 45.8% that age group and 21.9% of working individuals (ILO, 2008[28]). Labour participation rises with age: 32.6% of children aged 5-11 are in some form of employment compared with 62.3% of those aged 15-17. The overwhelming majority (95%) were employed in agriculture and produce for home consumption. By 2014/15, the number of employed children had fallen to 414 246, or 39.0% of the total population aged 5-17 (ILO, 2016[29]).

An increase in hazardous labour accompanied this drop in employment: the percentage of children working in dangerous jobs rose from 12.5% to 18.6% between 2007 and 2014. An additional 9.3% of children worked in non-acceptable forms of labour, meaning they were not at risk of physical harm but worked an excessive number of hours and/or did not attend school. Children in poor households, particularly those with low parental education levels, are at greatest risk of child labour (ILO/NSC, 2016[30]).

## Transition from school to work is especially hard for women

Approximately 15.4% of the entire youth population (aged 15-29) was not in education, employment or training (NEET) in 2013. The rate is much higher for females than for males: 22.7% of young women were classified NEET in 2013, versus 7.5% of young men. Figure 1.24 disaggregates NEET into inactivity and unemployment. Inactivity is a greater challenge than unemployment, especially among young women. In total, 13.5% of youth were inactive.

**Figure 1.24. Young women are more likely to be NEET**

Share of total youth population (aged 15-29) not in employment, education, or training by gender (2013)

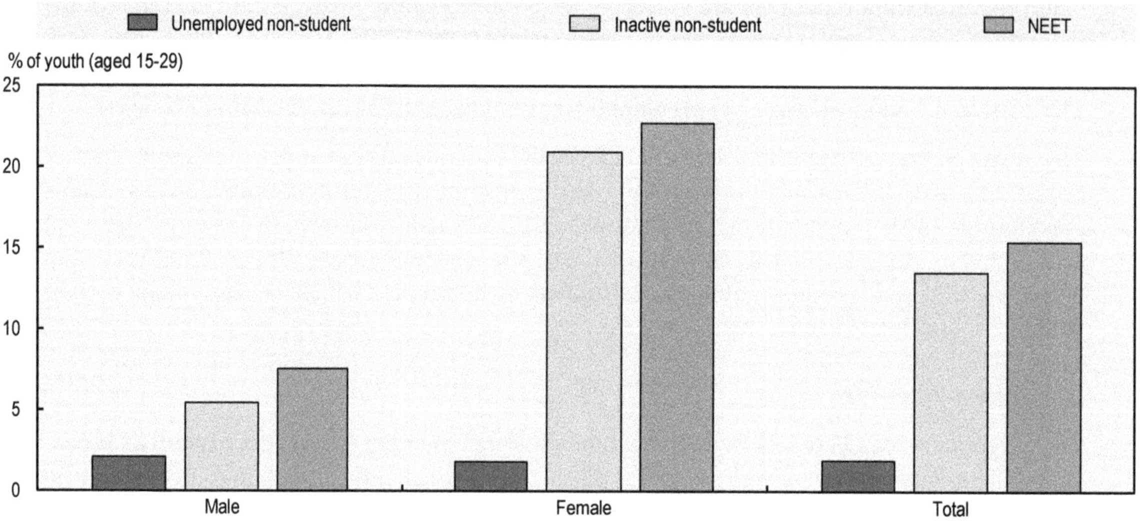


*Source*: ILO (2013[31]), *School-to-Work Transition Survey: Kyrgyzstan (2013)* (database), available at ilo.org/employment/areas/WCMS_234860.

In 2014, 12% of youth classified as economically active were unemployed, down from 14% in 2009. Unemployment varied by age, place of residence and education (Figures 1.24A and 1.24B). The unemployment rate is highest among urban youth aged 15-19 with only secondary education. Unemployment among tertiary graduates is above the average youth unemployment rate, likely reflecting the reduced quality of higher education and an oversupply in certain occupations, such as economists and lawyers. Lack of economic opportunities for youth is an important driver of emigration.

**Figure 1.25. Youth unemployment is highest in urban areas**

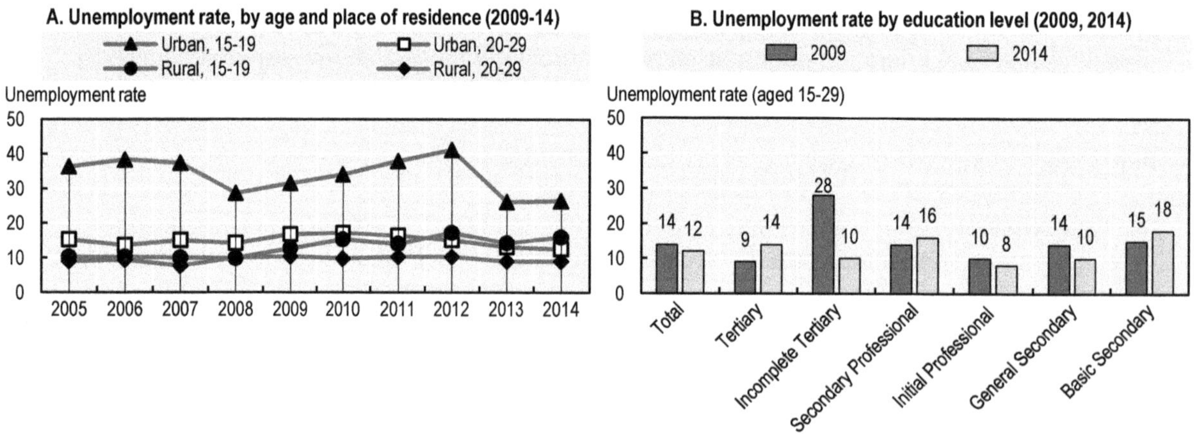


*Note*: Figure 1.24A shows the percentage of economically active population of the relevant age cohort.
*Source*: NSC (2014[10]), *Kyrgyz Integrated Household Survey* (database).

**Box 1.2. Under-age pregnancy is on the rise**

Childbirth among under-age women has increased steadily since 2000 and is rising particularly rapidly among urban women (Figure 1.26). Early maternity is a social phenomenon with historical, religious, ethnic and social roots. It is also driven by arranged marriages at early ages, bride-napping and polygamy.

**Figure 1.26. Teenage pregnancies are more common in urban areas**

Birth rate among girls aged 15-17 years, by area of residence

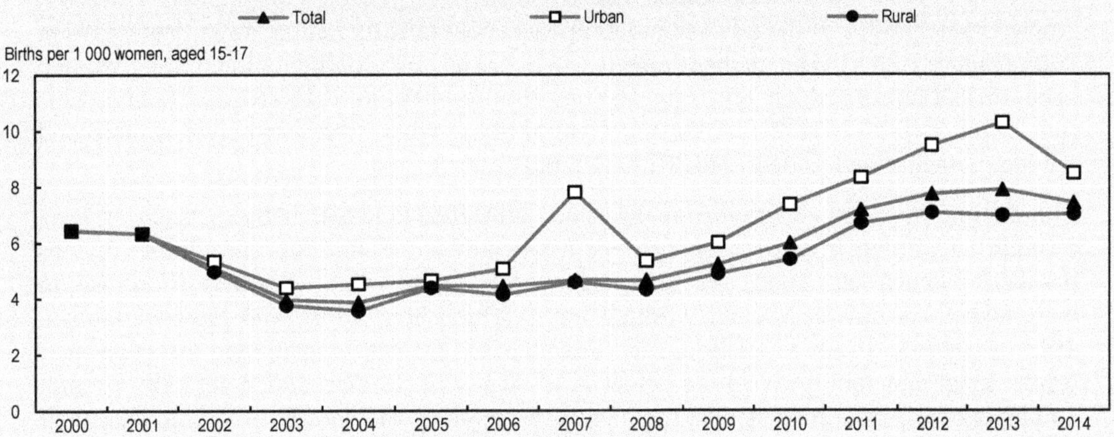


*Source*: NSC (2015[32]).

Unmet need for contraception among young, married women in the country is another likely factor behind these high rates, exacerbated by the high prevalence of early marriage and bride-napping. In 2012, unmet need affected 18% of married women aged 15-49 (Figure 1.27), the second highest rate among the benchmark countries after Tajikistan (NSC/MoH/ICF International, 2013[33]).

**Figure 1.27. Unmet need for contraception is high by regional standards**

Unmet need for contraception amongst married women aged 15-49

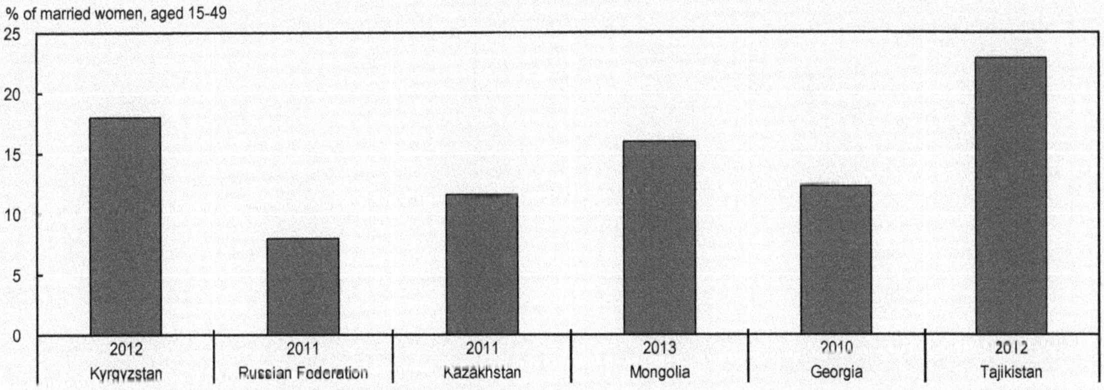


*Note*: No data was available for Uzbekistan.

*Source*: World Bank (2017[7]), *World Development Indicators* (database), available at data.worldbank.org/products/wdi.

Unmet need likely contributes to the high maternal mortality rate and worsening labour market outcomes. Evidence from 144 countries shows that risk of death from pregnancy is nearly one third higher for women aged 15-19 than those aged 20-24 (Nove et al., 2014[34]). Moreover, giving birth at an early age has been shown to negatively affect women's future wages.

## Working lives are characterised by unemployment, informality and migration

Individuals aged 30-60 accounted for 67% of Kyrgyzstan's population in 2014. Approximately 80% of the adult population was economically active, down from 84% in 2005 (Figure 1.28A). The decline reflects lower labour force participation among women aged 15 and above, which fell from 56% in 2000 to 49% in 2015 (Figure 1.28B). This runs counter to elsewhere in East and Central Asia, where the gap between male and female participation has decreased (ILO, 2016[35]).

The decline in female participation has been attributed to legal barriers, such as laws prohibiting women from performing certain types of work, limiting the number of jobs pregnant women can hold and allowing women with young children to refuse to undertake tasks outside normal working hours (Dubashov, Kruse and Ismailakhunova, 2015[36]). While these regulations are intended to protect women and balance their professional and family lives, the effect is to segregate women and potentially prompt employers to discriminate against them amid perceptions they are less flexible than their male counterparts. The pay gap between men and women stood at 29% in 2014, up from 22% in 2011 but below an average of 35% between 2000 and 2010 (NSC, 2014[10]).

**Figure 1.28. Female labour force participation has declined significantly**

Labour force participation

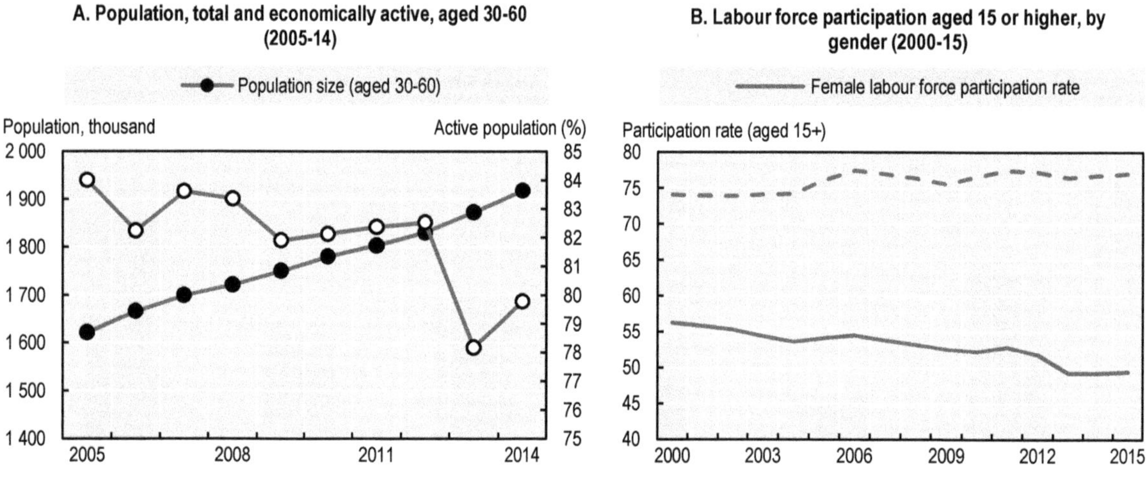


*Source*: NSC (2017[37]), "Economically active and inactive population"; ILO (2016[35]), *Key Indicators of the Labour Market, 9th edition* (database).

### *Unemployment*

The unemployment rate increased during the first decade of the 2000s. Despite sustained and relatively robust economic growth, the economy was not able to accommodate rapid growth in the supply of labour even though migration mitigated this growth to a certain extent (ADB, 2014[38]). Although unemployment declined after 2010, the rate was higher in 2014 (8.2%) than in 2004 (7.5%) (Figure 1.28A).

Unemployment is especially prevalent among lower consumption deciles: 3% of individuals in the top decile were unemployed in 2014 compared with 12% of those in the lowest decile. The discrepancy widened between 2004 and 2014. Between 2005 and 2014, unemployment among women was, on average, 1.5 percentage points higher than among men. In addition to the unemployed, approximately 20% of the workforce is employed for less time than desired: "time underemployment" is most pronounced among workers aged 25-34 (Figure 1.28B).

**Figure 1.29. Unemployment is higher than in 2004**

Unemployment and underemployment

**A. Unemployment by decile (2004, 2010, 2014)**

**B. Time underemployment by decile (2004, 2014)**

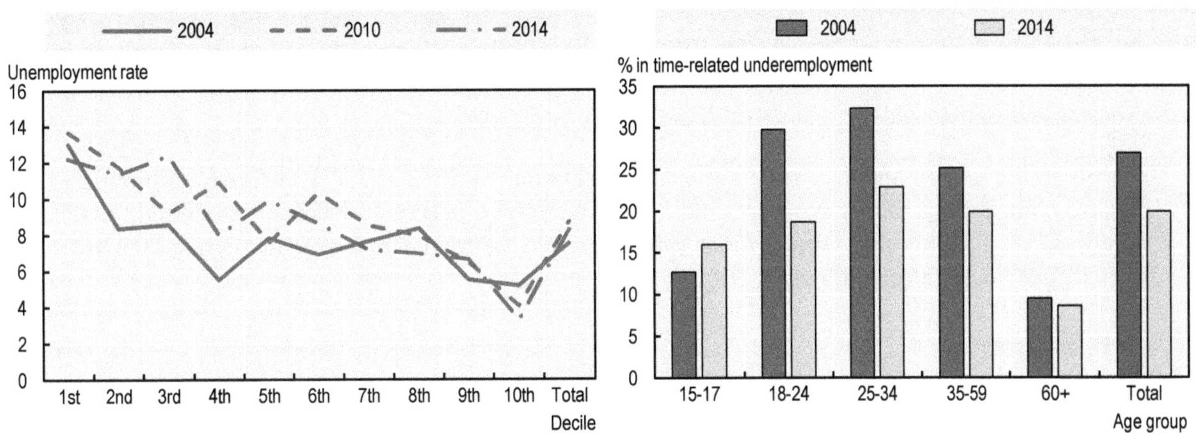


*Source*: NSC (2014[10]), *Kyrgyz Integrated Household Survey* (database).

In 2015, 25.9% of workers earned low pay, defined as less than two thirds the median hourly wage (Figure 1.29A). Although the rate of low pay earners has decreased by four percentage points since 2004, the labour market remains characterised by low-paying jobs that result in insufficient household income and contribute directly to poverty. In 2016, the minimum wage was KGS 1 060 per month, which was 41% of the poverty line in the same year (KGS 2 596 per month) and significantly lower than the average wage (KGS 14 847 per month).

A high proportion of individuals work excessive hours. According to 2014 KIHS data, 45.8% of workers aged 25-34 and 43.8% of those aged 35-59 worked more than 40 hours per week in 2014 (Figure 1.29B), the limit imposed by Kyrgyz labour law. The share working excessive hours has increased by 9.3 percentage points since 2004. Long working hours pose a health risk in the short term (as workers are more likely to suffer occupational injuries) and can increase the likelihood of major illnesses and disabilities in the long term (Dembe et al., 2005[39]). According to the Life in Kyrgyzstan Study, 21.2% of workers said their jobs exposed them to health risks, and 19.0% said they had to work at night.

**Figure 1.30. Low pay and long hours are widespread**

Low wages, by decile, and excessive work hours, by age

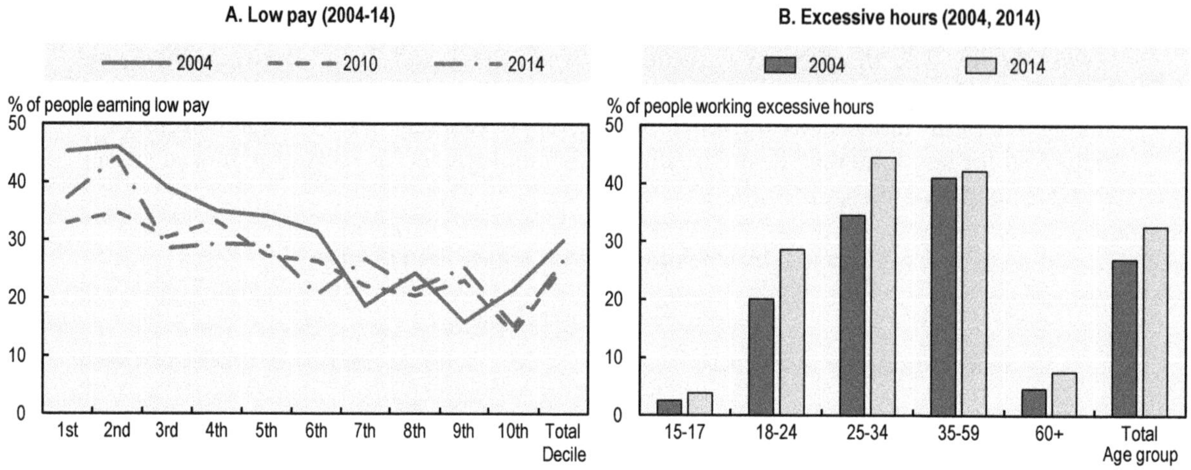


*Source*: NSC (2014[10]), *Kyrgyz Integrated Household Survey* (database).

Vulnerable employment is very high in Kyrgyzstan. In 2013, 12.7% of those employed were contributing family workers, and 28.9% were own-account workers. Combined, this represents a vulnerable employment rate of 41.6% of total employment, higher than in 2010 but lower than in the early 2000s.

## *Informality*

The informal sector is growing rapidly; it accounted for 71.8% of total employment in 2014, up from 60.2% in 2002 (Figure 1.31A). The rate is higher among men than women and higher in rural areas than in urban areas (Figure 1.31B).

**Figure 1.31. Informal employment is prevalent across different groups and rising**

Growth and profile of informal sector workers

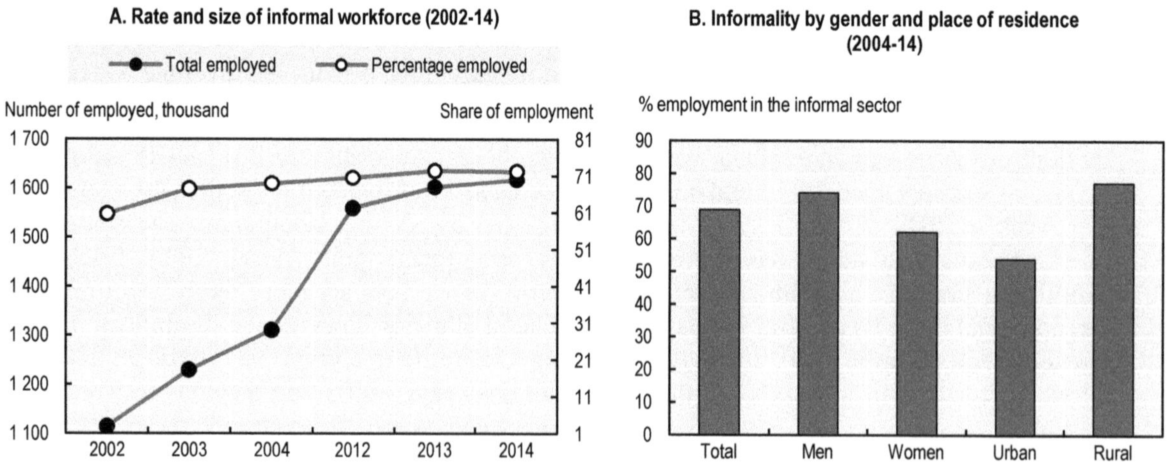


*Source*: NSC (2014[10]), *Kyrgyz Integrated Household Survey* (database).

Kyrgyzstan defines the informal sector as non-criminal, profit-yielding economic activities concealed to avoid taxation and/or social security contributions. The NSC considers workers informally employed if they work in enterprises not registered as legal entities. Agriculture accounted for 45.3% of informal employment in 2014, followed by trade (18.7%), construction (12.7%), transport (6.9%), manufacturing (5.9%), and hotels and restaurants (3.7%) (NSC, 2015[40]).

Social insurance contributions are an important driver of informality. According to an evaluation of the informal economy by the National Institute for Strategic Studies, 26.8% of entrepreneurs and 50.8% of entities cited contributions to the Social Fund and income tax payments as reasons for informal activities. Some 26.8% of individual entrepreneurs and 28.6% of firms chose informality to avoid providing social guarantees to workers, while 73.2% of entrepreneurs and 55.6% of legal entities cited the complexity of recruitment and dismissal procedures (NISS, 2014[41]).

Internationally, there is often extensive heterogeneity among informal workers, in terms of skills, income and vulnerability. There can also be important differences in how informality affects men and women. Moreover, households with a mix of formal and informal workers often experience different risks than those with all informal workers (OECD/ILO, 2018[42]).

### *Migration*

External migration plays a key role in the economy. Aside from the important contribution of remittances, emigration has reduced the supply of domestic labour, thereby keeping a lid on unemployment and putting upward pressure on wages. However, there are also profound costs to migrants, their families and society as a whole.

There was rapid growth in the number of Kyrgyzstan workers moving to Russia and Kazakhstan during the first decade of this century. This migration is expected to continue, thanks to Kyrgyzstan's accession to the Eurasian Economic Union (EEU) and Russia's shrinking labour force. Estimates indicate between 15% and 20% of Kyrgyzstan's population is currently working abroad (Vinokuriv, 2013[43]). Some 90% of Kyrgyzstan's migrants go to Russia and almost all the rest to Kazakhstan.

Kyrgyzstan migrants are attracted by the guarantee of work and higher wages abroad. By way of comparison, the average Kyrgyzstan wage was 74% of the Russian average in 1990 but fell to 20% by 2010. It recovered to 37% in 2015 due to a sharp fall in the value of the ruble (Denisenko, 2016[44]). The average wage in Kazakhstan was on a par with the Russian average in 2015, up from 80% in 2007.

Younger workers from small families are most likely to emigrate. The average age of Kyrgyzstan workers abroad is 29, and they most likely come from southern regions, where low economic development is a strong push factor. Some 43% of workers who emigrated to Russia received some post-secondary education, although not all graduated. Less than 6% of migrants intend to live in Russia on a permanent basis, but 44% see themselves working there for an extended period (Vinokuriv, 2013[43]), which limits their ability to contribute to the Kyrgyz social insurance system.

The benefits of these emigration patterns for the Kyrgyz economy are substantial. According to World Bank calculations, remittances equated to 34.5% of GDP in 2016, the highest level in the world as a proportion of the overall economy (World Bank, 2017[45]). Although remittances are primarily used for consumption, there is also evidence they are used to finance investment in small businesses. Additional benefits accrue to the

Kyrgyz economy when migrants return home with the money, know-how and networks to set up businesses.

However, there are also extensive costs to emigration. The legal rights of Kyrgyzstan migrants to Russia and Kazakhstan are not always respected, and they confront challenges in assimilating into Russian society, as well as accessing accommodation and utilities. Kyrgyzstan's accession to the EEU in August 2015 has simplified certain administrative procedures for migrants to Russia, but such workers are still not entitled to the same rights as Russian workers.

Access to social protection is a major concern for migrant workers. Although a treaty on pension coverage for migrant workers in EEU member states is currently under discussion, Kyrgyzstan workers are currently unable to access social protection programmes either in their own country or abroad. This renders migrants and their families vulnerable to an income shock and places them at high risk of poverty in old age. It also threatens the sustainability of Kyrgyzstan's pay-as-you-go pension arrangement, which is currently experiencing financing challenges due to the low proportion of the current workforce making contributions (discussed later in the report).

Meanwhile, large-scale emigration is associated with various social problems at home, including growing demographic disparities among regions and family breakdowns. It is also associated with social orphanhood (children with one or both living parents who are unable or unwilling to care for them), which is driving continued demand for residential institutions (discussed in Chapter 2).

Internal migration is also an important phenomenon in Kyrgyzstan, reflecting the country's uneven economic development. Changes in the structure of the economy have caused (and continue to cause) significant movement of people between urban areas and between rural and urban areas. Yet this process is not administratively straightforward: internal migrants need an official permit to settle in a new municipality. Individuals without a permit cannot apply for local services, including social protection.

## Kyrgyzstan faces a double disease burden

Kyrgyzstan suffers from a double burden of disease. Infectious diseases, such as tuberculosis (TB) and (increasingly) HIV/AIDS, are a persistent problem, but non-communicable diseases have become an even greater challenge. Demand for health services and the profile of disability are changing to reflect these burdens.

Table 1.1 indicates the main health challenges facing Kyrgyzstan. Disability-Adjusted Life Years (DALYs), a linear sum of potential years of healthy life lost due to premature mortality and disability, for most conditions rose between 1990 and 2005 but fell thereafter. Cardiovascular diseases are the largest contributor to years of healthy life lost: 11 105 per 100 000 in 2013, up from 10 210 in 1990 but down from 12 363 in 2005. HIV is a growing concern, with a 54% increase in DALY rates between 2005 and 2013, although the absolute number remains low. The burden of infectious diseases, maternal disorders, nutritional deficiencies and neonatal diseases has dropped since 1990.

Cardiovascular diseases are the leading cause of death for individuals of working age and account for 33% of all deaths (NSC, 2015[11]). Cancer accounts for 11%, while trauma, poisoning and other external factors account for 9%. Respiratory diseases account for 6% of deaths, the most common being TB. Over 70% of individuals who die from TB are men; 90% of men affected are of working age.

**Table 1.1. Cardiovascular diseases are the principal health threat**

Changes in principal causes of losses of Disability-Adjusted Life Years in the Kyrgyzstan population (1990-2013)

| | Age-standardised DALY rates (per 100 000) | | | | |
|---|---|---|---|---|---|
| | 1990 | 2005 | 2013 | Change (%) 1990-2005 | Change (%) 2005-13 |
| All causes | 46 214 | 43 121 | 38 214 | -6.7 | -11.3 |
| Cardiovascular diseases | 10 210 | 12 363 | 11 105 | 21.6 | -10.1 |
| Neoplasms | 3 666 | 2 999 | 2 823 | -18.5 | -5.7 |
| Mental and substance use disorders | 2 501 | 2 790 | 2 668 | 12 | -4.4 |
| Other non-communicable diseases | 2 561 | 2 547 | 2 396 | -0.3 | -6 |
| Neonatal disorders | 3 178 | 2 742 | 2 309 | -13.6 | -15.9 |
| Diarrhoea lower respiratory and other common infectious diseases | 7 644 | 3 099 | 2 076 | -59.5 | -33 |
| Diabetes urogenital blood and endocrine diseases | 1 693 | 2 179 | 2 048 | 29.8 | -6.2 |
| Musculoskeletal disorders | 1 870 | 1 912 | 1 930 | 2.1 | 1 |
| Cirrhosis | 928 | 1 975 | 1 789 | 112.6 | -9.3 |
| Chronic respiratory diseases | 2 494 | 2 227 | 1 760 | -12.9 | -21.3 |
| Unintentional injuries | 2 859 | 2 005 | 1 678 | -31.6 | -16.6 |
| Neurological disorders | 1 466 | 1 585 | 1 550 | 8.1 | -2.3 |
| Transport injuries | 1 514 | 1 165 | 1 040 | -23.1 | -10.7 |
| Self-harm and interpersonal violence | 1 278 | 1 065 | 942 | -21 | -12.3 |
| Tuberculosis | 457 | 857 | 592 | 105.2 | -30.9 |
| Nutritional deficiencies | 667 | 542 | 526 | -18.4 | -3.4 |
| Digestive diseases | 517 | 456 | 387 | -13.5 | -15.1 |
| HIV/AIDS | 17 | 154 | 237 | 1 064.2 | 54.0 |
| Neglected tropical diseases and malaria | 146 | 100 | 91 | -30.7 | -8.9 |
| Maternal disorders | 112 | 79 | 66 | -29.2 | -17.3 |

*Source*: IHME (2016[19]), *Global Burden of Disease* (database).

The prevalence of diabetes has risen steadily since the early 2000s and was nearly twice as high in 2014 as in 1990 (WHO, 2016[46]). The rapid growth in new cases is likely a result of improved diagnosis. The prevalence of HIV/AIDS among individuals aged 15-49 increased from 0.1% to 0.3% between 2007 and 2014. Accompanying this rise was an increase in antiretroviral therapy (ART) coverage: only 1% of HIV/AIDS cases had access to treatment in 2006, but this share has risen steadily in the last decade to 19% of people living with the disease receiving ART in 2014.

Inequalities in health outcomes exist but are not highly significant. Hypertension among the poorest three quintiles is 7.3% on average, versus 6.5% for the richest two quintiles. The prevalence of diarrhoea episodes among children under age 5 is 5.5% for the poorest three quintiles and 4.5% for the richest two quintiles (NSC/MoH/ICF International, 2013[33]).

Health care is not equally accessible to all segments of the population. The KIHS shows that 2.3 million individuals (58% of whom were women) required medical assistance during 2015. Those reporting they needed medical assistance were not distributed evenly: 49% of individuals in the highest decile said they required medical help during the year compared with only 28% of those in the lowest decile (Figure 1.32). It is widely known that self-reported need for health care leads to underestimations of health status by the poorest population groups and thus does not reflect inequalities in health outcomes but more likely the history of use of health services for diagnosis and treatment (WHO, 2000[47]).

**Figure 1.32. Individuals at lower income levels tend not to seek medical assistance**

Distribution of individuals reporting need for medical assistance (2014)

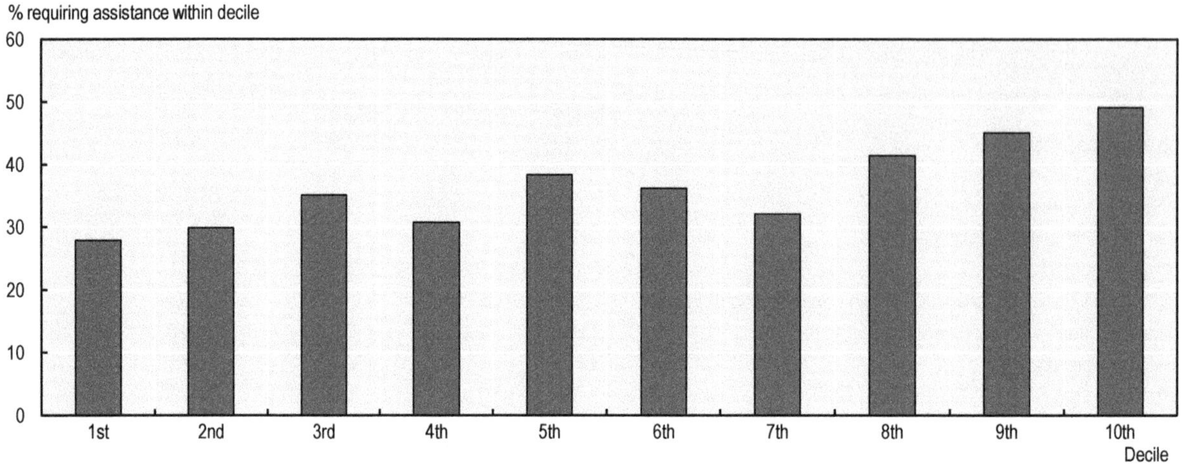


*Source*: NSC (2014[10]), *Kyrgyz Integrated Household Survey* (database).

Inpatient care has decreased rapidly since the dissolution of the Soviet Union. Inpatient care discharges fell from a peak of 25.8 per 100 people in 1988 to 14.1 in 2015. The drop reflects the policy objective of shifting provision of care away from hospitals towards family medicine-based primary health services. Such services are receiving increased government funding as part of a restructuring of the health sector (Ibraimova A., Akkazieva and Ibraimov, 2011[18]). However, with challenges in retaining health workers in rural areas, this policy move towards primary care has not ensured equity in access (Ibraimova A., Akkazieva and Ibraimov, 2011[18]).

## Disability rates are moderating

According to the 2015 KIHS, 0.9% of the total population lives with some disability. Poverty is more prevalent among households that include people with disabilities. While 21.9% of households were below the consumption poverty line in 2014, the rate was 26.9% of households with at least one member with a disability. Individuals with disabilities face great difficulty in finding employment: 2.3% were in some form of employment, with the majority registered as pensioners.

Between 2005 and 2012, the number of registered children under age 18 with disabilities rose from 18 519 to 25 346, a 36.9% increase. Possible explanations include poor health among children and improved reporting, which might be encouraged by improved access to social protection or higher benefits.

Health care comes at a considerable cost to those with disabilities. To pay for treatment, 5 080 individuals borrowed money, 23 120 used savings, and 11 135 received help from relatives (NSC, 2015[11]). All individuals with a disability are eligible for some form of social protection, either through social assistance, compensations for privileges or contributory social insurance. However, there are numerous types of benefit with considerably different values. Moreover, the process of applying for the different benefits can lack transparency (discussed in Chapter 3).

Despite the rising need for education facilities adapted to children with disabilities, a majority still attend regular facilities. In 2012, 2 350 children with disabilities were enrolled in regular pre-school while only 1 674 attended special facilities for this age-group. The disparity grows for school-age children: 2 477 children attended boarding schools specialised for disability care, while 9 945 children with disabilities were registered at regular schools (UNICEF, 2012[48]).

## Old-age poverty is low thanks to the pension system

The contributory pension system acts as a crucial buffer against poverty. As discussed in Chapters 2 and 3, pension coverage among the current elderly population is nearly universal – a legacy of near-full employment before the collapse of the USSR. The average pension benefit in 2014 was KGS 4 710 per month, equivalent to 106% of the subsistence minimum calculated for pensioners, almost twice the overall poverty line (KGS 2 485 in 2014) and more than triple the EPL (KGS 1 466).

However, this average masks significant variations in incomes among the elderly. Pension levels are much lower for those who did not belong to the Social Fund throughout their careers or whose contribution rates were very low. Workers who did not contribute to the Social Fund at all are entitled to a very low monthly income from the MSB, a non-contributory arrangement.

Approximately 20% of individuals aged 60 and above are economically active. According to NSC figures, approximately 60% of those employed in this age group are in the informal sector. The elderly amount to 3% of the employed population, and unemployment among the elderly is lower than among the workforce as a whole.

Older people face challenges affording necessities, especially health care. The 2013 Life in Kyrgyzstan Study showed that 29.6% of individuals over 59 could not afford treatment, while 19.8% reported borrowing money to make health payments (DIW/SIPRI, 2014[49]). Similarly, 52.6% of respondents in the 2015 KIHS over 59 reported moderate difficulties in paying for health services and 11.9% reported great difficulty. Some 27.7% who required medical assistance self-medicated.

Skip-generation households consisting of older people and children face particular hardships. They often report insufficient income, especially in winter, and reliance on credit. These households prioritise food and heating, frequently at the expense of children's education (HelpAge International, 2009[50]).

## Subjective well-being indicators are mixed

Different surveys provide different evidence of the subjective well-being of Kyrgyzstan's population. Gallup's nationally representative survey of individuals aged 15 and above indicates the population is among the least positive of the benchmark countries. Life satisfaction (on a scale of 10) declined between 2013 and 2015 (Figure 1.33) after increasing between 2006 and 2009, and the average has remained steady at around 5, in contrast to the fluctuations in other benchmark countries.

Local surveys tell a more positive story. The 2014 MICS showed that 70.8% of women aged 15-24 believed their lives improved in the year before the survey, while 95.3% believed their lives would improve in the upcoming year. Overall, 96.1% were satisfied with their lives, 93.1% with their family lives and 95.5% with their health, although only 77.7% reported satisfaction with their income level.

**Figure 1.33. Gallup data shows subjective well-being in decline**

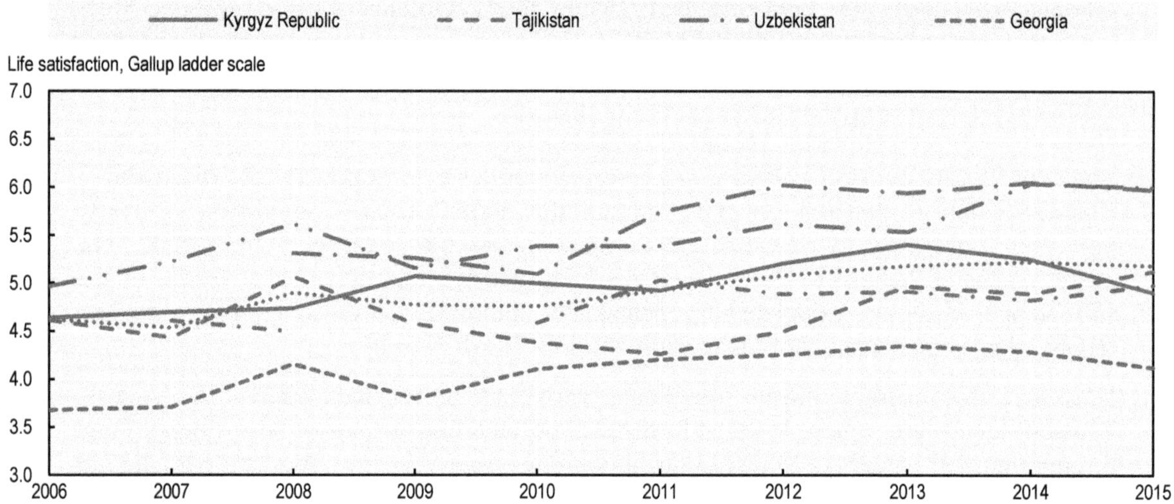


*Note*: The Gallup ladder scale is an adaptation of the Cantril Self-Anchoring Striving Scale. Participants aged 15 and above are asked to "imagine a ladder with steps numbered from zero at the bottom to 10 at the top", and to position themselves on the ladder, where "the top of the ladder represents the best possible life for [them] and the bottom of the ladder represents the worst possible life for [them]."
*Source*: Gallup (2016[51]), *Gallup World Poll* (database), gallup.com/analytics/213704/world-poll.aspx.

The Life in Kyrgyzstan Study also provides subjective well-being information. Asked to rate level of worry about their economic situation on a scale of 10, 18.3% of 2013 respondents reported being extremely worried. Overall, 44.1% reported some improvement in their economic situation over the past year, and 46.5% reported no change. At the same time, 51.3% expected some progress in their situation, 7.1% expected strong improvement, and 39.9% expected no change.

## Emerging risks and uncertainties will affect demand for social protection

The context for social protection will change considerably in the coming decades due to a wide range of factors. Demographics and climate change will be fundamental forces; both are likely to have a negative impact on the economy and affect demand for social protection. There are mixed signals for the macroeconomic context. The political situation is stabilising but there is significant uncertainty around the economy, particularly regarding the energy sector.

### *Changing demographics*

Changes in the age structure of Kyrgyzstan's population have so far favoured economic growth. The dependency ratio declined from 75.9 in 1994 to 52.5 in 2010 (or two people of working age to every dependant under age 15 or above age 60), meaning Kyrgyzstan has a relatively large working-age population (Figure 1.35).

Kyrgyzstan's demographics will continue to improve relative to other countries in the region. While its dependency ratio was the second highest among the benchmark countries in 2010 due to its high fertility rate, it will be the second lowest by 2070, if current trends persist (Figure 1.34).

**Figure 1.34. Kyrgyzstan has one of the highest fertility rates in the region**

Total fertility rate (1960-2015)

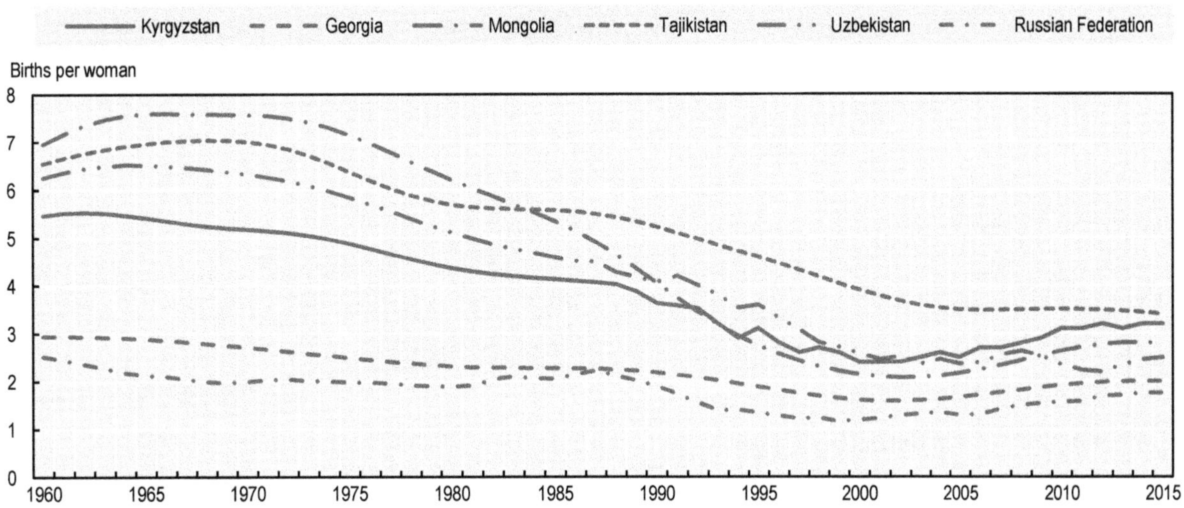


*Source*: World Bank (2017[7]), *World Development Indicators* (database), available at data.worldbank.org/products/wdi.

However, the population is also ageing. The old-age dependency ratio will more than triple over the next 50 years, from 7 in 2015 to 23 in 2065 (Figure 1.35), while the child dependency ratio will decline, albeit at a slower rate. Population ageing will result in increased demand for social spending targeted at the elderly, including pensions and health care. This might be partially offset by reduced pressure on education budgets and social protection for children, although pensions already account for the majority of social protection expenditure (discussed in Chapter 4).

**Figure 1.35. The dependency ratio will fluctuate in the future**

Dependency ratios of Kyrgyzstan and benchmark countries (1970-2070)

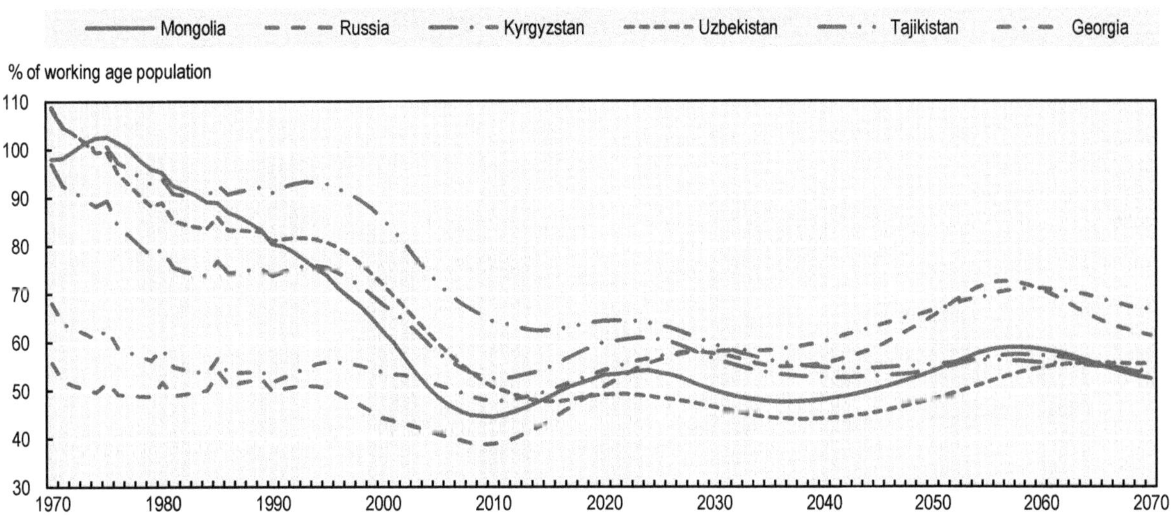


*Source*: UN DESA (2017[52]), *World Population Prospects, 2017 revision* (database), available at esa.un.org/unpd/wpp.

**Figure 1.36. The old age dependency is starting a rapid increase**

Decomposition of Kyrgyzstan's dependency ratio, 1970-2070

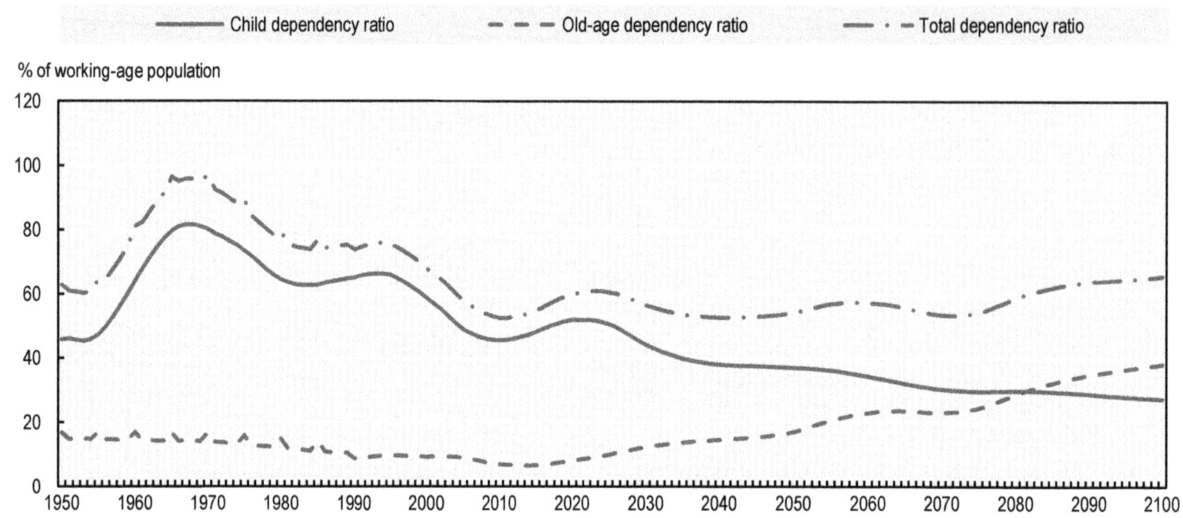


*Source*: UN DESA (2017[52]), *World Population Prospects, 2017 revision* (database), available at esa.un.org/unpd/wpp.

Kyrgyzstan's population will remain predominantly rural until around 2050. Projections by the United Nations Population Division indicate that the urban and rural populations will continue to grow until 2030, at which point the number of people residing in rural areas will start to decline (Figure 1.37) (UN DESA, 2017[52]). The urban population will continue to grow after this point but will not overtake the rural population until around 2050. Overall population growth will increase pressure to improve the quality of services in both rural and urban areas. Addressing the current gaps in rural services will be a particular challenge.

**Figure 1.37. Kyrgyzstan's population will remain mostly rural until 2050**

Rural versus urban population (1985-2045)

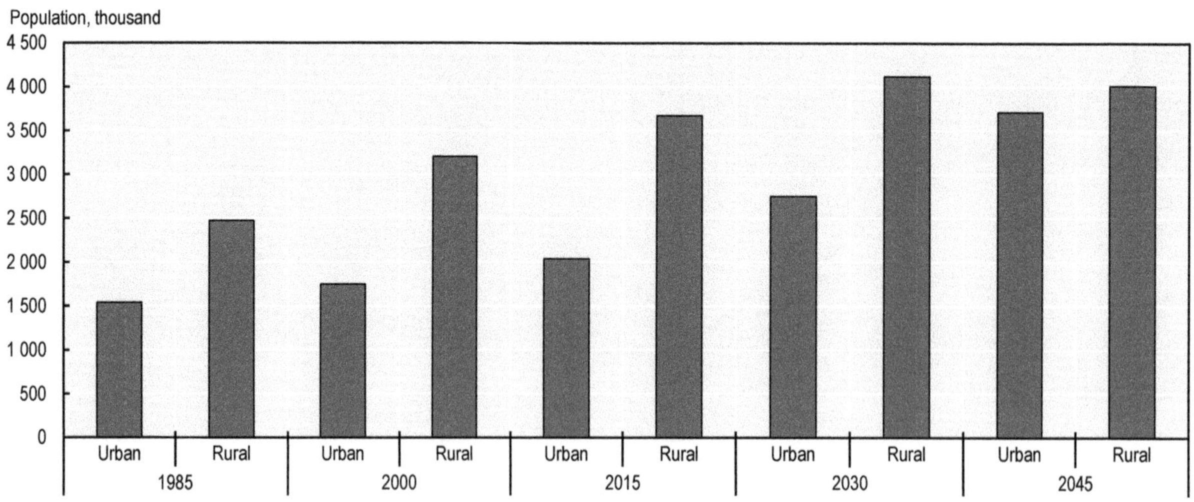


*Source*: UN DESA (2014[53]), *World Urbanization Prospects, 2014 revision* (database).

## *Climate change*

Climate change will have a dramatic long-term effect on Kyrgyzstan and is already inflicting a heavy human cost. As a result of increased temperatures, up to 95% of Kyrgyzstan glaciers are expected to disappear by 2100, leading to water shortages both within Kyrgyzstan and in countries downstream.[3] As a result of melting glaciers, river run-off will peak in 2020 then fall until the end of the century, with severe implications for crop irrigation.

With 31.7% of the workforce employed in some form of agriculture, the long-term effects could be disastrous, although livestock farmers, who account for the majority of the rural workforce, are more resilient to water shortages than crop farmers. Hydropower generation will also be negatively affected, as a result of reduced waterflows in the Naryn cascade.[4]

Melting glaciers also increase the likelihood of flooding and landslides (CAMP Alatoo, 2013[54]). This risk is exacerbated by the impact of heavy mining since the Soviet era, which has altered the geography of the seismically sensitive mountains, increasing the frequency of landslides, earthquakes and avalanches (UNISDR, 2011[55]). From 2001 to 2014, the frequency of all types of natural emergencies increased significantly (Figure 1.38). Landslides were responsible for the highest number of deaths from climate-related natural disasters during the same period. Almost all these landslides occurred in the southern part of the country.

**Figure 1.38. Natural emergencies are on the rise**

Natural emergencies, by type (2001-14)

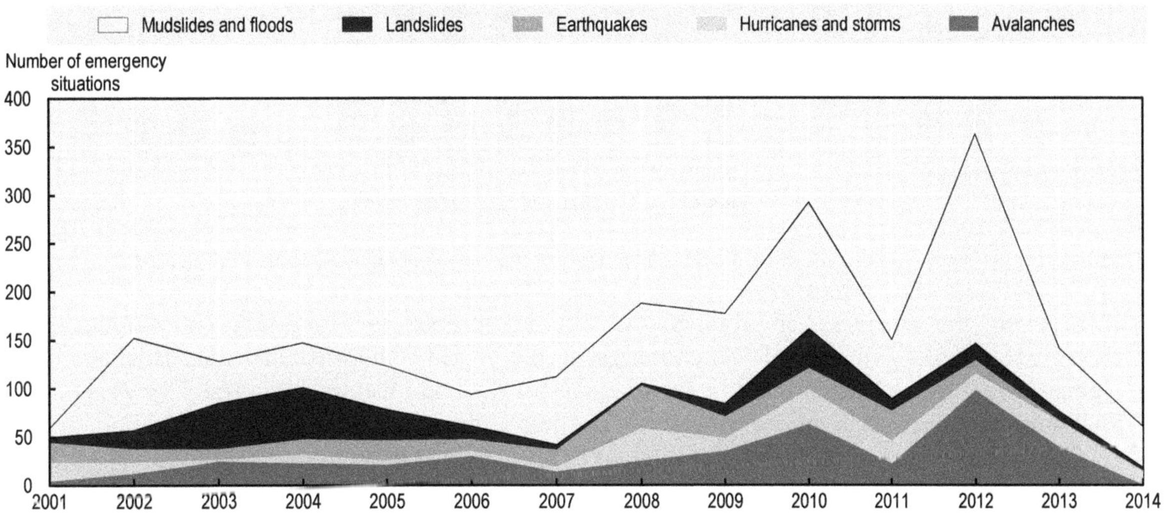


*Source*: NSC (2015[32]).

## *Macroeconomic context*

Kyrgyzstan's political and economic systems have undergone major upheavals at various points since independence. Elections in 2015, 2016 and 2017 occurred without incident or contestation, giving cause for optimism regarding the country's long-term political stability and promising greater policy continuity and long-term planning in government.

However, the risk of conflicts between ethnic Kyrgyz and Uzbeks – recurrent since independence – persists.

The long-term prospects for the economy are highly uncertain, although it has shown great resilience in recent years. As a small, highly-liberalised economy it is susceptible to political and economic crises outside its borders (Dubashov, Kruse and Ismailakhunova, 2015[36]) and needs to maintain strong business relationships with Russia, China and other Central Asian countries. Kyrgyzstan's recent accession to the EEU ties its economic fortunes even more closely to those of Russia.

Perhaps the greatest domestic impediment to long-term growth is the country's low productivity by regional standards (Figure 1.39). Low skill levels related to poor education outcomes and relatively high wage growth hamper Kyrgyzstan's international competitiveness (ADB, 2014[38]). Low productivity in the agriculture and service sectors is of particular concern given their predominance in output and employment.

**Figure 1.39. Labour productivity is very low by regional standards**

Labour productivity in the benchmark countries (2000, 2010, 2020)

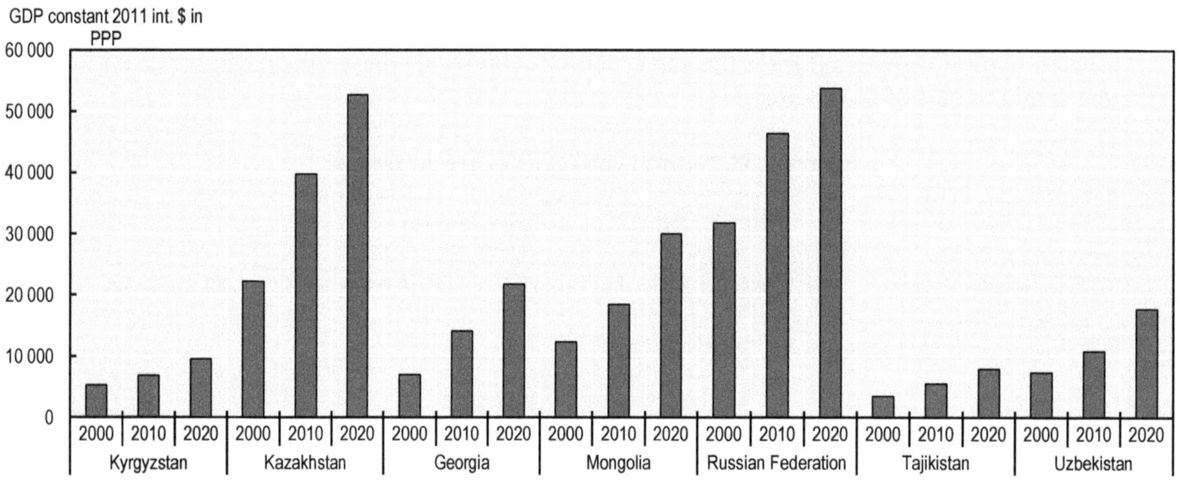


*Source*: ILO (2016[35]), *Key Indicators of the Labour Market, 9th edition* (database), accessed 4 Dec 2017.

Moreover, the business environment is not favourable for long-term investment. Kyrgyzstan ranks 77th (out of 180 countries) in the World Bank Ease of Doing Business Index (2018[56]) with a score below the average for East and Central Asia (65.7 vs 71.3). Although it ranks 29th in the world for starting a business and 8th for registering a property, it ranks 151st for ease of paying taxes and 164th for access to electricity.

Challenges in the energy sector – electricity in particular – are a major constraint to growth and a drain on the government's resources. Tariffs for residential consumers are kept artificially low to ensure access but this is leading to major losses in the energy sector that are subsidised by the Government. The World Bank (2017[45]) calculated the debt of the energy sector at around 20% of GDP in 2016.

At the same time, the sector cannot keep up with the demand generated by the low tariffs, leading to supply problems, particularly outside Bishkek, that are a major constraint on economic activity. Significant investment is required to update ageing infrastructure and build new generating capacity but this is not forthcoming given the perilous financial state of the energy sector.

Measures adopted under the Medium-Term Tariff Policy 2014-17 have improved the situation. However, it will not be possible to balance supply and demand without residential consumers paying more for their electricity. Given the reliance on electricity, especially in bitterly cold winter months, a price shock of this nature could push the large vulnerable population into poverty.

Thus, the tariffs, while highly regressive, are politically contentious. Previous attempts to increase tariffs contributed directly to the turmoil in 2010 (discussed in Chapter 2), in spite of the administration's attempt to compensate for the increase with higher social protection benefits.

## Notes

[1] Latent Class Analysis has been employed in various fields, ranging from marketing to epidemiology. For LCA applied in a similar context, please see the Cambodia SPSR (OECD, 2017[57]), Latent Class Analysis of the Out-of-Work Population in Greece, 2007–11 (World Bank, 2015[58]) and Profile of the Disabled Population in Albania (Ferré, Galanxhi and Dhono, 2015[59]).

[2] Currently, the mandatory prophylactic immunisation programme includes vaccines against ten infections: Polio, TB, Diphtheria, Pertussis, Tetanus, Measles, Mumps, Rubella, Hepatitis B and Haemophilus Influenza.

[3] These projections are taken from the Agreement between the Republic of Kazakhstan, Kyrgyzstan, the Republic of Tajikistan, Turkmenistan and the Republic of Uzbekistan on Cooperation in the Field of Joint Management on Utilisation and Protection of Water Resources, signed in 1992.

[4] These projections are taken from the Agreement between the Republic of Kazakhstan, Kyrgyzstan, the Republic of Tajikistan, Turkmenistan and the Republic of Uzbekistan on Cooperation in the Field of Joint Management on Utilisation and Protection of Water Resources, signed in 1992.

## References

ADB (2015), *Assessment of higher education: Kyrgyz Republic*, Asian Development Bank, Manila, https://www.adb.org/documents/assessment-higher-education-kyrgyz-republic. [24]

ADB (2014), *The Kyrgyz Republic: Strategic Assessment of the Economy*, Asian Development Bank, Manila, http://, https://www.adb.org/publications/kyrgyz-republic-strategic-assessment-economy. [38]

CAMP Alatoo (2013), *Testing of Climate Risk Assessment Methodology in Kyrgyzstan*, CAMP Alatoo, UNDP Central Asia Climate Risk Management Program, https://cdkn.org/wp-content/uploads/2013/08/Climate-Risk-Profile-Fin-clear.pdf. [54]

Carneiro, P. and J. Heckman (2003), "Human Capital Policy", *Discussion Paper*, No. 821, Institute for the Study of Labor (IZA), Bonn. [22]

Dembe, A. et al. (2005), "The impact of overtime and long work hours on occupational injuries and illnesses: new evidence from the United States", *Occupational and Environmental Medicine*, Vol. 62/9, pp. 588-598. [39]

Agnieszka Pikulicka-Wilczewska Greta Uehling (ed.) (2016), *Migration to Russia and the Current Economic Crisis*, E-International Relations Publishing, Bristol. [44]

DIW/SIPRI (2014), *Life in Kyrgyzstan Study, 2011-2013, Version 1.0*, German Institute for Economic Research (DIW Berlin) and Stockholm International Peace Research Institute (SIPRI), http://dx.doi.org/10.15185/izadp.7055.1. [49]

Dubashov, B., A. Kruse and S. Ismailakhunova (2015), *Kyrgyz Republic - Biannual economic update: resilience amid turbulence - special focus: meeting the jobs challenge*, World Bank, Washington DC. [36]

Ferré, C., E. Galanxhi and O. Dhono (2015), *Profile of the disabled population in Albania*, United Nations Support to Social Inclusion in Albania Programme, United Nations Development Programme (UNDP) in Albania, http://al.undp.org/content/albania/en/home/library/profile-of-the-disabled-population-in-albania.html.. [59]

Gallup (2016), *Gallup World Poll*, http://gallup.com/analytics/213704/world-poll.aspx. [51]

HelpAge International (2009), *Constant Crisis: Perceptions of vulnerability and social protection in the Kyrgyz Republic*, HelpAge International, Bishkek. [50]

Hoen, H. (2010), "Transition strategies in Central Asia: is there such a thing as "shock-versus-gradualism"?", *Economic and Environmental Studies*, Vol. 10/2, pp. 229-245. [2]

Hou, D. (2011), "Education Reform in the Kyrgyz Republic - Lessons from PISA", *Europe and Central Asia Knowledge Brief*, No. 40, World Bank, Washington, DC. [27]

Ibraimova A., B. Akkazieva and A. Ibraimov (2011), *Kyrgyzstan: Health System Review*, European Observatory on Health Systems and Policies, Brussels. [18]

ILO (2016), *Key Indicators of the Labour Market, 9th edition*, http://ilo.org/employment/areas/WCMS_234860. [35]

ILO (2016), *Results of National Child Labour Survey presented in Bishkek*, International Labour Organization, Geneva, http://ilo.org/moscow/news/WCMS_449678/lang--en/index.htm. [29]

ILO (2013), *School-to-Work Transition Survey: Kyrgyzstan (2013)*, International Labour Organization, Geneva, http://ilo.org/employment/areas/WCMS_234860. [31]

ILO (2008), "Working Children in Kyrgyzstan: Results of the 2007 Child Labour Force Survey", International Labour Organization, Bishkek. [28]

ILO/NSC (2016), *Working children in the Kyrgyz Republic: Child Labour Survey 2014-2015*, International Labour Organization (ILO) and National Statistical Committee of the Kyrgyz Republic, Bishkek, http://ilo.org/wcmsp5/groups/public/---europe/---ro-geneva/---sro-moscow/documents/publication/wcms_533504.pdf. [30]

IMF (2017), *World Economic Outlook*, http://imf.org/external/datamapper/datasets/WEO (accessed on 01 April 2017). [6]

IMHE (2016), *Global Burden of Disease 2015*, Institute for Health Metrics and Evaluation, Seattle. [19]

NISS (2014), *Informal Employment in Kyrgyzstan*, National Institute for Strategic Studies of the Kyrgyz Republic, Bishkek. [41]

Nove, A. et al. (2014), "Maternal mortality in adolescents compared with women of other ages: evidence from 144 countries", *The Lancet Global Health*, Vol. 2/3, pp. 155-164, http://dx.doi.org/10.1016/S2214-109X(13)70179-7. [34]

NSC (2017), *Basic consumer price index in the Kyrgyz Republic (core inflation)*, http://stat.kg/en/statistics/uroven-zhizni-naseleniya. [8]

NSC (2017), *Economically active and inactive population*, National Statistics Committee of the Kyrgyz Republic, Bishkek, http://stat.kg/en/statistics/uroven-zhizni-naseleniya. [37]

NSC (2017), *Number of households with incomes below subsistence level*, http://stat.kg/en/statistics/uroven-zhizni-naseleniya. [5]

NSC (2017), *Poverty rate*, National Statistics Committee of the Kyrgyz Republic, Bishkek, http://stat.kg/en/statistics/uroven-zhizni-naseleniya. [4]

NSC (2016), *Poverty rate*, National Statistics Committee of the Kyrgyz Republic, Bishkek, http://stat.kg/en/statistics/uroven-zhizni-naseleniya. [13]

NSC (2015), *Employment and Unemployment. The Results of Integrated Survey of Household Budgets and Labor Force in 2014*, National Statistics Committee of the Kyrgyz Republic, Bishkek. [40]

NSC (2015), *Kyrgyz Integrated Household Survey*, National Statistics Committee of the Kyrgyz Republic, Bishkek. [11]

NSC (2015), *Living Standards of Population in the Kyrgyz Republic, 2010-2014*, National Statistics Committee of the Kyrgyz Republic, Bishkek. [32]

NSC (2014), *Kyrgyz Integrated Household Survey*, National Statistics Committee of the Kyrgyz Republic, Bishkek. [10]

NSC (2004), *Kyrgyz Integrated Household Survey*, National Statistics Committee of the Kyrgyz Republic, Bishkek. [9]

NSC/MoH/ICF International (2013), *Kyrgyz Republic Demographic and Health Survey 2012*, National Statistical Committee of the Kyrgyz Republic, Ministry of Health of the Kyrgyz Republic, and ICF International, http://dhsprogram.com/publications/publication-FR283-DHS-Final-Reports.cfm. [33]

OECD (2017), *Social Protection System Review of Cambodia*, OECD Publishing, Paris, http://dx.doi.org/10.1787/9789264282285-en. [57]

OECD (2010), *Reviews of National Policies for Education: Kyrgyz Republic 2010: Lessons from PISA*, OECD Publishing, Paris, http://dx.doi.org/10.1787/9789264088757-en. [26]

OECD/ILO (2018), *Tackling vulnerability in informality: a household perspective*, OECD Publishing, Parss. [42]

OPHI (2016), *Country briefing 2016: Kyrgyzstan, Multidimensional Poverty Index (MPI) At a Glance*, Oxford Poverty & Human Development Initiative, http://ophi.org.uk/policy/multidimensional-poverty-index. [15]

Pomfret, R. (1999), "Living Standards in Central Asia", *MOCT-MOST Economic Policy in Transitional Economics*, Vol. 9/4, pp. 395-421. [1]

Schweitzer, A. et al. (2015), "Improved coverage and timing of childhood vaccinations in two post-Soviet countries, Armenia and Kyrgyzstan", *BMC Public Health* , Vol. 15, pp. 1-9, https://doi.org/10.1186/s12889-015-2091-9. [20]

UN DESA (2017), *World Population Prospects: The 2017 Revision*, United Nations Department of Economic and Social Affairs, New York, http://un.org/en/development/desa/population/publications. [52]

UN DESA (2014), *World Urbanization Prospects: The 2014 Revision*, United Nations Department of Economic and Social Affairs, New York, http://esa.un.org/unpd/wup. [53]

UNDP (2016), *Human Development for Everyone: Briefing note for countries on the 2016 Human Development Report*, United Nations Development Programme, New York, http://hdr.undp.org/sites/all/themes/hdr_theme/country-notes/KGZ.pdf. [12]

UNESCO (2016), *UNESCO Institute for Statistics*, United Nations Educational, Scientific and Cultural Organization. [23]

UNICEF (2013), *Situation analysis of children in the Kyrgyz Republic*, United Nations Children's Fund, Bishkek, http://unicef.org/kyrgyzstan/sitan_eng.pdf. [25]

UNICEF (2012), *Childcare services in Kyrgyzstan*, United Nations Children's Fund, Bishkek, http://unicef.org/ceecis/KY_Country_profile_eng_29July_FINALproofed.pdf. [48]

UNISDR (2011), "Emerging Risks", in *Global Assessment Report on Disaster Risk Reduction, United Nations International Strategy for Disaster Reduction*, http://preventionweb.net/english/hyogo/gar/2011/en/what/drivers.html. [55]

Vinokuriv, E. (2013), "The Art of survival: Kyrgyz labor migration, human capital, and social networks", *Central Asia Economic Paper* 7, http://papers.ssrn.com/sol3/papers.cfm?abstract_id=2741639, pp. 1-9. [43]

WHO (2016), *Diabetes country profiles, Kyrgyzstan*, World Health Organization, Geneva, http://who.int/diabetes/country-profiles/kgz_en.pdf. [46]

WHO (2016), *Global Health Observatory*, World Health Organization, Geneva. [21]

WHO (2000), *The world health report 2000 - Health systems: improving performance*, World Health Organization, Geneva, http://who.int/whr/2000/en/whr00_en.pdf?ua=1. [47]

WHO/UNICEF/UNFPA/World Bank Group/United Nations Population Division (2015), *Trends in maternal mortality: 1990 to 2015 – Estimates by WHO, UNICEF, UNFPA, World Bank Group and the United Nations Population Division*, World Health Organization, Geneva, http://who.int/reproductivehealth/publications/monitoring/maternal-mortality-2015/en. [16]

Wiegers, T., W. Boerma and O. de Haan (2010), "Maternity care and birth preparedness in rural Kyrgyzstan and Tajikistan", *Sexual & reproductive healthcare: official journal of the Swedish Association of Midwives*, Vol. 1/4, pp. 189-194, http://dx.doi.org/10.1016/j.srhc.2010.08.004. [17]

World Bank (2018), *Doing Business 2018: Reforming to Create Jobs*, World Bank, Washington DC. [56]

World Bank (2017), *Kyrgyz Republic Economic Update, Spring 2017: A Resilient Economy... on a Slow Growth Trajectory*, World Bank, Washington DC, http://openknowledge.worldbank.org/handle/10986/27523. [45]

World Bank (2017), *World Development Indicators*, http://data.worldbank.org/products/wdi (accessed on 01 June 2017). [7]

World Bank (2015), *Kyrgyz Republic: Poverty profile for 2013*, World Bank, Washington DC. [14]

World Bank (2015), *Latent Class Analysis of the Out-of-Work Population in Greece, 2007−2011*, World Bank, Washington DC, http://documents.worldbank.org/curated/en/837771468246370480/pdf/918830WP0P14360240PoLME0Full0Report.pdf. [58]

World Bank (2015), *Poverty and economic mobility in the Kyrgyz Republic - Some insights from the "Life in Kyrgyzstan Survey"*, World Bank, Washington DC. [3]

# Chapter 2. Social protection coverage in Kyrgyzstan

*This chapter charts the evolution of social protection in Kyrgyzstan. It outlines the economic, political and legislative context for social protection, which is still undergoing transition from a Soviet-era system predicated on full employment, to a system more appropriate for a market-based economy with chronic unemployment and long-term poverty. It inventories existing social protection schemes, analyses their key design features and scale of operation, and discusses how well they meet the present and future needs identified in Chapter 1.*

Social protection is perceived as a basic right of all citizens in Kyrgyzstan – a vestige of cradle-to-grave social protection provision under the Soviet Union. Transition to a market economy and the economic upheavals of the past three decades have undermined the feasibility of the old model, prompting a succession of major reforms to the social protection system.

The Government of Kyrgyzstan (GoK) spends more on social protection than on any other area. A broad range of programmes exits across the main pillars (social assistance, social insurance and labour market policies), along with the health care system. However, these pillars are not equally well developed and have evolved at different times in response to different demands, leading to fragmentation. Social insurance programmes achieve much greater coverage than social assistance and active labour market policies, which were established only after the collapse of the Soviet Union.

Moreover, the challenges identified in Chapter 1 are undermining existing social protection provision. Informality and declining labour force participation threaten the sustainability of the social insurance system, while fiscal and structural constraints limit the impact of social assistance on poverty and the effectiveness of labour market policies.

## Kyrgyzstan's social protection system has shrunk since the Soviet era but remains large

In 1990, approximately half the population of Kyrgyzstan received either pensions or family allowances. In the same year, expenditure on social protection was 29% of gross domestic product (GDP), a level of spending only sustainable due to transfers from the Soviet Union (World Bank, 1993[1]). When these transfers disappeared in 1992, the existing system of social protection became unviable.

A second shock occurred when the country embarked on a programme of rapid liberalisation, which fundamentally changed the structure of the economy and led to increases in poverty, inequality, unemployment and inflation. Closure of state-owned enterprises not only destroyed large quantities of jobs but also removed an important provider of social protection.

The first phase of social protection in Kyrgyzstan thus consisted of keeping the Soviet-era system from collapsing as well as protecting large portions of the population from destitution. Contributions to social insurance arrangements shrunk and demand for social assistance increased, especially instruments aimed at protecting children from poverty, reflecting the fact that approximately half the population was under the age of 20. The GoK was also required to support the incomes of unemployed workers and assist them in finding new work and acquiring new skills (World Bank, 1993[1]).

At the same time, the GoK was bound by severe fiscal constraints. Revenues declined dramatically due to the contraction of the economy, the decline in labour force participation and the abrupt end to transfers from the USSR. Government spending shrunk significantly as a result: expenditure on education and health was cut repeatedly in the early- to mid-1990s and social protection spending was also reduced, principally via reductions to family allowances.

Expenditure on the seven different types of family allowances fell from 6.7% of GDP in 1991 to 2.6% of GDP in 1992 (World Bank, 1993[1]). Pension spending nearly halved over the same period, falling from 7.0% of GDP to 3.6% of GDP, even though a large number of workers took early retirement. Importantly, GDP fell significantly in real terms over this period, compounding the decline in spending. Subsidies – food subsidies in particular – also decreased, despite high levels of food poverty (World Bank, 2000[2]).

When the macroeconomic performance improved and fiscal conditions stabilised from 1995 onwards, the GoK embarked on a second phase of longer-term structural reforms to social protection. It implemented major reforms to public health care and the pension system in the latter half of the 1990s, and introduced the first poverty-targeted social assistance programme: the Unified Monthly Benefit (UMB).

Social assistance was established in law, in recognition that social insurance coverage in the new market economy would not be universal, i.e. that benefits previously provided on a contributory basis would need to be replaced by non-contributory programmes. A large-scale "residual" social protection instrument for people excluded from the economy was needed.

Unlike the Monthly Social Benefit (MSB), which was established to provide the same categorical coverage as the social insurance system to people outside the formal labour market, the UMB was a departure from the family allowances. Family allowances were eliminated, and the UMB paid benefits at much lower levels, with much less coverage and at much lower cost to the GoK (World Bank, 2000[2]). The concept of a guaranteed monthly income – initially called the guaranteed minimum consumption level – was introduced as a benchmark for benefit levels and as a threshold for eligibility for social assistance payments.

However, these reforms only partially resolved the central dilemma facing the GoK for the past 25 years: how to respond to a fundamental shift in the demand for social protection brought about by the economic transition, in a context of limited resources and high levels of informality, without reneging on entitlements generated by the previous system? Initial reforms did not go far enough to adapt to the new socio-economic conditions, and parametric reforms implemented subsequently have not changed the structure of social protection provision.

Moreover, reforms to the social insurance arrangements and the introduction of new social assistance and labour market programmes were not carried out in a systemic fashion. As a result, there was a significant fragmentation of social protection provision and policy making that has obtained to this day.

Many post-Soviet countries have faced the challenges of transitioning from a social protection system predicated on full employment. Kyrgyzstan is unique for the extent to which it has sought to maintain entitlements established by the Soviet system despite the costs, both in overall expenditure on pensions and the crowding-out of other social protection spending.

Kyrgyzstan spends more on social protection than the other benchmark countries (Georgia, Mongolia, Russian Federation, Tajikistan and Uzbekistan) for which data exist, with the exception of Mongolia, whose GDP per capita has tripled since 1992 (Figure 2.1). In contrast to Mongolia and Georgia, social insurance accounts for the vast majority of Kyrgyzstan's social protection spending. Spending on labour market policies is extremely low across the benchmark countries.

**Figure 2.1. Kyrgyzstan's social protection spending is high relative to the benchmark countries**

Spending on social protection across the benchmark countries (2011-13)

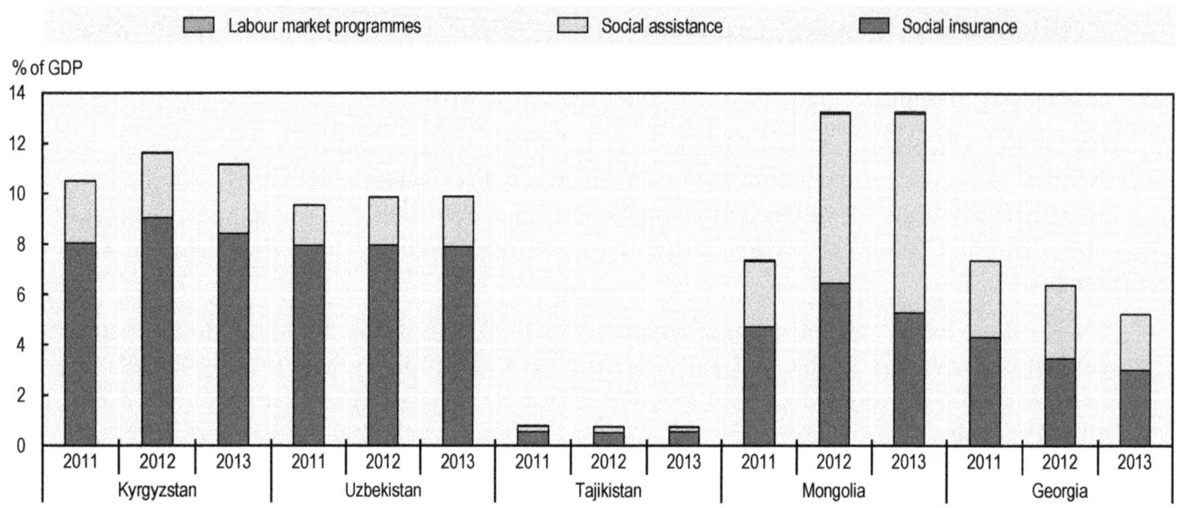


*Note*: No information available for the Russian Federation or Kazakhstan.
*Source*: ADB (2013[3]), *Social Protection Index* (database), hdl.handle.net/11540/79, accessed December 2017.

## Social protection is enshrined in the Constitution

The current system of social protection is enshrined in the 2010 Constitution, which was promulgated following the change of government in that year. Article 9 stipulates state obligations to:

- Establish decent conditions of life and free personal development as well as assistance to employment.
- Ensure support to socially vulnerable categories of citizens, guaranteed minimal level of labour remuneration, protection of labour and health.
- Develop a system of social services and medical services and establish state pensions and benefits as well as other social security safeguards.

Article 53 expands on what social protection entails:

- Social security in old age, in case of disease and in the event of disability or loss of the breadwinner shall be guaranteed to the citizens;
- Pensions and social assistance in accordance with the economic resources of the state shall ensure a standard of living not lower than the minimum subsistence level established by the law.

The specific inclusion of social assistance in the 2010 Constitution was a departure from the 1993 Constitution. Articles 27 and 28 of the 1993 Constitution committed the state to provide income support in the event of a worker's retirement, disability or illness and to provide a standard of living not below the minimum wage established by the law, subject to the resources it has at its disposal. This constitution also acknowledged the state's responsibility to provide protection against unemployment. The Constitutions of 1993 and

2010 identify a clear role for local government in supporting the implementation of social protection programmes.

Social protection featured prominently in the GoK's National Poverty Reduction Strategy (NPRS) in 2002, which was part of the Comprehensive Development Framework of the Kyrgyz Republic to 2010 – the county's first national development plan. The NPRS placed an emphasis on targeted social assistance and on strengthening the link between individuals' contributions to the pension system and their retirement benefits to ensure the system's sustainability.

There were two major structural reforms to social protection towards the end of the first decade of the 2000s: the inclusion of a fully funded component in the pension system and the monetisation of in-kind benefits for certain "privileged" groups. The GoK also introduced new subsidies and increased the benefit levels of existing social protection programmes to compensate for substantial increases in electricity prices in 2009/10.

These latter measures did not quell popular anger about the tariff increases or numerous other public services- and governance-related issues. Revolution ensued in April 2010 (Wooden, 2014[4]). The resultant change in government was a pivotal moment for the country's democratic development, and social protection was at the forefront of the new government's priorities. One of its first actions was to roll back the tariff increases, leaving in place measures to compensate the population for their impact. The combined impact of monetising the privileges, the electricity subsidy and the increased benefit levels caused a step-change in social protection spending.

The present analysis of social protection provision principally concerns the period since 2010. The GoK has published its first two social protection strategies, covering 2012-14 and 2015-17, respectively. These strategies were based around the identification of vulnerable groups. The first strategy identified four such groups: families and children in a difficult life situation; people with disabilities; elderly citizens; and homeless people. The second strategy specified three vulnerable groups; these were the same as in the previous strategy with the exception of homeless people.

Between these two strategies, the GoK launched the National Sustainable Development Strategy for the Kyrgyz Republic for the Period of 2013-2017, a development plan whose recommendations for social protection closely follow the first social protection strategy.

At the time of writing, a third social protection strategy and a new development plan are under development. The new social protection strategy focuses on programmes rather than vulnerable groups. It will feed into the national development strategy called *40 Steps to a New Era,* which covers the period 2018-2022. Social protection is included under Step 28: "Equal opportunities - base for development of the society".

This chapter begins by examining the most important programmes within the three main pillars of the social protection system in order of their size: social insurance, social assistance and active labour market policies. It examines the coverage of different programmes and recent policy developments with reference to the needs identified in Chapter 1.

## Social insurance coverage is almost universal among the elderly

Social insurance dominates the social protection system both in terms of coverage and expenditure, a legacy of the Soviet economic system whereby full employment entailed universal coverage by social insurance. The contributory system in place at the end of the

Soviet Union consisted of a Pensions Fund, a Social Insurance Fund and an Employment Fund that provided a full range of social protection instruments except for poverty-related income support (which in theory would not be necessary in a context where employment was guaranteed).

During the Soviet era, social insurance provision was divided between a complex system of government agencies and state enterprises. Nowadays, the state pension system provides a more limited range of benefits and is overseen by the Social Fund, a Ministry-level institution established in 1993 to co-ordinate the different social insurance arrangements established prior to the collapse of the Soviet Union. The Social Fund initially reported to the Ministry of Labour and Social Protection (MLSP) but in 1998 it was granted full autonomy and in 2000 was made responsible to the President alone (Andrews et al., 2006[5]).

The Social Fund's responsibilities, as codified in 2004, are to design social insurance policy, provide pension payments to the insured population and ensure the financial sustainability of the social insurance system (GoK, 2004[6]). Not all the benefits that are paid by the Social Fund are contributory: it also pays pensions or top-ups to certain groups on a non-contributory basis based on categorical status rather than contributions:

- pensions for military personnel
- pensions for Heroine mothers and mothers of children with disabilities
- top-ups for individuals working in highland conditions or remote areas
- increments for persons with disabilities
- increments for outstanding military and civil service
- a compensatory increment for the increase in electricity tariffs

Full, formal employment in the Soviet era not only ensured high social insurance coverage but also the financial sustainability of the system through a large contribution base. Until 2000, social security contributions worth 39% of wages were required (33% employer/6% employee), a rate that proved a major impediment to formal job creation following the transition to a market economy and which could therefore not be sustained. Thereafter, the contribution rate was reduced progressively. As of 2018, the rate for formal workers is 27.25% of salaries, of which 25.00% is for pensions, 2.00% for health insurance and 0.25% for an occupational injury arrangement.

Pension coverage of the elderly is almost universal: the World Bank (2014[7]) calculated that pension coverage as a proportion of the population over age 65 was 142% in 2011, reflecting coverage rates among that age group in excess of 90% and significant early retirement from the system. According to Social Fund data, there were 661 000 beneficiaries (including retirement, disability and survivor pensioners) in 2016, up from 466 000 in 2011 – a 42% increase (Social Fund of the Kyrgyz Republic, 2018[8]).

Recent data for the number of contributors are not available, but this figure appears to be growing far more slowly: the number of contributors increased by 15% between 2010 and 2013, from 1.16 million to 1.33 million. This disparity in growth rates means that the number of contributors per beneficiary – a key variable for the sustainability of a pay-as-you-go pension system – is already below two beneficiaries per worker and is expected to decline further.

Moreover, the proportion of contributors in the formal sector declined from 63.1% of contributors in 2011 to 59.1% in 2014. This implies that the number making full contributions is declining. The majority of self-employed workers contribute at a rate equivalent to 10% of the economy-wide average wage (9% to pensions and 1% to health), although there are special categories of the self-employed with contribution rates of 12%, 6% or 3% of the average wage. Farmers' contributions vary by the amount of land they own, with many contributing 1% of their income or less. In 2011, farmers accounted for 34% of contributors and salaried workers accounted for 60%, with the self-employed comprising the balance.

Because of these high coverage levels, pensions are the principal means of poverty alleviation not only among the elderly but also among younger generations, as shown by the Latent Class Analysis in Chapter 1. However, high coverage is not synonymous with generosity and pension receipt is no guarantee against poverty (discussed in Chapter 3).

Successive administrations have been unable to arrest the decline in pensioners' purchasing power. In part, this is a function of challenges identified in Chapter 1: a decline in per capita incomes, contraction of the formal labour force and growth in the elderly population since the collapse of the USSR. A reduction in the contribution rate has also contributed to the fall in pension values. However, the design of the pension system is also responsible for the decline, as will be discussed below.

A high contribution rate is an endogenous challenge to pension coverage. Unfunded pension arrangements need a certain level of contributions to meet their commitment to older workers, but if the contribution rate is so high as to deter workers from contributing then the adverse impact is felt for current and former workers alike: payments to current beneficiaries cannot be made and current workers will not be eligible for pensions when they retire.

### *Old-age pensions*

The pension system in place at the collapse of the Soviet Union has undergone major reforms since 1992. These measures have sought to improve the sustainability of the pension system without affecting the entitlements accrued prior to reforms or significantly altering the structure of the system. As a result, the pension system confronts major structural challenges to its sustainability and is increasingly reliant on support from the Republican Budget (discussed in Chapter 4).

The largest reforms took place in 1997. In response to recurrent deficits in the Social Fund, which reached 1.7% of GDP in 1996, the Government committed to increasing the retirement age by three years for men and women over a nine-year period (to age 63 and 58, respectively) and a new pillar was introduced to the pension system (IMF, 2000). The Soviet-era defined benefit arrangement, which has become known as the SP1 component, was closed to new members and to further contributions from existing members, but the entitlements it generated for workers who had contributed up to that point remained valid. This part of the system will remain operational until around 2035-40 (Schwarz et al., 2014[9]).

At the same time, a new pillar – the SP2 component – was introduced for contributions made from 1997 onwards and is commonly assumed to cover individuals born after 1980. This arrangement is run on a notional defined contribution (NDC) basis, meaning contributors are no longer guaranteed a certain level of benefits in retirement but generate an accumulation throughout their working careers that will be converted into an annuity at retirement. In both systems, contributions by today's workers are used to finance the benefits of current retirees. This move to an NDC system was consistent with the approaches taken in various other countries in the region around the same time (World Bank, 2012[10]), most notably Latvia (Müller, 2005[11]).

The 1997 reform sought to retain a strong link between a pensioner's benefits in retirement and their income during their career at a time when replacement rates (the proportion of the former to the latter) were low and declining. This principle was reinforced by the introduction of a defined contribution pillar in 2010, which is currently financed by contributions worth 2% of a worker's salary. This arrangement works on a funded basis, meaning workers contributions are invested and the capital plus interest will be paid to a worker upon retirement. The Social Fund initially proposed funded individual accounts in 2002 but this was opposed by the World Bank on the grounds that Kyrgyzstan's financial markets were not sufficiently well developed to accommodate such arrangements (World Bank, 2014[7]), a concern that remained more than a decade later (Andrews et al., 2006[5]).

These arrangements are built on a basic pension component, which is set at a maximum rate of 12% of the economy-wide average wage. The basic pension is quasi contributory insofar as it is payable to individuals according to the duration of their contributions but not the value of their contributions nor the rate at which they contributed. For individuals with shorter contribution histories than the statutory minimum, the basic pension payout is pro-rated.

The design of the basic pension component means that it is highly redistributive between workers at different income levels. This is an important means of incentivising individuals to contribute but it allows people to game the system by opting for one of the lower contribution rates.

As well as a basic pension, a social pension exists for elderly individuals who did not contribute to the social insurance system while they worked, although the eligibility age is higher than the statutory retirement age governing receipt of the pension. This social pension is contained within the MSB (discussed below).

Table 2.1 shows the structure of the pension system. As of 2018, an individual's pension in retirement comprised the basic pension plus their entitlement to SP1 and SP2. For the SP1, the benefit is calculated as the length of service multiplied by the average monthly wage over the five years in which their earnings were highest and by an accrual rate of 1%. For the SP2 component, the benefit is calculated as the (notional) accumulated contributions multiplied by an actuarial factor that reflects an individual's age of retirement and life expectancy across the population.

**Table 2.1. Structure of the contributory pension system**

| | Basic pension | SP1 pension | SP2 pension | Fully funded defined contribution |
|---|---|---|---|---|
| Financing source | Republican Budget | 23% contribution rate | | 2% contribution rate |
| Benefit type | Flat benefit (12% of economy-wide average wage) | Earnings-related (defined benefit) | Notional defined contribution | Fully funded defined contribution |

*Note*: Adapted from World Bank (2014[12]).

The decline in average pension levels reflects the design of the insurance components (SP1 and SP2) rather than the value of the basic pension, which is indexed to average earnings. For the SP1 contributions, the 1% accrual rate is not very generous; it implies that workers who contributed for 40 years receive a pension from this component worth 40% of their highest earnings, which is not particularly high given the level of contributions. However, the SP1 is more generous than the SP2 component, the pensions from which are constrained by the way past earnings are indexed: the Social Fund adjusts the value of pension contributions over the most recent year to reflect the impact of price rises but not the value of the entire (notional) accumulation, meaning the value of previous contributions reduces significantly over time in real terms.

By allowing inflation to erode the value of pension accumulations, the SP2 has protected the solvency of the Social Fund but has also contributed to the decline in pension values. According to World Bank calculations, the average pension will decrease from 43% of the average wage in 2011 to 25% of the average wage over the subsequent three decades unless the indexation method is changed. The pension for groups whose contributions are set at a lower rate, such as the self-employed and farmers, will be below this level.

In part, the GoK is able to address low pension levels by adjusting their value post retirement. At present, such adjustments are made in an ad hoc manner and typically link pension increases to wage growth in the economy, a strategy that is costlier than indexing to prices and thus reinforces the need to restrict the value of pension accumulations.

Moreover, the Social Fund is increasingly reliant on the Republican Budget to subsidise pension expenditure (discussed in Chapter 4). This reflects not only a policy decision that the basic pension should be fully financed by transfers from the Republican Budget but also the growing burden of military pensions.

There are two principal concerns with military pensions beyond the fact they are non-contributory. The first relates to the very low retirement ages, whereby individuals are able to retire upon attaining 20 years of service or reaching age 50 (for men) and 45 (for women) – whichever happens first. The second relates to the fact it is not only members of the military who are covered; employees from a wide range of government agencies with a security component are also eligible (GoK, 1993[13]).

### *Disability and survivor pensions*

In addition to old-age pensions, the Social Fund provides benefits to contributing workers in the event of disability and pays survivor benefits to a worker's household in the event of death before retirement. In 2011, the proportion of beneficiaries for each of the three components was 71% for old age, 19% for disability and 10% for survivorship (World Bank, 2014[12]).

Disability pensions follow the same structure as old age pension system and are payable until vocational rehabilitation or for life. Contributors to the Social Fund are entitled to a disability pension provided they have contributed for the following periods at the age of onset:

- aged 23 years or younger: 1 year
- aged 23-26 years: 2 years
- aged 26-31 years: 3 years
- aged 31 years and older: 5 years.

The level of disability payment depends on the degree of disability: Group I (total disability and requiring constant attendance), Group II (total disability with an 80% loss of mobility) or Group III (partial disability with some loss in working capacity). The GoK assigns disability pensions equal in value to the basic and insured (SP1 and SP2) old-age pensions for those with disabilities in groups I and II and 50% of the old-age pension for people with disabilities in Group III.

A contributor's dependants are eligible for pension payments should a contributor die before retirement age. The following categories are eligible for survivor pensions:

- children up to age 16 (over age 16 if they have disabilities)
- siblings or grandchildren up to 16 years of age
- parents or spouse, if they have reached the pensionable age or have disabilities by the time of the contributor's death.

The survivor pension benefit is a sum of the basic and insured (SP1 and SP2) pension components for disability Group II, assigned at the following rates:

- one dependent: 50%
- two dependents: 90%
- three dependents: 120%
- four or more dependents: 150%.

## Social assistance is small in scale and caught between categorical benefits and poverty-targeting

Social assistance is implemented on a much lower scale than social insurance, reflecting the legacy of the Soviet social protection system. As the World Bank (1993[1]) noted in its report on social protection in Kyrgyzstan: "At present there is no system of social assistance in Kyrgyzstan...To date, [it] has been largely synonymous with charity, caring for orphans, the elderly, the infirm, the disabled, and so forth."

Social assistance is managed by the Ministry of Labour and Social Development (MoLSD), which also has responsibility for labour-market programmes. As of 2015, the two largest programmes were the poverty-targeted Monthly Benefit for Poor Families with children (MBPF, previously called the UMB) and the MSB, a categorical benefit for people with disabilities and other vulnerable groups. Combined expenditure on these programmes was 1.2% of GDP in 2015, versus 7.4% of GDP spent on pensions in the same year.

### *Monthly Benefit for Poor Families*

As of 2017, the MBPF provided a monthly cash transfer to households with contain children under age 16 (or under age 18 if they are still in education) whose per capita income does not exceed the value of the guaranteed minimum income (GMI). According to official data, the programme covered 304 000 children in 2015, or around 5% of the total population.

Applying for the MBPF is a complex process involving a range of institutions and documentation. Households apply for the benefit to the MoLSD branches at rayon (district) level or, if they reside in rural areas, to the aiyl okmotu (community government). When applying for the benefit, households must supply information regarding their income, household and assets, including the amount of land they own. This information forms the basis of an official document known as the social passport for poor families (SPPF), which is filled in either by MoLSD staff or social protection specialists employed by the aiyl okmotu. A commission from the aiyl okmotu then visits the household to verify the information it provided (CASE/MoLSD/UNICEF, 2008[14]).

Once the information is verified, the rayon-level branch of the MoLSD calculates whether a household's per capita income falls below the means test threshold. This calculation takes into account cash income as well as imputed or in-kind income from land and possession of durable goods and livestock. The MoLSD aims to visit 30% of new recipients to double-check they meet eligibility requirements. Should a household be deemed eligible, it receives the MBPF for one year, after which it must reapply. Payments are made via the post office; beneficiaries typically collect these payments themselves but in some cases they will receive them by post.

Since 2015, the value of the benefit has been set equal to the value of the GMI. Previously, it was calculated as the difference between a household's aggregate per capita income and the value of the GMI. This link between the value of the GMI and the MBPF is not legislated: the value of the latter can vary (either up or down), according to government resources.

Benefits values are multiplied by an altitude coefficient which is applied to all public payments (including social protection benefits and public-sector wages) according to the altitude at which each rayon is situated. This represents a belief that individuals living at high altitudes are in greater need of support from the state. The altitude coefficient ranges from 1 to 1.95, meaning that the value of MBPF is almost twice as high for individuals living in extremely mountainous areas than the standard value of the benefit.

The MBPF's predecessor, the UMB, was established to eliminate extreme poverty. The connection between the MBPF and extreme poverty remains codified in the design of the programme even though extreme poverty has almost been eliminated. The income eligibility threshold is set at the same level as the GMI, which was introduced at a level around 50% of the extreme poverty line (EPL) for affordability reasons, with the intention of equalising the two benchmarks. This increase never transpired; in fact, the GMI dropped as low as 21% of the EPL before returning to its original level in 2015. This highly restrictive targeting means that the MBPF has in fact been aimed at only the poorest of the extreme poor.

The restrictive targeting criteria and the near-elimination of extreme poverty have driven a decline in the number of beneficiaries. Between 2005 and 2015, the number of beneficiaries fell from 440 000 to 304 000 (Figure 2.2). This represents a reduction in coverage of just over 30% in absolute terms and an even larger decline in relative terms, since the number of children grew over this period.

**Figure 2.2. MBPF benefits have risen but coverage has declined**

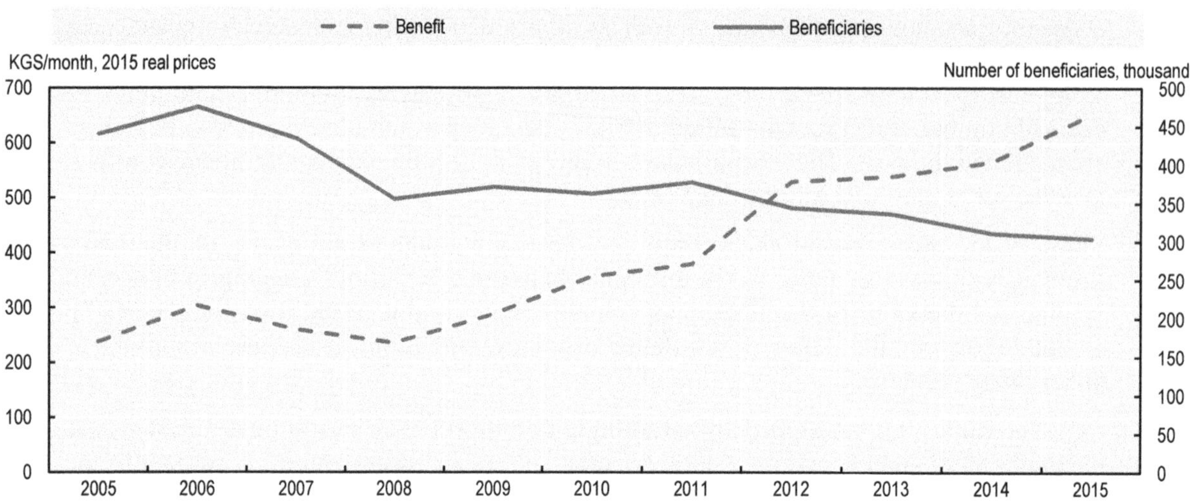


*Source*: Authors' calculations based on NSC (2015[15]), *Kyrgyz Integrated Household Survey* (database).

The sharpest decline in coverage occurred between 2005 and 2008, when the poverty rate also declined by 10 percentage points. Changes to the design of the MBPF might also have contributed to the decline: targeting criteria were tightened by including durable goods and livestock in the proxy means test and updating valuations of revenue from land.

The decline in coverage has been accompanied by increases in benefit levels. Between 2005 and 2015, the average benefit level more than doubled in real terms (in 2015 prices). The overall effect has been to increase spending on the MBPF, which overtook the MSB as the largest social assistance programme in expenditure terms in 2015. The increase in benefit levels magnifies the cost of targeting errors.

The MBPF's impact in reducing poverty is diminished by both errors of inclusion (ineligible households receiving the MBPF) and exclusion (eligible households not receiving it). In the strictest terms, inclusion error is built into the programme, given it is targeted at extremely poor households with children, the number of which has fallen declined to very low levels. Yet, even by this strict definition, exclusion errors occur.

As in many other countries, identifying and enrolling the very poorest households is a major challenge. It is a particular challenge in the case of the MBPF given the complexity of the income assessments, the low capacity of the local-level of social workers employed to implement these assessments and the remoteness of the locations where many poor individuals reside.

How agricultural incomes are imputed is a major weakness of the programme. As Kyrgyz agriculture is semi-subsistence, and virtually all produce sales are cash-based, direct accounting for household income from agricultural activities is challenging. The means test uses imputed agricultural income norms that are usually very low and rarely adjusted for inflation, leading to an underestimation of the imputed income from land that allows the GMI (the means test threshold) to be kept very low. This effectively excludes urban households from the programme, such that more than 90% of MBPF beneficiaries reside in rural areas.

Targeting errors might also be driven by the fact that livestock provisions do not take household size into account. A household with two residents is granted the same livestock allowance under the income assessment as one with eight. The means test's failure to account for income from remittances might exacerbate inclusion errors, while its failure to take into account household labour potential might do the same for exclusion errors; a household's landholdings might exclude it from the MBPF even if no resident can use the land.

Potential MBPF beneficiaries face high application costs. Registering often requires multiple documents and travel to rayon (district) centres to collect them – a more significant impediment for those with the lowest incomes. The absence of an electronic document circulation system among government agencies increases application costs for beneficiaries. The complexity of the application process and the number of role players involved also creates room for corruption.

### *Monthly Social Benefit*

The MSB is a descendent of invalidity pensions (also known as social pensions) paid out during Soviet times, which has since expanded to include seven groups considered vulnerable or living in difficult conditions:

1. children under age 18 with disabilities
2. children of mothers living with HIV/AIDS, until 18 months
3. persons with lifelong disabilities (Groups I, II and III), if not eligible for a pension
4. persons with systemic disabilities (Groups I, II and III), if not eligible for a pension
5. senior citizens who are not eligible for a pension
6. mothers of seven or more children who are not eligible for a pension (known as Heroine mothers)
7. orphaned children, if not eligible for a survivor pension.

In 2015, 78.5% of MSB beneficiaries were people with disabilities; among this group, 45% were children (Figure 2.3). Each of the disability categories is sub-divided. For adults, lifelong and systemic disability are divided into Groups I, II and III. For individuals under age 18, there are different categories, including general disabilities, cerebral palsy and those with HIV/AIDS.

**Figure 2.3. People with disabilities account for the majority of MSB beneficiaries**

MSB beneficiary categories, percentage (2015)

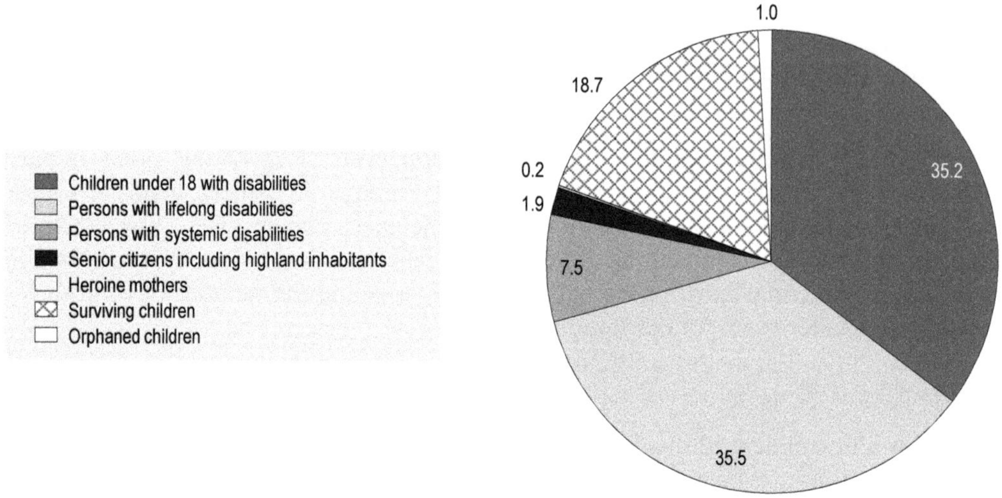


*Source*: Authors' calculations based on NSC (2015[15]), *Kyrgyz Integrated Household Survey* (database).

The number of people covered by the MSB has grown steadily, from 53 900 in 2005 to 80 500 in 2015 (Figure 2.4), the 2015 figure representing about 1.3% of the population or about one-quarter of the number of MBPF beneficiaries. Despite the disparity in coverage between the two programmes, the MSB was the largest social assistance programme in expenditure terms until 2015, reflecting the fact that MSB benefits have historically been higher than those of the MBPF.

**Figure 2.4. MSB coverage and benefits are on the rise**

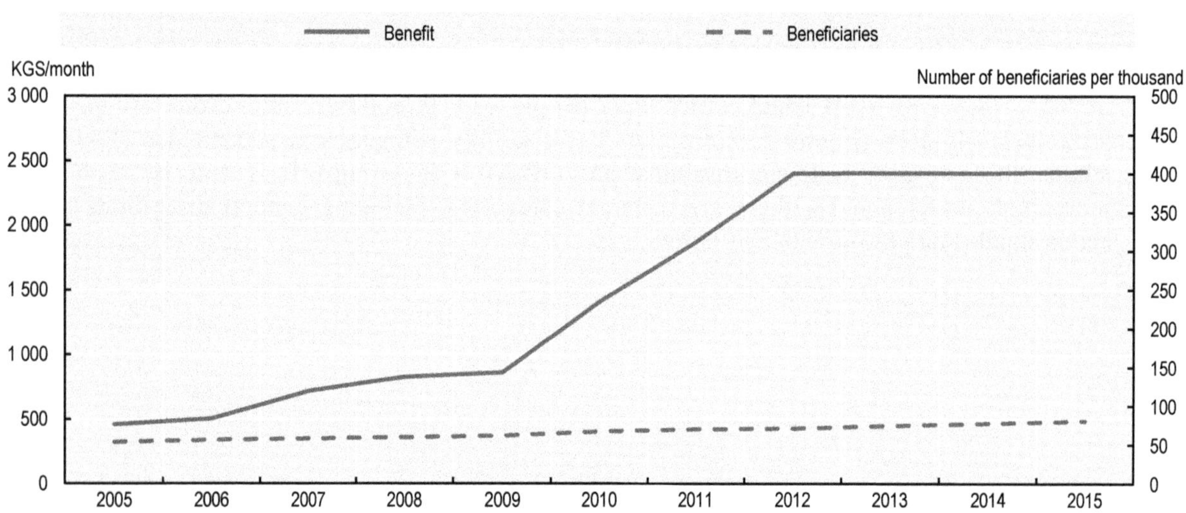


*Source*: Authors' calculations based on NSC (2015[15]), *Kyrgyz Integrated Household Survey* (database).

There is overlap between the categorical benefits covered by the MSB and the compensations for privileges for special population groups (Box 2.1). Although these transfers, which are a legacy of the Soviet era, are financed through the budget of the

MoLSD, they are treated separately from state benefits. This reflects their history: until 2010 the privileges were in-kind payments to groups on the basis of merit rather than need. As a result, not all privileges can be considered as social protection instruments; reprioritising funding towards state benefits would be a political choice that has so far been resisted.

**Box 2.1. The dwindling role of privileges for special population groups**

One of the most contentious features of the Kyrgyz social protection system are the state privileges to compensate certain groups for vulnerabilities or contributions to the previous regime. Before 2010, this system was governed by ten laws (ADB/IMF/World Bank, 2010[16]), providing 40 types of privileges to 39 categories of beneficiaries (World Bank, 2014[7]). Privileges were usually price discounts for utilities, housing, health services and sanatoriums, and various other municipal services.

A 2010 reform reduced the number of privileged groups to 25 and replaced price discounts with monetary benefits, known as compensations for privileges. Under the new system, the value of cash benefits varies between categories[1], from a minimum of KGS 1 000 to a maximum of KGS 7 000 per month. Recipients remain eligible for early retirement or pension top-ups that existed under the previous system and are financed by the Republican Budget, paid through the Social Fund.

As of 2017, beneficiaries of the compensations for privileges include veterans of the Second World War, survivors of concentration camps, heroes of the Soviet Union or the Kyrgyz Republic and individuals involved in clean-up operations following the Chernobyl nuclear disaster. However, less venerated groups, such as people living in mountainous areas and people with disabilities, account for the majority of recipients.

The monetisation of privileges led to a spike in the cost of the programme, in part because many beneficiaries were unable to access services that they would have received at a subsidised cost. In 2010, spending on compensations was approximately 75% of combined spending on the MSB and the MBPF, leading to intense pressure to reprioritise from privileges to state benefits.

The burden of the compensations has diminished considerably since then (discussed in Chapter 4). The value of benefits was frozen at their 2010 level, leading to a significant decline in their real value. Moreover, the death of elderly beneficiaries is likely to further reduce spending into the future.

### *Supplementary Monthly Social Benefit*

The Supplementary Monthly Social Benefit (SMSB) is a categorical benefit awarded to the families of those killed and injured in the violence that occurred in 2010, regardless of income or access to other social benefits.

### *Maternity benefit*

In the Soviet and early post-Soviet era, maternity benefits were paid from the Social Insurance Fund. The link between contributions and eligibility was weak: all women who gave birth to a live child were eligible for a one-time, flat-rate payment set at two months of the minimum wage. Maternity leave was also paid to all employees for a period of

126 days (140 days in certain circumstances) at 100% of salary, regardless of length of service. The expense was considered a deterrent in hiring women (World Bank, 1993[1]).

Today's maternity dispensation is much less generous. As of 2017, there was no once-off benefit for the birth of a child, although a reform of state benefits in 2018 might reintroduce it. Entitlement to paid maternity leave is also restricted to women who pay tax or are registered as unemployed, thus excluding the informal sector.

According to a 2011 government decree, the duration of paid maternity leave is 126-180 days, depending on the difficulty of delivery, the number of births and the region. Only employed women living in mountainous areas are entitled to a benefit worth 100% of salary throughout their maternity leave. Otherwise, women in formal wage employment are eligible for 100% of their salary for just ten days, whereupon the benefit drops to ten times the so-called imputed rate[2], paid by the Republican Budget. Women who are (formally) self-employed, who work in farm enterprises or who are registered as unemployed are entitled to a benefit equivalent to ten times the imputed rate for the duration of their maternity leave.

In 2015, the average maternity benefit was KGS 7 660). The benefit payable to women who are either self-employed, members of farm enterprises or registered as unemployed was KGS 3 500. The benefit payable to women residing and working in mountainous and remote areas exceeded KGS 30 700.

### *Funeral benefit*

Kyrgyzstan citizens are entitled to a funeral benefit, the level of which varies according to a range of factors stipulated in the 2011 decree that also governs maternity payments. For different categories of deceased individual, the benefit is calculated with reference either to the average wage, the imputed rate or the basic pension. Annex 2.AB details the different benefit levels. The benefit is not paid for Kyrgyzstan workers who die abroad.

### *School meals*

The Ministry of Education and Science is integrating social protection into its plans as a means of making education more pro-poor. The sectoral budget for 2012-2020 allocates resources for catering services in primary schools with a view to increasing enrolment of low-income students. The World Food Programme is supporting the school feeding initiative for children in grades 1-4 by funding the purchase of kitchen equipment to provide hot meals using the KGS 7-10 per child provisioned by the Republican Budget in 275 schools.

### *Natural disasters*

The MoLSD provides assistance for those affected by natural disasters in the form of grants and loans. However, the Ministry has no specific capacity for emergency assistance and does not have a mandate to support affected individuals or communities recover from livelihood losses caused by natural disasters.

## Social services still consist mostly of residential care

The state has an obligation to provide social services to poor and vulnerable groups, such as children, the elderly and people with disabilities, as codified in Article 5 of the 2010 Constitution. In practice, only a very small proportion of vulnerable individuals or households have access to social services, due to a lack of resources, low capacity at local level and the absence of a clear statutory framework for social services. As a result, residential institutions remain the foremost social services intervention in Kyrgyzstan, despite the GoK's commitment to making the enrolment of vulnerable individuals in such institutions a last resort (Box 2.2).

The extremely low provision of social services represents a major gap in the social protection system and severely constrains the impact of other social protection interventions. For instance, it will not be possible to enhance the impact of state benefits without enhancing the capacity of social workers at local government level, since they are responsible for identifying poor households.

Improving social services nationally is complicated by the fact that social services are a core function of the aiyl okmotu, the administrations of the aiyl aimak. Aiyl okmotu are responsible for implementing economic development and social protection programmes and for ensuring the welfare of poor and vulnerable residents. They are also responsible for verifying and updating the information contained in SPPFs and thus play a critical role in the payment of state benefits. In reality, however, social protection is one of the functions of local government that is not executed due to a lack of resources Mukanova (2007[17]).

Aiyl okmotu must employ one social protection worker for every 5 000 inhabitants (GoK, 2011[18]). However, training opportunities are limited and a very low proportion of social protection experts at a local level are qualified: according to GiZ (2012[19]), only 6% of social workers have a basic education in social work. An important part of enhancing capacity is standardising the status and responsibilities of these social workers, which in turn relies on an overarching legal and regulatory framework for the sector. There is not even uniformity regarding key terms used in the design and implementation of social services.

In recent years, the MoLSD at rayon level has sought to play a greater role in the provision of social services. The Ministry must employ one member for each of the 459 aiyl aimaks to implement sector policies, such as the identification of poor households, maintain the SPPF and develop capacity among local social workers. However, the budget allocated to their activities is extremely small.

It is critical that a state guaranteed minimum level of social services provision be established in law. From this starting point it will be easier to allocate roles and responsibilities for the provision of social services between the MoLSD and local government and thence to allocate budgetary resources and manpower accordingly.

There is significant scope for local and international non-governmental organisations to support the GoK in the provision of social services; however, the modalities for them to do so are largely absent. More of the NGOs in Kyrgyzstan are active in the provision of social protection than in any other activity (ADB, 2011[20]). However, the institutional and financial arrangements required to harness these activities in support of an overarching vision for social services are extremely limited, not least by the absence of such a vision.

The MoLSD is responsible for accrediting NGOs and monitoring their activities. It can also outsource the provision of social services by contracting with NGOs. However, the Ministry is only able to finance these services on budget rather than by creating a results-based spending modality that would have the potential to increase financing for the sector in line with improved performance.

**Box 2.2. Optimising residential care for children in Kyrgyzstan**

Residential care for orphaned or abandoned children and people with disabilities accounts for the majority of social services provided in Kyrgyzstan. Although such institutions play a less central role in social protection than in Soviet times, the number of children enrolled remains high. While there have been substantial improvements in the quality of these institutions in recent years, they are still associated with a range of adverse developmental impacts (Ismayilova and Huseynli, 2014[21]).

The state's responsibility to raise children who are orphaned or deprived of parental care is enshrined in Article 36 of the Constitution. The number of children in institutional care increased by 69% between 1991 and 1994 (Tobis, 2000[22]). As of 2012, 10 908 children were in residential care across 117 different institutions (Ismayilova and Huseynli, 2014[21]). The number of children in residential care increased between 2005 and 2010, a period of rapid declines in poverty and in MBPF coverage.

Chronic poverty is a strong underlying factor for enrolment in the majority of cases. According to a 2005 study, children from single-parent families, large families or families vulnerable for other reasons are most likely to be enrolled; only 6% had lost both their parents. Children tend to stay for as long as they are age-eligible rather than leave as soon as conditions at home improve.

Although residential homes provide a full range of child services, budget constraints and overcrowding severely limit the level of care. As a consequence, children who attend these institutions often experience major challenges integrating into society.

This challenge is especially serious for children with disabilities, who accounted for 29% of all children in residential care in 2014 (UNICEF, 2014[23]). In the Soviet Union, almost all children with disabilities were put in residential care and faced higher levels of social exclusion as a result of their care tenure; conditions in institutions for disabled children were grim relative to other residential institutions. While the situation has improved since the collapse of the Soviet Union, progress has been hampered by resource constraints, lack of capacity among social workers and stigmatisation.

State provision of residential institutions is highly fragmented. Boarding schools, run at the local level, account for 27% of these institutions and 40% of children in residential care. The MoES runs 20% of these institutions, with 34% of children in residential care, while the Ministry of Health (MoH) runs three institutions for 200 infants. The MoLSD and the Ministry of Internal Affairs are also responsible for residential institutions. Privately-run institutions, which operate outside government control and without accreditation, run 33 residential institutions of different types, providing care for 13% of all children in residential care.

Since the introduction of the Child Code in 2012, the number of children enrolled in public institutions has declined due to the introduction of gatekeeping measures to ensure care in public residential institutions is a last resort and sanctioned by a court. The Code also gives local government greater responsibility for protecting children. However, private institutions are still able to take children on demand.

At the time of writing, a major policy push to reform residential institutions is drawing to a close. The Government Decree "On the Optimization of the Management and Financing of Residential Child Care Institutions of the Kyrgyz Republic 2013-2018", signed in

2012, has two objectives: to reduce the number of residential institutions for children and to promote community-based and kinship care services whereby at-risk children are placed with extended family members or cared for in the community rather than in institutions.

While this approach is to be encouraged, it is unlikely to address many of the factors that drive demand for residential institutions. As discussed in Chapter 5, a systemic approach to vulnerable children (and their wider households) involving state benefits, social services and access to education and health care is needed to reduce reliance on public institutions to provide care.

Residential care for the elderly is much less prevalent than the institutionalisation of children, in large part for cultural reasons. Some 6 000 elderly receive social care at home compared with 400 in institutions. As the population ages, the number of elderly living with chronic medical conditions increases and pension levels continue to deteriorate, demand for social services is likely to increase significantly.

## Labour market policies are underdeveloped, especially for women

Kyrgyzstan's labour system was transformed by the collapse of the Soviet Union and the transition to a market-based economy. With the end of the command economy, the GoK was no longer responsible for the provision or allocation of labour. At the same time, the economic contraction that followed the end of the Soviet Union and the demise of many large-scale enterprises sparked massive unemployment.

As with its social assistance programmes, Kyrgyzstan's labour market policies were introduced in response to high demand but in a context of severe fiscal constraints that have limited their growth. While labour market conditions have eased in the subsequent two decades, there remains a clear need for such programmes: unemployment remains relatively high, labour market participation among women has declined and productivity levels across the economy are low. Labour market conditions are a key driver of migration, both internal and external.

Despite this need, labour market policies are a very small component of social protection provision in terms of both coverage and expenditure. They are also poorly aligned with other social protection programmes, despite oversight by the same ministry. This is partly a function of the fact that the current labour market strategy – the Programme for Promoting Employment and Regulating Internal and External labour Migration until 2020 – was drawn up when the labour portfolio was under the Ministry of Labour, Migration and Youth (MoLMY), (GoK, 2014[24]).

### *Public Employment Services*

Public Employment Services (PES) are the gateway for labour market policies. PES date back to Soviet times, when they allocated labour across the economy. From 1991, their mandate changed to matching labour supply and demand, and helping unemployed workers – often the victims of mass lay-offs by a state enterprise – find work. PES functions include registering unemployed workers, matching employers to jobseekers, and referring unemployed workers to active labour market policy instruments, such as training, micro-credit agencies or public works programmes.

The vacancy registration service attempts to simplify the process of vacancy notifications, provide recruitment assistance, systematise communications between PES and employers, and facilitate job searches. However, there is a mismatch between the supply of vacancies registered at PES – mostly low-paid jobs in the public sector – and the employment demanded by jobseekers. Registered vacancies are mostly in urban areas, leaving rural areas (where informal employment is the norm) underserved by PES (Schwegler-Rohmeis, Mummert and Jarck, 2013[25]). Only 15% of all jobseekers found work through PES in 2010; personal referrals by friends and relatives are a much more common means (Schwegler-Rohmeis, Mummert and Jarck, 2013[25]).

PES provide free training for registered unemployed individuals across all regions, but training mostly takes place in urban areas. It is also apparent that the MoLSD lacks adequate information regarding national labour market trends (GoK, 2014[24]). Participants receive a stipend of 1.2 times (120%) the unemployment benefits. Training is implemented through public providers or in partnership with private institutions. Between 2009 and 2011, 8 000 to 8 600 participants per year received training. In 2014, participants comprised 24% (8 352 participants) of the 34 800 beneficiaries of the active labour market policies.

PES also directs the registered unemployed towards the ministerial micro-credit agencies. Ala-Too Finance, an agency overseen by the MoLSD, assesses eligibility and processes the application (Schwegler-Rohmeis, Mummert and Jarck, 2013[25]). In 2014, 4% of all active labour market policy beneficiaries participated in the micro-credit programme, nearly half of whom were women (Schwegler-Rohmeis, Mummert and Jarck, 2013[25]).

**Box 2.3. World Food Programme pilots new approaches to labour market policies**

In 2016-17, the World Food Programme (WFP) implemented large-scale pilots in two parts of Kyrgyzstan (Kochkor and Bazar-Korgon) to identify options for expanding active labour market policies. The pilots were undertaken for more than 8 000 households in collaboration with MoLSD, the Ministry of Agriculture, Ministry of Finance, Ministry of Emergency Situations, State Agency on Environmental protection and Forestry, State Agency on Local Self-Government, State Material Reserve and WFP.

One aspect of the pilots seeks to extend the state system of short-term agricultural training to residents of rural areas who would ordinarily not be able to attend vocation training courses that are currently on offer. Some 70 training courses (designed in collaboration with the MoES, the Agency on Vocational Education and Kyrgyz National Agrarian University) will be available, chosen according to local demand. The focus of these courses, which will be overseen by the Ministry of Agriculture, is on improving yields and reducing crop losses.

### *Public works programmes*

PES also serve as an entry point for public works programmes, which are by far the largest active labour market policy in terms of coverage and expenditure. However, provision is carried out at the local level, without an overarching national policy framework. Participants in public works programmes are not linked to other social protection instruments once they exit a programme.

Participation in public works programmes is open to all registered unemployed. However, priority is given to those registered with the authorised government agencies for more than six months, who have more than three dependents under age 16 and/or are not receiving unemployment benefits. Jobseekers cannot be compelled to participate. The majority of enrolled individuals are men.

Public works programmes provide temporary employment for approximately 23 000 to 26 000 participants per year. Average monthly wages in 2011 were KGS 750. In 2014, some 24 000 individuals were enrolled in public works programmes, representing 26% of those registered with the employment service or 12% of the total unemployed population. Such programmes accounted for 72% of all beneficiaries of the three main active labour market policies.

Public works programmes are managed by local state administrations, in collaboration with local enterprises and authorised government agencies. Temporary, low-skill employment on social infrastructure improvement projects in the region is provided on an ad hoc and contractual basis. Enrolment takes into account workers' health, age, professional and other individual characteristics. Individuals may terminate the fixed-term employment contract before it expires if they obtain other work.

Remuneration must exceed 50% of the unemployment benefits but cannot exceed four times that amount. Remuneration includes a base wage from the employer and co-payment from the authorised government agencies' funds, according to a procedure established by the GoK. Participants are covered by standard labour and social insurance laws and regulations.

Despite receiving the largest share of funding among active labour market policies, the annual per beneficiary spending in 2011 was much less (USD 39) than that for the micro-credit and training schemes (USD 102 and USD 88, respectively).

### *Unemployment benefits*

A very small proportion of the unemployed population receives unemployment benefits. In the first instance, unemployed workers must have contributed to the Social Fund for at least 12 months during the last three years to be eligible. Moreover, they can only access unemployment benefits once they have passed through other labour-market programmes. As a result, Kyrgyzstan ranks 24th out of 27 Eastern European and Central Asian countries in the proportion of unemployed individuals receiving unemployment benefits (Kuddo, 2011[26]).

The basic unemployment benefit is KGS 250 (USD 3.90) per month to a maximum of KGS 500 or 10% of the subsistence minimum. Individuals can receive the benefit for a maximum of six calendar months in a year but for no more than 12 months over a period of three years. The low level of benefits and the eligibility requirements combine to constrain both demand for and access to unemployment benefits. There were just 463 beneficiaries in 2015.

## Health-care reforms have improved coverage and efficiency but quality and access lag behind

The health sector has undergone three major reforms since the collapse of the USSR, and the system now bears little resemblance to the system in place prior to 1992. These reforms included the Manas (1996-2005), the Manas Taalimi (2006-10) and the Den

Sooluk (2012-16) programmes, whose main goal is to curb unofficial, private payments through official co-transfers in order to reduce the financial burden on patients and improve the system's efficiency and responsiveness (MoH, 2012[27]).

Specific measures within these broader processes included the introduction of a Mandatory Health Insurance (MHI) contribution and the Mandatory Health Insurance Fund (MHIF) in 1997, as a first step in moving from subsidising the supply of health care to subsidising strategic purchasing of health services (Falkingham, Akkazieva and Baschieri, 2010[28]).[3] In 2001, a single-payer system was introduced, pooling transfers from the government budgets and MHI contributions under the MHIF. This move consolidated financing for the health services and pharmaceuticals delivered by health care institutions.

Also in 2001, a State Guaranteed Benefits Package (SGBP) clarifying entitlements and co-payments for health services was introduced. The co-payments currently apply for in-patient services and for certain laboratory and diagnostic tests. With the introduction of the SGBP and co-payments, an exemption mechanism was also established. This exemption mechanism has gradually been expanded to cover 16 categories related to medical conditions (such as HIV, TB or maternal care) and 30 socially vulnerable groups. The latter includes children under the age of five or individuals older than 70, households in possession of a social passport, recipients of state benefits and beneficiaries of compensations for privileges.

Health protection in Kyrgyzstan thus includes three kinds of insurance:

- The SGBP, which entitles all patients to primary health care services free at the point of service regardless of their insurance status and also defines the exemptions from co-payments.
- The MHI programme, maintained under the MHIF, which covers certain co-payments for contributing members.
- Voluntary health insurance.

### *The Mandatory Health Insurance Fund (MHIF)*

The MHIF manages two programmes with revenues transferred from MHI premiums and government budgets: the SGBP and the Additional Drug Package (ADP) for the insured population.

The MHIF has several tasks:

- Ensure the financial sustainability of the Basic State Health Insurance and MHI system, as well as create conditions for levelling the volume and quality of care to achieve fair and equitable access to preventive, medical and pharmaceutical services.
- Accumulate funds to ensure financial sustainability of the single-payer and health insurance systems.
- Supervise the rational and targeted use of single-payer system funds.
- Create equal conditions of payment for medical services to health care organisations, public or private, under the SGBP from single-payer system funds.
- Improve the quality of preventive, medical and pharmaceutical services delivered by providers in the health sector.

### *State Guaranteed Benefits Package*

The SGBP has two components:

- A universal package of services provided to the entire population (Basic Mandatory Health Insurance)
- An additional package of services for individuals covered by the social health insurance system (Additional Mandatory Health Insurance) that includes co-payments for selected health services.

The SGBP provides the following types of health services:

- primary health care
- outpatient emergency care
- emergency consultation services (air ambulance)
- specialised outpatient health care
- inpatient health care
- health services financed by the high-tech medical care fund
- dental care
- medicines and vaccines
- immunisation

Primary health care facilities that include family group practices (FGPs)[4] or Feldsher-Obstetrical Ambulatory Points (FAPs)[5] provide free health services to all individuals assigned to them. Patients needing specialised care are referred to specialists in family medicine centres (FMCs), operating as outpatient diagnostic departments of hospitals.[6] The provision of laboratory testing and medical advice is free under the SGBP.

### *Additional Drug Package*

The ADP provides subsidised drugs through its network of pharmacies, meeting two notable targets:

1. provision of medicines for individuals insured under the Additional Mandatory Health Insurance programme, implemented since 2000;
2. provision of medicines for the privileged category of patients under the SGBP programme, implemented since 2006: patients with bronchial asthma, epilepsy, paranoid schizophrenia, affective disorders and oncologic patients (GoK, 2012).

The ADP guarantees discounts on the purchase of medicines for a certain list of active ingredients. The ADP list of medicine is largely based on the Essential Medicine List. This list of medicine covered under ADP is updated regularly and new medicines have been added to the list over time. For example, medicines for mental conditions were recently added after successful campaigning by some non-governmental organisations.

## Young people, migrants and the urban poor fall between the gaps in social protection coverage

Kyrgyzstan's social protection system covers a wide range of risks and receives a significant proportion of government spending (discussed in Chapter 4). However, it has evolved in an uncoordinated manner, and the allocation of resources between these different risks is very uneven. As a result, the impact and coherence of the system is limited (discussed in Chapters 3 and 5, respectively).

Two groups are at greatest risk of exclusion from the social protection system: young people and migrants working abroad. Young people's best chance for employment lies in the informal sector, but this diminishes the likelihood of coverage by the social insurance system. Moreover, the youth unemployment rate is higher than that of the overall economy but labour market policies are not implemented at sufficient scale to help large numbers of youth into formal employment.

Labour migrants are unable to contribute to the Kyrgyz social protection system and are at great risk of poverty should they lose their jobs abroad, where they are unlikely to be protected by public social protection policies. Moreover, they will not be able to fall back on informal social protection networks without returning to households in Kyrgyzstan for which they might have been the main breadwinner.

In addition to the gaps between programmes, there are also major gaps within them. The urban poor, for example, are largely excluded from the MBPF by the targeting criteria, even though the disparities between rural and income poverty have reduced considerably in recent years. The MBPF also has a relatively narrow focus on income poverty rather than multidimensional deprivation; the two do not always coincide.

Labour-market policies cover only a small proportion of the unemployed population and are thus ineffective in addressing the mismatch between the supply of labour and demand, particularly from the formal sector. This is further undermining the sustainability of the social insurance system and will adversely affect the retirement outcomes of today's workers. While pension coverage is high for existing elderly populations, today's labour force is less likely than older generations to contribute to the Social Fund, and those who do might not be contributing the full amount. As a consequence, the current generation of workers is likely to receive much lower pensions than today's pensioners – a likelihood reinforced by the failure of the pension system to protect the value of workers' contributions.

Labour market policies for women need to be significantly improved. Chapter 1 showed that young women are the most likely not to be in education, employment or training, teenage pregnancy is one the rise, and overall labour force participation rates for women are low. Elevated school enrolment rates for girls are not translating into good labour market outcomes, and what little assistance exists to get women into the labour force operates on a very low scale. Public works programmes are the main labour market policy but are overwhelmingly accessed by men and do not have a clear social protection rationale.

## Notes

[1] Benefits for merit groups are outlined in Annex 2.A.

[2] The imputed rate is a value used to calculate different benefits, fees, fines, etc., which are usually set as multiples of this rate. Originally, this was a minimum monthly wage but subsequently became a separate value. In 2015, the imputed rate was KGS 100.

[3] The MHIF, located in Bishkek, is responsible for the collection of contributions for the Additional Mandatory Health Insurance programme (through the Social Fund) and is the sole purchasing agency for health services within the Kyrgyz health care system.

[4] FGPs are the main providers of primary health services.

[5] FAPs provide the most basic services, such as prenatal and postnatal care, immunisations and health education.

[6] FMCs are the largest outpatient health care providers in the country.

## References

ADB (2013), *Social Protection Index*, Asian Development Bank, Manila, http://hdl.handle.net/11540/79. [3]

ADB (2011), *Civil Society Briefs: The Kyrgyz Republic*, Kyrgyz Republic Resident Mission, Asian Development Bank. [20]

ADB/IMF/World Bank (2010), *The Kyrgyz Republic Joint Economic Assessment: Reconciliation, Recovery and Reconstruction*, Asian Development Bank, International Monetary Fund, World Bank, http://imf.org/external/np/pp/eng/2010/072110.pdf. [16]

Andrews, E. et al. (2006), *Pension reform and the development of pension systems : an evaluation of World Bank assistance*, World Bank, Washington DC, http://documents.worldbank.org/curated/en/629861468166150111/Pension-reform-and-the-development-of-pension-systems-an-evaluation-of-World-Bank-assistance. [5]

CASE/MoLSD/UNICEF (2008), *Effectiveness of Benefits to Families and Children in the Kyrgyz Republic*, Center for Social and Economic Research (CASE), Ministry of Labor and Social Development of the Kyrgyz Republic (MoLSD), United Nations Children's Fund (UNICEF), https://www.unicef.org/kyrgyzstan/sites/unicef.org.kyrgyzstan/files/2018-02/Effectiveness_Benefits_Families_Children_Eng.pdf. [14]

Falkingham, J., B. Akkazieva and A. Baschieri (2010), "Trends in out-of-pocket payments for health care in Kyrgyzstan, 2001–2007", *Health Policy Plan*, Vol. 25/5, pp. 427-436. [28]

GIZ (2012), *Исследование для изучения возможностей системы государственного управления, образования для создания системы повышения квалификации, переподготовки специалистов социальной защиты [Study to study the possibilities of the system of public administration, education to create a system of professional development, retraining of specialists in social protection]*, Healthcare in Central Asia regional program, German Development Organisation - Deutsche Gesellschaft für Internationale Zusammenarbeit (GiZ). [19]

GoK (2014), *Programme for Promoting Employment and Regulating Internal and External labour Migration until 2020*, Government of Kyrgyzstan, Bishkek, http://cbd.minjust.gov.kg/act/view/ru-ru/94692?cl=ru-ru. [24]

GoK (2011), *Government Resolution No. 451 of August 5, 2011 On approval of model structure and staffing level of the executive body of local self-government of the Kyrgyz Republic*. [18]

GoK (2004), *Law of the Kyrgyz Republic of 02 August, 2004 No. 103 About Social fund of the Kyrgyz Republic*. [6]

GoK (1993), *Law of the Kyrgyz Republic of 07 May, 1993, No. 1194-XII On provision of pensions for military personnel*. [13]

Ismayilova, L. and A. Huseynli (2014), "Reforming child institutional care in the Post-Soviet bloc: The potential role of family-based empowerment strategies", *Children and Youth Services Review*, Vol. 47, pp. 136-148, http://dx.doi.org/10.1016/J.CHILDYOUTH.2014.09.007. [21]

Kuddo, A. (2011), *Unemployment Registration and Benefits in ECA Countries*, World Bank, Washington DC. [26]

MoH (2012), *Den Sooluk National Health Reform Program in the Kyrgyz Republic for 2012-2016*, Ministry of Health, Government of Kyrgyzstan. [27]

Mukanova, K. (2007), *Local self government in Kyrgyzstan—myth or reality?*, http://nispa.org/conf_paper_detail.php?cid=16&p=1154&pid=7003. [17]

Müller, K. (2005), "Post-Socialist Pension Reform: Contributory and Non-Contributory Approaches", *Public Finance & Management* , Vol. 5/2, pp. 290-309. [11]

NSC (2017), *National Statistics Committee of the Kyrgyz Republic.* [29]

NSC (2015), *Kyrgyz Integrated Household Survey*, National Statistics Committee of the Kyrgyz Republic, Bishkek. [15]

Schwarz, A. et al. (2014), *The Inverting Pyramid: Pension Systems Facing Demographic Challenges in Europe and Central Asia*, World Bank Group, Washington DC, http://documents.worldbank.org/curated/en/514831468029365694/Main-report. [9]

Schwegler-Rohmeis, W., A. Mummert and K. Jarck (2013), *Labour Market and Employment Policy in the Kyrgyz Republic: Identifying constraints and options for employment development*, Deutsche Gesellschaft für Internationale Zusammenarbeit (GIZ) GmbH, Eschborn/Bishkek. [25]

Social Fund of the Kyrgyz Republic (2018), *Social Fund of the Kyrgyz Republic*, http://socfond.kg/ (accessed on 01 May 2017). [8]

Tobis, D. (2000), "Moving from residential institutions to community-based social services in Central and Eastern Europe and the former Soviet Union", *A World Free of Poverty series*, World Bank, Washington DC. [22]

UNICEF (2014), *TransMonEE: Transformative Monitoring for Enhanced Equity*, http://transmonee.org/wp-content/uploads/2016/07/TM_2014_brochure_v1.pdf (accessed on 09 May 2017). [23]

Wooden, A. (2014), "Kyrgyzstan's dark ages: framing and the 2010 hydroelectric revolution", *Central Asian Survey* , Vol. 33/4, pp. 463-481, https://doi.org/10.1080/02634937.2014.989755. [4]

World Bank (2014), "Kyrgyz Republic Public Expenditure Review Policy Notes: Pensions", in *Public Expenditure Review Report No. 89007*, World Bank, Washington DC. [12]

World Bank (2014), "Kyrgyz Republic Public Expenditure Review Policy Notes: Social Assistance", in *Public Expenditure Review Report No. 89022*, World Bank, Washington DC. [7]

World Bank (2012), *The First Wave of NDC Reforms: The Experiences of Italy, Latvia, Poland, and Sweden Nonfinancial Defined Contribution Pension Schemes in a Changing Pension World*, World Bank, Washington DC. [10]

World Bank (2000), *Kyrgyz Republic - Fiscal sustainability study*, World Bank, Washington DC. [2]

World Bank (1993), *Kyrgyzstan - Social protection in a reforming economy*, World Bank, Washington DC. [1]

# Annex 2.A. Inventory of social protection programmes

## Annex Table 2.A.1. Existing social protection programmes

| Programme | Type of transfer | Eligibility criteria | Coverage (individuals in 2015)/% of total population | Responsible ministry/agency | Legal basis |
|---|---|---|---|---|---|
| Monthly benefit for poor families with children (MBPF) | Monthly unconditional cash transfer | Families must have the following: at least one child under age 16; a gross monthly per capita family income not exceeding the guaranteed minimum income | 304 000/ 5.16% | MoLSD | Law No. 318 of 29 December 2009 on state benefits in the Kyrgyz Republic |
| Monthly social benefit (MSB) | Monthly unconditional cash transfer | Paid to the following categories: children under age 18 with disabilities; children with mothers living with HIV/AIDS, until 18 months; persons with lifelong disabilities (Groups I, II and III), if not eligible for a pension; persons with disabilities (Groups I, II and III), if not eligible for a pension; senior citizens, if not eligible for a pension; Heroine mothers, if not eligible for a pension; surviving children, orphaned children, if not eligible for a pension | 80 500/1.37% | MoLSD | Law No. 318 of 29 December 2009 on state benefits in the Kyrgyz Republic |
| Supplementary Monthly Social Benefit (SMSB) | Monthly unconditional cash transfer | Paid to families of those killed and injured in the events of April June 2010. Eligible categories: natural and adopted children of deceased citizens, from the death of the parent until age 18; parents of deceased citizens, from the date of reaching the retirement age (if the deceased was the only child, his/her parents are entitled to the SMSB for life); people with disabilities, from onset of disability until the expiration of the corresponding disability certificate issued by the board of medical-social experts (Disability Board of Review) | 637/0.01%<br>Of them:<br>427 children under age 18;<br>210 people with disabilities | MoLSD | Law No. 173 of 22 October 2012 on social protection of family members of the victims of the April June 2010 events |
| Maternity Benefit | Lump sum cash transfer | Maternity benefit (for pregnancy and delivery) paid to women for the period of maternity leave: 126 180 calendar days, depending on the difficulty of delivery, the number of births and the region of work (mountainous/remote areas) | 40 859/0.69% | MoLSD | Regulation on the assignment, payment and amount of benefit on sick and maternity leave.<br>Last version of the regulation approved by Government |

| | | | | | |
|---|---|---|---|---|---|
| | | | | | Decree No. 192 of 3 April 2015 |
| Funeral (burial) benefits | Lump sum cash transfer | Provided to citizens of the Kyrgyz Republic at death. The amount depends on the employment status of the deceased or the caregiver of a deceased dependent. The benefit is not paid upon the death of Kyrgyzstan labour migrants who lived and worked abroad. | 3 593/0.06% | MoLSD* | Regulation on the assignment, payment and the amount of the burial benefit.<br>Last version of the regulation approved by Government Decree No. 308 of 4 June 2014 |
| Unemployment benefit | Monthly unconditional cash transfer | Provided to individuals who are officially registered unemployed for at least 12 months aggregately for a maximum of 6 calendar months in a year but for no more than 12 months in 3 years | 463/0.008% | MoLSD | Law No. 3 of August 2015 on facilitation to the population's employment |
| Privileges for categories of citizens | Multiple types, including monthly cash payments (compensations for privileges), annual payments, lump sum payments, non-monetary benefits, and loans | Paid to 25 categories of beneficiaries, including veterans and family members, Chernobyl victims and people with lifelong sight or hearing disabilities | 63 900/1.08% | MoLSD | Government Decree No. 795 of 22 December 2009 on payment of monthly monetary compensations instead of privileges |
| Pensions | Monthly cash transfer (Contributory) | • Old-age: paid to men aged 63+ with the qualifying period (length of pensionable service) of 25 years and to women aged 58+ with the qualifying period of 20 years<br>• Disability: paid to insured people recognised as persons with disabilities with the qualifying period by onset of disability<br>• Survivor: paid to unemployable family members who were dependent on the deceased, if the deceased had the qualifying period for disability pension by time of death | In 2014:<br>634 000/10.98% | Social Fund | Law No. 57 of 21 July 1997 on state pension, social insurance |
| Active labour market programmes | Various | • Paid for vocational training/re-training<br>• Paid for public works<br>• Paid for micro-credits | Start of 2016†:<br>34 800/0.58%<br>In 2014:<br>34 200/24% (vocational training); 4% (recipients of micro-credits‡); 72% (public works) | MoLSD | Law No. 3 of August 2015<br>On facilitation to the population's employment |
| Social services in institutions (15 institutions) | Transfer from the MoLSD to the institutions' banking accounts | • Provided for children with mental disabilities<br>• Provided for adults with mental disabilities | As of end of 2014‖<br>Adults with disabilities and the elderly: | MoLSD | Law No. 111 of 19 December 2001 on foundations of social services in the |

| | | | | | |
|---|---|---|---|---|---|
| | | • Provided for people with Group I and II disabilities<br>• Provided for elderly people and family couples who need external assistance§ | 1 915/0.03%<br>Children with disabilities: 428/0.007% | | Kyrgyz Republic |
| Social services provided at home | Services provided free of charge | • Provided for single elderly people<br>• Provided for single people with disabilities | In 2014#: 3 000/0.27% (disabilities); 6 000/0.55% (elderly) | MoLSD | Law No. 111 of 19 December 2001 On foundations of social services in the Kyrgyz Republic |
| Housing allowances | Transfer to utility enterprises | Targeted means-tested social benefit provided for low-income families in Bishkek to help pay for utility services. Eligibility criterion: allowable utility charges exceed 10% of family income. Allowable amount is based on living area of 14 $m^2$ per person but not more than 70 $m^2$ per family (or 35 $m^2$ for one- to two-person families). | 7 120 families (Moiseeva, 2015) | Bishkek city kenesh (council) | Decree of Bishkek City Kenesh No. 316 of 12 June 2012 Regulation on the utility allowances for people living in Bishkek |
| State Guaranteed Benefits Package (SGBP) | • A range of free basic health services<br>• Copayments** for additional health services such as preventive services, medicines, rehabilitation, and recreation activities | • Basic health care provided – for all citizens<br>• Additional health care provided for mandatory health insurance (MHI) programme beneficiaries | Whole population | MoH (Mandatory Health Insurance Fund [MHIF]) | Manas<br>Manas Taalimi<br>Den Sooluk<br>Law No. 6 of 9 January 2005 on Health Protection of the Citizens of the Kyrgyz Republic |
| Additional Drug Package (ADP) | Provision of medicines | • MHI programme beneficiaries | In 2012: 76.6% of the total population was enrolled in MHI | MoH (MHIF) | Manas<br>Manas Taalimi<br>Den Sooluk<br>Law No. 6 of 9 January 2005 on Health Protection of the Citizens of the Kyrgyz Republic |

* Families of all pensioners who received pensions from the Social Fund also receive this benefit also from the Social Fund.

† For all labour market policies. Source: Author (year), Medium-Term Budgetary Framework for 2017 - 2019, URL.

‡ On average, one unemployed individual may receive KGS 10-30 000 for one year with an interest rate of 10-15%.

§ As per service standards.

|| Source: NSC (2017[29]).

# Source: MoLSD (2015), Social Protection System Development Programme, 2015-2017.

** Some socially and medically vulnerable groups, such as those suffering with diseases requiring frequent health care service visits, are exempt from co-payments.

# Annex 2.B. Funeral benefits

**Annex Table 2.B.1 Funeral benefits by category**

| Category of deceased at death | Rate of benefit | Amount of benefit in 2015, KGS | Amount of benefit in 2015, USD |
|---|---|---|---|
| Employed person | 100% of the average wage | 12 285 | 190.60 |
| Individual entrepreneurs working on the basis of a patent or tax contract<br>Head or adult member of an unincorporated peasant farm enterprise<br>Unemployed person registered with Public Employment Services<br>Dependent family member supported by an employed person | 50% of the average wage | 6 142 | 95.30 |
| Dependent family member supported by an individual entrepreneur<br>Dependent family member supported by a household head or adult member of a peasant farm enterprise<br>Dependent family member supported by an unemployed person | 20% of the average wage | 2 457 | 38.10 |
| Person entitled to the Monthly Social Benefit | 30 of the IR | 3 000 | 46.50 |
| Unemployed person | 20% of the average wage | 2 457 | 38.10 |
| Pensioner | 10 times the baseline pension | 15 000 | 232.70 |
| Dependent family member supported by a pensioner | 3 times the baseline pension | 4 500 | 69.80 |

# Chapter 3. The effectiveness of social protection

*This chapter evaluates the effectiveness of the largest components of the social protection system according to their coverage rates, adequacy, equity and efficiency, using administrative and household survey data. It examines the Monthly Benefit for Poor Families with children (MBPF), the Monthly Social Benefit (MSB) and contributory pensions paid by the Social Fund, as well as the overall effectiveness of the pension and the health-care systems in responding to the population's needs. It also analyses the impact of possible reforms to the state benefits for children.*

Chapter 2 identifies the wide range of social protection instruments protecting different groups of people in Kyrgyzstan. However, these programmes are not always well aligned with the needs of the population identified in Chapter 1, and they vary considerably in size. The next step in the SPSR is to understand the effectiveness of the different programmes in order to determine which represent best value for money and which might require reform.

This chapter analyses the impact of Kyrgyzstan's major social protection programmes in greater detail. It considers their effectiveness across three dimensions: coverage, equity and the efficiency with which they reduce poverty. This analysis includes preliminary analysis of a proposed new system of state benefits for children that combines categorical and poverty-targeted components.

## The MBPF's impact is hampered by low coverage, low benefits and targeting errors

The MBPF is intended to mitigate the effects of extreme poverty among households with children. This programme is of utmost importance given 48.5% of the poor population is aged under 18. However, its low coverage rates and low benefit levels constrain its effectiveness.

### *Coverage*

Coverage of the MBPF is low and declining. According to the GoK, coverage rates of children under age 18 declined from 21% in 2005 to 13.6% in 2015 (Figure 3.1). Survey data suggest coverage at a household level is much lower. According to the 2015 Kyrgyz Integrated Household Survey (KIHS), 8.5% of all households received a benefit through the programme, while only 4.9% of the population lived in MBPF-eligible households.

**Figure 3.1. Official figures show a decline in coverage**

Coverage rate of children under 18 through the MBPF

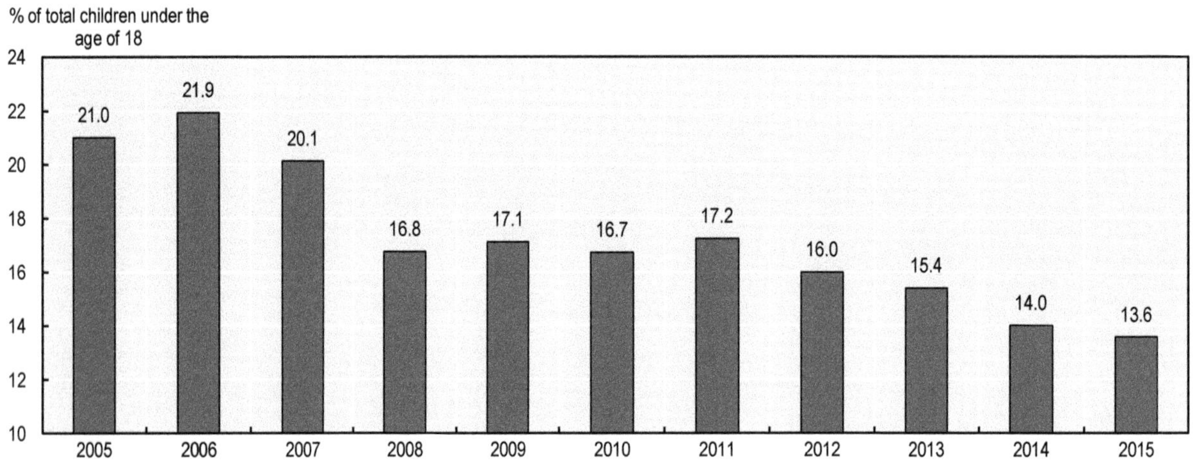


*Source*: MoLSD, NSC (2015).

This level of coverage is far below the proportion of households with children that are classified as poor. However, it is higher than the proportion of households who are (*de jure*) eligible for the programme, which is targeted at the extreme poor by using the guaranteed monthly income (GMI) as a threshold even though extreme poverty has almost been eradicated (Box 3.1).

The MBPF's impact is undermined by significant exclusion errors. Data from the 2015 KIHS show an overall take-up rate among eligible households of 22.7%, meaning some 77.3% of people living in MBPF-eligible households did not receive any benefits. Only 24.8% living in eligible households in the first decile did receive the benefit. This is consistent with other analysis indicating that the MBPF excludes over 80% of extremely poor children (Gassmann and Trindade, 2016[1]).

It is apparent that the GMI is not an appropriate means test threshold (Box 3.1). Assuming the GoK retains a poverty-targeting component to the child benefits, it might need to establish an eligibility threshold that is both measurable and affordable. A cost-neutral option would be to allow coverage of the MBPF to increase while reducing benefit levels (thereby reversing the tendency of the last decade). As is discussed below, however, the value of the MBPF already falls below critical welfare measures.

**Box 3.1. The link to the GMI limits both the cost and effectiveness of the MBPF**

The GMI plays a critical role in determining eligibility for the MBPF as well as the value of the benefit. As such, it serves to ration coverage and limit adequacy. In both cases, the low level of the GMI; it thus serves as a major impediment to the effectiveness of Kyrgyzstan's only poverty-targeted programme.

When the GMI was established in 1998, it was set at 50% of the EPL, with the intention of gradually raising it to 100% of the EPL. Instead, the GMI fell as a proportion of the EPL to as low as 21% in 2008 before recovering to breach 50% for the first time in 2015. The result is that the value of the MBPF, which is connected to the value of the GMI, is very low.

It also means that the eligibility threshold for the MBPF is not meaningful; only a very small proportion of the households have a per capita income below the GMI. The only way to retain the GMI is to artificially deflate the imputed income of rural households so that it falls below the level of the GMI. This option doesn't exist for urban households, whose income is much less likely to be in-kind; this contributes to the overwhelming bias of the MBPF towards rural households.

### *Adequacy*

At the end of 2015, the value of the MBPF benefit was KGS 705 per month.[1] This benefit value was not high enough to guarantee households with children an income above the EPL even though it was three times higher in real terms than it had been previously.

As is the case with the low coverage of the MBPF, the fact that the value MBPF is not adequate is also a function of its link to the GMI. Until 2014, the benefit a household received was intended to fill the gap between their current income and the level of the GMI. In 2015, this system was simplified such that the value of the benefit was set at the level of the GMI. It should be remembered that benefit values vary according to the altitude coefficient discussed in Chapter 2.

The MBPF is too low to cover beneficiaries' basic needs. Its average level in 2015 was 16.0% of the required subsistence minimum for children,[2] 46.4% of the EPL and 26.8%

of the overall poverty line (OPL) (Figure 3.2). A significant increase in benefit levels (either by increasing the value of the GMI or cutting the link with this threshold) would therefore be required to make the MBPF more adequate according to these thresholds. However, the cost of the programme would rise commensurately with such an increase.

**Figure 3.2. The MBPF falls short of key poverty benchmarks**

The value of MBPF relative to key poverty thresholds (2005-15)

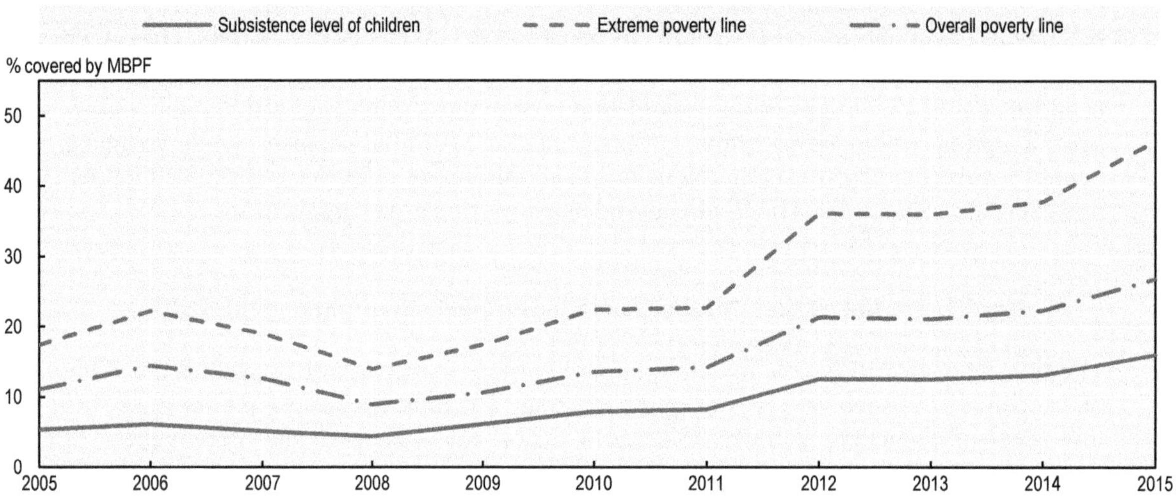


*Source*: Authors' calculations based on NSC (2015[2]), *Kyrgyz Integrated Household Survey* (database).

## *Equity*

In addition to its coverage and adequacy, a social protection programme's effectiveness is determined by the distribution of benefits. A programme is considered pro-poor if the distribution of benefits and beneficiaries displays higher incidence in the lower deciles of the population.

The MBPF is pro-poor. A World Bank expenditure review of social assistance (2014[3]) found that over 70% of MBPF recipients who received over 80% of the total MBPF benefits belonged to the poorest 40% of the population in 2011. In 2015, 36.4% of benefits distributed through the programme were transferred to households in the first decile of the income distribution, and 61.9% of MBPF recipients who received over 71.7% of the total MBPF benefits, belonged to the poorest 40% of the population.

In contrast, the combined benefits to the top three deciles accounted for less than 4% of total benefits in 2015 (Figure 3.3, right-hand column). The trend is similar, although less pronounced, in the incidence of beneficiaries (Figure 3.3, left-hand column), which show one-fifth of all beneficiaries were in the first decile of the population. In 2015, 62% of MBPF recipients who received over 72% of the total MBPF benefits belonged to the poorest 40% of the population.

**Figure 3.3. The MBPF is pro-poor but there is leakage to higher income groups**

Incidence of MBPF beneficiaries and benefits (2015 KIHS)

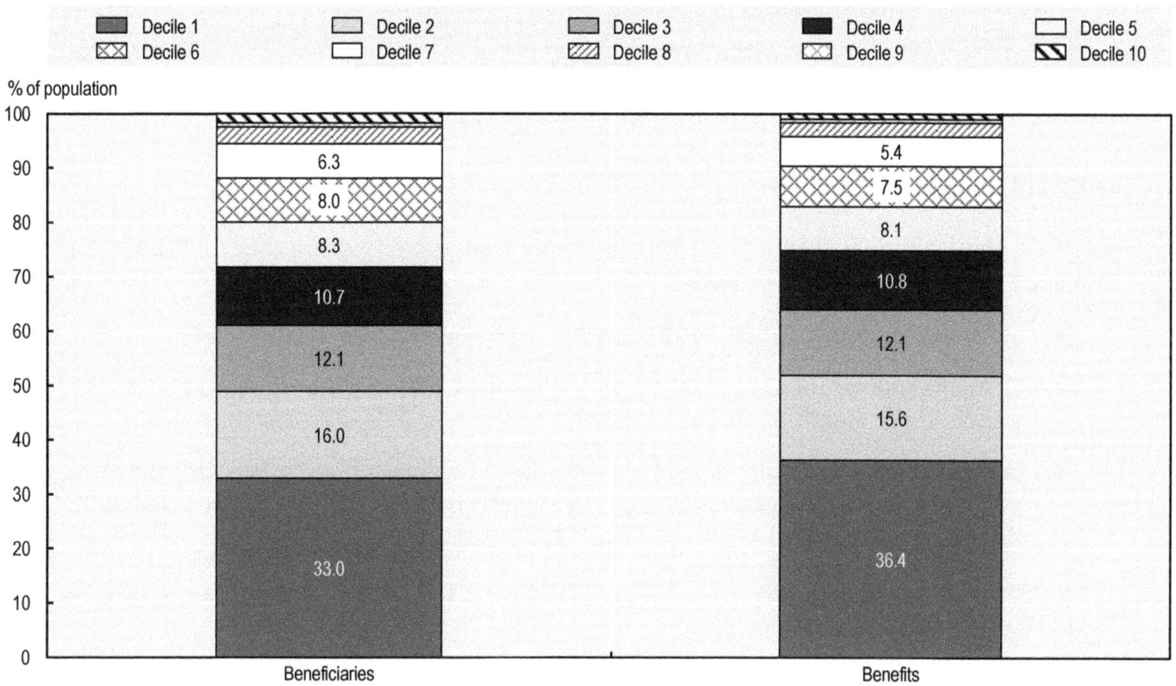


*Source*: Authors' calculations based on NSC (2015[2]), *Kyrgyz Integrated Household Survey* (database).

## *Efficiency*

Measured against the extreme and overall poverty lines, the MBPF has relatively low effects on poverty alleviation. However, the exact effect depends on a key assumption in the simulations: the marginal propensity to consume (MPC). Previous analysis of social assistance in Kyrgyzstan (Gassmann and Trindade, 2015[4]) has assumed a very low MPC, of around 33%. This implies that the income boost associated with receiving a benefit is lower than the value of the benefit itself, perhaps because some other source of income is reduced as a consequence (such as transfers from another household).

The impact of transfers on poverty at the household level can be sensitive to the size and composition of the household. Children might have lower consumption requirements than adults, and there might be economies of scale in larger households. Equivalence scales can be applied to poverty analysis results to capture these factors. Although mindful of the analysis of equivalence scales by the World Bank (2013[5]), this report will not apply an equivalence scale as the GoK does not do so when calculating the official poverty rate.

Analysis of the 2015 KIHS based on these assumptions shows that MBPF benefits achieve a 4% reduction in the poverty headcount, displaying a poverty gap reduction efficiency of 60% (a cost of KGS 1.66 led to a poverty gap reduction of KGS 1).[3] The extreme poverty gap reduction efficiency of 8.25% is considerably lower (a cost of KGS 12.12 led to an extreme poverty gap reduction of KGS 1).[4]

**Table 3.1. Poverty-reducing efficiency of the MBPF**

| Cost (KGS, million) | Poverty headcount reduction (%) | Extreme poverty headcount reduction (%) | Poverty gap reduction (KGS, million) | Extreme poverty gap reduction (KGS, million) | Poverty reduction efficiency (%) | Extreme poverty reduction efficiency (%) |
|---|---|---|---|---|---|---|
| 2 180 | -3.91 | -37.5 | -1 309.8 | -179.76 | 60.08 | 8.25 |

*Source*: Authors' calculations based on (2015[2]), *Kyrgyz Integrated Household Survey* (database).

## Reforming the MBPF to balance impact and cost is a major challenge

In 2017, the GoK published a Draft Law on State Benefits proposing that the MBPF be replaced by three categorical benefits:

- A once-off payment at the birth of every child equivalent to KGS 4 000
- A monthly benefit for all children under the age of three, with a value of KGS 700 per child per month.
- A monthly grant for any household with three or more children between the ages of three and sixteen, paying a monthly benefit of KGS 500 per child per month, starting from the third child.

This proposed design encountered strong resistance from different groups. Objections focused on two issues in particular:

- The adverse impact on existing beneficiaries: The requirement that only households with three or more children would receive the benefit for children aged over 3 years old, and that only the third child onwards would be eligible, meant that current recipients of the MBPF would invariably be worse-off.
- Cost: Categorical benefits would cost significantly more than the MBPF.

In response to these concerns, a hybrid model has been discussed that retains three components but envisages a continued role for the MBPF. The components are:

- A once-off payment at the birth of every child, equivalent to KGS 4 000
- A monthly benefit for infants up to 2 years old, with a value of KGS 700 per child per month (with an altitude coefficient applied)
- The MBPF for children aged between 2 years old and 16 years old whose per capita household income falls below the GMI, payable at a rate of KGS 810 per child per month (altitude coefficient applied)

This section of the SPSR compares the distributional implications, impact on poverty and cost of each component. It also analyses a lower MBPF value set at the average level of benefit paid in 2015 (KGS 653) to show how differences in the value of the MBPF affect its impact. Poverty impact is calculated based on the poverty rate in 2015; in that year, the national poverty rate would have been 33.1% if MBPF payments were excluded from household consumption.

### *Poverty-reducing impact of the new and old schemes*

The three components of the proposed benefits benefit the poorer deciles more than those with higher incomes (Figure 3.4). The MBPF is the most progressive in the sense that coverage falls most steeply across income deciles: from 20.7% in the first decile to 11.2%

in the third. However, the universal infant benefit achieves the highest level of coverage in the first and second deciles, at 41.3% and 29.0% respectively. Coverage of the infant benefit declines after the fifth decile but exceeds 20% up to and including the eighth decile. While receipt of the infant benefit declines with income, there is significant leakage to higher deciles, as is to be expected for a universal benefit.

**Figure 3.4. The MBPF is more progressive than categorical benefits**

Beneficiary incidence of three possible components of a hybrid scheme

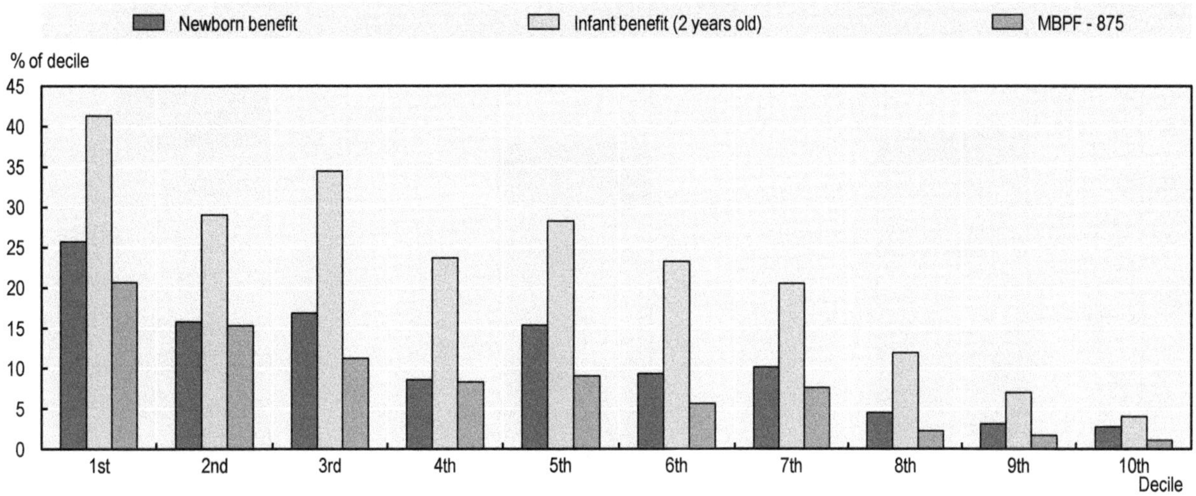


*Note:* Deciles are calculated based on pre-MBPF consumption.
*Source*: Authors' calculations based on NSC (2015[2]), *Kyrgyz Integrated Household Survey* (database).

Figure 3.5 shows how the beneficiary population is distributed across the income distribution. This is a more accurate reflection of the distributional implications of the different components, since it strips out the discrepancies in absolute coverage of the MBPF and universal benefits respectively. There is less disparity between the universal benefits and the MBPF in terms the proportion of beneficiaries in each decile.

**Figure 3.5. A majority of categorical beneficiaries are in the lowest income deciles**

Distribution of beneficiaries for the three components by decile

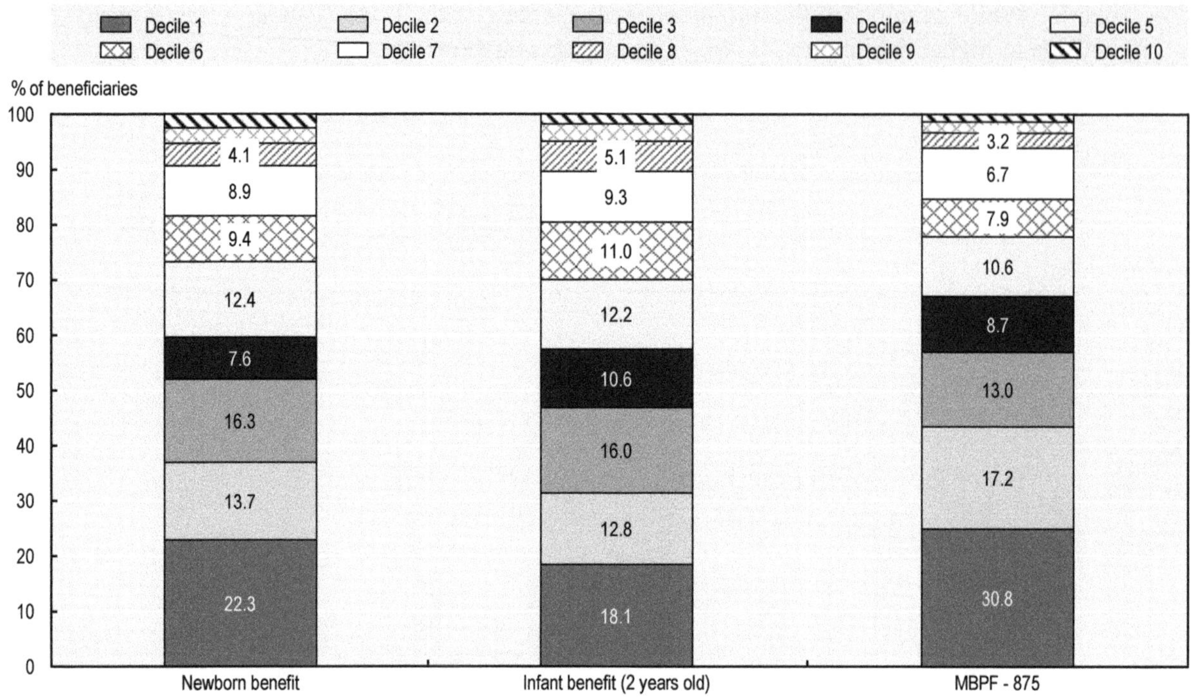


*Note:* Deciles are calculated based on pre-MBPF consumption.
*Source:* Authors' calculations based on NSC (2015[2]), *Kyrgyz Integrated Household Survey* (database).

Benefit incidence shows similar trends to the beneficiary incidence. However, in this case, there is an even steeper decline for the MBPF: 30.8% of total MBPF benefits are transferred to the first decile, versus 13.0% in the third decile (Figure 3.6). Leakage of the MBPF to non-poor households is again evident: 39.0% of benefit expenditure goes to income deciles four and above. However, this is much lower than the equivalent figure of 53.1% for the infant benefit and 47.2% for the newborn benefit.

**Figure 3.6. Over half of MBPF benefits would go to the first two income deciles**

Benefit incidence of the three components by decile

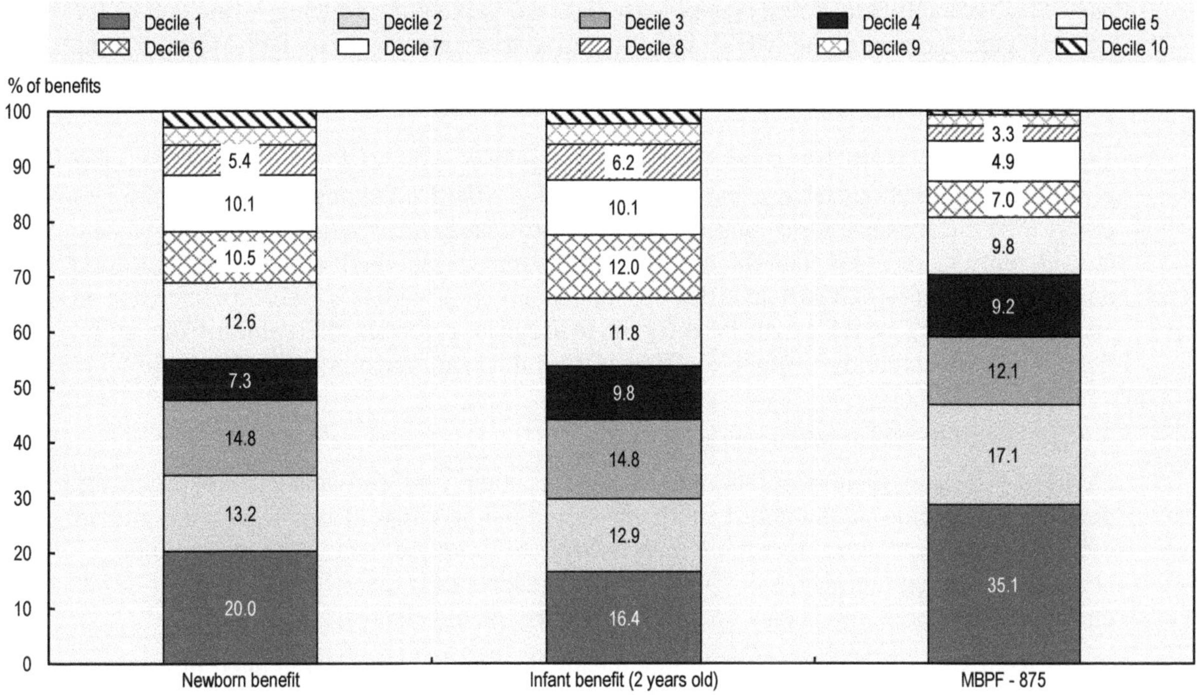


*Note:* Deciles are calculated based on pre-MBPF consumption.
*Source:* Authors' calculations based on NSC (2015[2]), *Kyrgyz Integrated Household Survey* (database).

**Table 3.2. Estimated coverage, cost and poverty impact of hybrid state benefits**

| Benefit | Value | Total number of beneficiaries | Total disbursement (KGS million) | Total disbursement (% of GDP) | Reduction in the poor population (%) | Reduction in poverty rates (percentage points) |
|---|---|---|---|---|---|---|
| Newborn benefit | KGS 4 000, without coefficient | 119 184 | 462.6 | 0.11 | 0.24 | 0.08 |
| Infant benefit (up to second birthday) | KGS 700 per month, with coefficient | 254 718 | 2 311.5 | 0.53 | 4.10 | 1.35 |
| Low MBPF (up to 2 years old) | KGS 653 per month, without coefficient | 232 219 | 1 819.8 | 0.42 | 4.13 | 1.37 |
| High MBPF (2-16 years old) | KGS 810 per month per capita, with coefficient | 232 219 | 2 438.7 | 0.56 | 4.80 | 1.59 |

*Source*: Authors' calculations based on NSC (2015[6]), *Kyrgyz Integrated Household Survey* (database).

The overall impact on poverty of the three components is shown in Table 3.2. This includes the "low benefit" for the MBPF by way of comparison. With a higher level of the MBPF benefit, the new hybrid programme has the effect of reducing poverty from 33.1% to 30.1%. Coverage levels of the universal and the poverty-targeted components are striking: the infant benefit reaches more children than the MBPF (eligible to children aged 2 to 16 years old) despite the disparity in overall cohort size.

The lower-value MBPF is 21.3% less expensive than the universal infant benefit while the higher-value MBPF is 5.5% more expensive. The infant benefit is less efficient at reducing poverty than either the high value MBPF or the low value MBPF. The low value MBPF is more efficient at reducing poverty than the high value, which is a function of the poverty gap: increasing the MBPF's value above a certain level has less impact on the overall poverty rate because the benefit is more than sufficient to exit recipients from poverty.

The overall cost of the proposed hybrid programme is estimated at 1.2% of GDP. The cost drops to 0.96% of GDP using the lower value MBPF. Although this would be less costly than the proposal for a complete shift towards categorical benefits, both options are considerably more costly than the MBPF in its current form, which received an allocation equivalent to 0.6% of GDP in 2015. As discussed in Chapter 4, such an increase in spending on state benefits will be difficult to finance; reducing the value of the infant benefit or eliminating the altitude coefficient from this component might be necessary.

### *Future demand for a categorical benefit*

Demand for categorical programmes, as well as their cost and impact, are driven by demographic factors. Assuming benefit levels remain constant in real terms, the cost of the categorical components of the proposed hybrid option would be determined by changes in the age structure of the population. Depending on whether more or fewer children are covered, the impact on national poverty would also vary.

Kyrgyzstan's relatively high fertility rate means the number of children aged under 20 is expected to grow from 2.3 million to 2.7 million between 2015 and 2025. However, the fertility rate is declining: the number of individuals under age five is projected to fall over this period, from 747 691 to 656 180 (Figure 3.7). This has the potential to reduce the cost of state benefits, and in particular categorical benefits aimed at newborns and infants.

**Figure 3.7. The proportion of infants in the population is declining**

Children under age 20, by five-year cohort (2015, 2020, 2025)

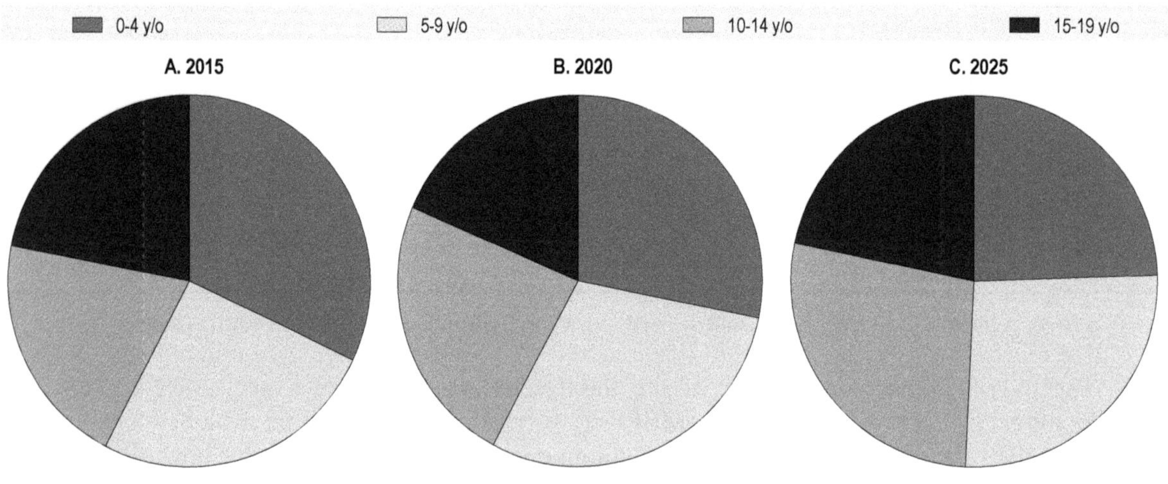


*Source*: UN DESA (2017[7]), *World Population Prospects* (database).

The analysis of the proposed hybrid programme lacks a counterfactual of the MBPF's impact under different conditions. For example, to gauge their respective impact on poverty, it might be interesting to allocate the same budget to the MBPF as to the new programmes and simulate the results. However, this disregards the structural problems with the MBPF that might limit its capacity to scale up, not least its rural bias.

Moreover, such an exercise might also require a revision of the eligibility criteria so that coverage of the MBPF is expanded at the same time; otherwise the impact of a higher allocation to this programme would merely be to (significantly) increase the benefits paid to households that are already receiving the benefit. Interestingly, anecdotal evidence has indicated that increases in the value of the MBPF (that have coincided with significant declines in coverage) have been associated with considerably higher leakage.

By combining categorical and poverty-targeted benefits, the hybrid programme modelled here addresses the two main shortcomings of the proposed shift to universal benefits: exclusion of existing recipients and excessive cost. As such, it represents a practical way forward that will enhance the poverty-reducing impact of state benefits at a lower cost than the initial proposal.

This analysis shows there is a weak rationale for continuing the recent trend of reducing coverage of the MBPF while simultaneously increasing benefit values, even though these remain far below important welfare measures. Assuming that the programme's budget is fixed in real terms, a greater impact on poverty would be achieved by widening access (by increasing the income threshold) while keeping benefit levels unchanged in real terms.

## Coverage of the MSB is growing but it has challenges with transparency

The MSB is a categorical rather than means-tested benefit. In recent years, there have been different dynamics at play for different groups, reflecting both demographic factors and political priorities. As a result, the MSB has evolved into an umbrella programme comprising benefits for various vulnerable groups, some of which have benefited from parametric adjustments while others have been left worse off. In general, benefits that have analogues in the social insurance system have been reduced while those that do not have increased.

### *Coverage*

Coverage of the MSB has steadily increased, from 53 900 beneficiaries in 2005 to 80 500 in 2015, growing at a much faster rate (a 50% increase) than Kyrgyzstan's population as a whole, which increased by 15% over this period. Nonetheless, the coverage rate in 2015 was just 1.3% of the total population in 2015 (up from 1.0% in 2010).

While overall coverage has increased, there are disparities in growth among categories. Strongest growth appears among children under age 18 with HIV/AIDS, orphaned children and persons with Group III systemic disabilities[5] (Table 3.3). However, while the relative increase was highest among children with HIV/AIDS, there were 445 beneficiaries of this category in 2015, up from 100 beneficiaries in 2010.

Among the adult disability categories, it is notable that strongest growth has occurred among adults with systemic disabilities and that the increases in lifelong and systemic disabilities have been highest among Group III beneficiaries – the group still able to work. The high growth among Group III claimants coincides with a proportionally higher increase in the benefit level relative to other categories and previous years (World Bank, 2014).

The Disability-Adjusted Life Years findings of Chapter 1 do not explain the increase in claimants for other categories, suggesting the possibility of latent demand for disability benefits: the increase in the size of the benefit has motivated eligible individuals to invest time and money to enrol. The increase in claimants might also be linked to employment patterns. There is evidence in other countries that workers vulnerable to difficult labour market conditions enrol for disability benefits, a trend likely pronounced when there is disparity between the value of unemployment benefits and disability benefits, as is the case in Kyrgyzstan.

The decrease in the number of MSB beneficiaries among older persons is a temporary phenomenon associated with an upwards adjustment in MSB entitlement ages, from 63 to 65 years for men and from 58 to 60 years for women. The purpose of this reform was to restrict access to the benefit so that workers would be incentivised to belong to the contributory pension system rather than rely on the social pension.

There was a significant increase in the number of MSB beneficiaries among orphaned children and children without an income-generating adult in the household, which likely reflects two factors: diminishing coverage of the contributory pension system among today's workforce and the impact of labour migration on childcare. The increased coverage of children with disabilities masks significant exclusion errors: the number of children with disabilities receiving MSB increased by 6 700 between 2011 and 2015, while the number of children with disabilities increased by 17 500.

**Table 3.3. The number of children eligible for the MSB is growing**

Level and growth in MSB beneficiaries, by category

| Category | Category composition | Increment in the number of beneficiaries in 2015 vs. 2010, (%) | 2010 | 2015 |
|---|---|---|---|---|
| Children under 18 with disabilities | Cerebral palsy | 26.2 | 3 435 | 4 335 |
| | Other disabilities | 33.7 | 17 211 | 23 011 |
| | HIV and AIDS | 481.4 | 62 | 362 |
| | Congenital HIV/AIDS in children | 256.5 | 23 | 83 |
| Persons with lifelong disabilities | Group I | 22.2 | 3 604 | 4 404 |
| | Group II | 13.8 | 14 493 | 16 493 |
| | Group III | 47.6 | 4 832 | 7 132 |
| Persons with systemic disabilities | Group I | 89.3 | 336 | 636 |
| | Group II | 86.7 | 1 961 | 3 661 |
| | Group III | 167.4 | 597 | 1 597 |
| Senior citizens, including highland inhabitants | | -16.6 | 1 807 | 1 507 |
| Heroine mothers | | 8.3 | 120 | 130 |
| Surviving children | | 25.6 | 11 719 | 14 719 |
| Orphaned children | | 166.6 | 300 | 800 |

*Source*: Authors' calculations based on NSC (2015[2]), *Kyrgyz Integrated Household Survey* (database).

As discussed in Chapter 2, coverage of MSB-eligible populations is characterised by exclusion and inclusion errors, which are attributable to unequal access to medical certification and non-transparent practices in the certification process.

Almost 49 000 individuals over the age of 18 were classified as disabled in 2015 according to the KIHS, while administrative data show that 34 000 individuals received a disability transfer through the MSB (Table 3.3). The MSB does not provide targeted support for the examination, diagnosis, treatment and rehabilitation of persons with disabilities in low-income households, which is particularly hurtful for children with higher chances of full rehabilitation contingent on timely medical treatment.

Main exclusion errors in the MSB relate to poor diagnosis of individuals in need of disability assessment by primary health care institutions and financial barriers to inclusion among low-income families. Increasing employment in the informal sector, where occupational safety requirements are not observed, is also believed to have driven increases in systemic disabilities.

Inefficiencies in the board of medical-social experts (Disability Board of Review) – especially inaccuracies in awarding benefits to disability Group III, often due to favouritism – is a major source of inclusion errors in the MSB. These beneficiaries have privileged admission to hospitals (entitled to free treatment) and maintain the right to work while receiving benefits (IVEST, 2016[8]).

### *Adequacy*

The benefits under the MSB are generous relative to the MBPF, with six out of the 14 beneficiary categories receiving benefits matching or exceeding the OPL in 2015 (Figure 3.8). These six categories all correspond to the group of disabled children or adults, although persons with systemic disabilities receive benefits below the OPL.

Until 2005, the value of the MSB was the same across all categories of beneficiary and set at the same level as the GMI.[6] Benefits were uniformly raised above the GMI in 2006, and in 2007, the GoK varied the MSB by category, disrupting the consistency across different components of the programme. The value of the MSB was officially delinked from the GMI from 2010, when the benefit value was also increased by around 50% to compensate for the electricity tariff increases.

On average, the value of the MSB almost doubled between 2005 and 2015. However, benefit levels have increased unevenly across categories since 2010; the benefit for children and adults with disabilities has increased, while it has not done so for other categories.

Benefits are smallest for surviving children, elderly without pensions, Heroine mothers and orphan children, ranging from 30% to 80% of the OPL. Benefits for these categories declined as a proportion of the OPL between 2010 and 2015.

The decline in real benefit levels for elderly individuals reliant on social assistance is in stark contrast to the treatment of Social Fund pensions, which are typically indexed on an annual basis with reference to wage inflation (consistently been higher than price inflation in Kyrgyzstan).

**Figure 3.8. The adequacy of the MSB differs by component**

Adequacy of MSB benefits, by category

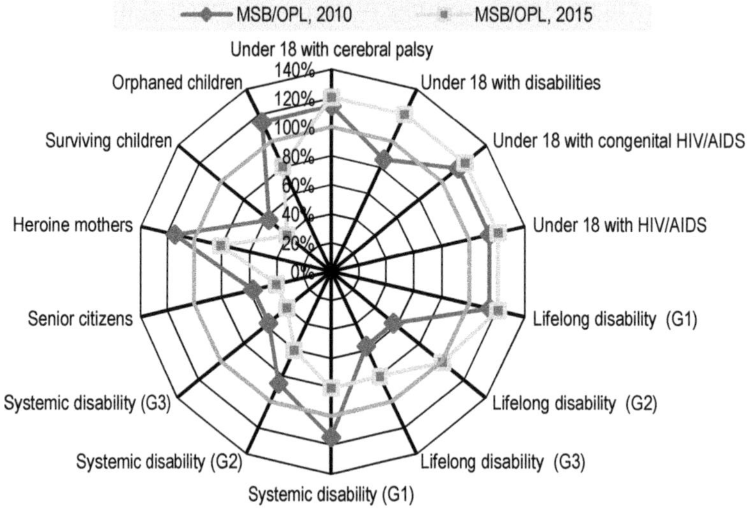


*Note*: G1, G2, and G3 refer to Group 1, Group 2, and Group 3, respectively.
*Source*: Authors' calculations based on NSC (2015[2]), *Kyrgyz Integrated Household Survey* (database).

### *Equity*

Since it is not poverty-targeted, the MSB is not pro-poor by design, except insofar as the prevalence of beneficiary categories declines with income. The relatively small number of beneficiaries makes it difficult to capture the incidence of benefits and beneficiaries through household survey data. However, eligible low-income individuals are at a higher risk of exclusion from the MSB due to high financial and access burdens associated with the examination and certification of disability.

The equity principle also relates to how vulnerable groups are treated by different social protection programmes. By providing more favourable eligibility conditions and benefit adjustments for contributory pensions than for the MSB, the GoK is undermining this principle. Given the structural challenges facing the contributory system it might be necessary to find other means of maintaining contributions to the Social Fund.

## High pension coverage will be difficult to sustain

The State Pension Social Insurance programme is the largest social protection programme in Kyrgyzstan. Contributors to the Social Fund, which is responsible for its management, are eligible for old-age, disability and survivor pensions, while military personnel receive pensions on a non-contributory basis.

### *Coverage*

Pension coverage among the elderly was nearly universal in 2015, and 45.2% of the population lived in pension beneficiary households. In that year, pensions covered nearly 647 000 individuals through the contributory components, up from 536 000 in 2005, versus 2 000 who received the MSB.[7] The increase in beneficiaries reflects demographic trends: coverage as a share of the population remained stable at around 10.5% between 2005 and 2015 (NSC, 2015).

The composition of pension beneficiaries changed between 2005 and 2014. While the share of old-age pensioners (76% and 74%, respectively), survivor pensioners (11% and 8%) and military pensioners (0.5% and 0.3%) decreased, the share of disability pensioners increased from 14% to 18% (Figure 3.9).

**Figure 3.9. The proportion of disability pensioners is growing**

Composition of Social Fund beneficiaries (2005 and 2014)

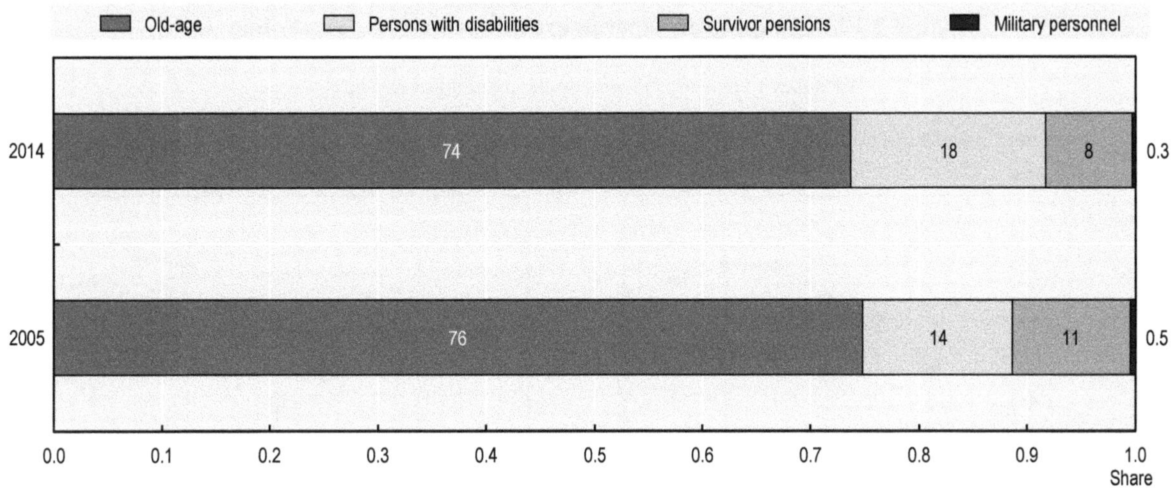


*Source*: Authors' calculations based on NSC (2015[2]), *Kyrgyz Integrated Household Survey* (database).

In 2011, the ratio of old-age pensioners to the population over age 65 exceeded 100% due to a combination of 91% coverage of the population over age 65 and significant early retirement (World Bank, 2014). Over 17% of old-age pension recipients in 2013 had taken early retirement, reflecting special dispensations for groups such as Heroine mothers and individuals living in high-altitude areas, who are able to retire 5 years and 10-13 years before the statutory retirement age, respectively.

However, the proportion of the current labour force contributing to the Social Fund is much lower than the proportion of the retired workforce receiving benefits. Just over half the labour force contributed to the Social Fund in 2013, which not only suggests pension coverage among the elderly will decline over time but also threatens the solvency of the pay-as-you-go component of the Social Fund.

Low coverage among the current workforce is partly a function of the high contribution rate. However, evidence suggests strong public desire to be covered by the Social Fund, albeit at a lower cost (discussed in Chapter 2).

### *Adequacy*

The average benefit from all forms of contributory pensions exceeds the OPL, meaning the programme plays a critical role in reducing poverty. However, there are variations in the level and trajectories of the different components.

The average value of the old-age pension rose from 105.2% of the OPL in 2005 to 208.1% in 2013 but fell to 192.0% thereafter (Figure 3.10, left-hand panel). The average disability pension has exceeded the OPL since 2010 and, in 2015, stood at 135.0% of the threshold. The average survivor pension benefit exceeded the value of the OPL for the first time in 2014 but showed the strongest growth over the preceding decade: in 2015, it was almost 3.5 times its 2005 level as a proportion of the OPL.

However, pension payments are much lower when indexed against the SM for pensioners (Figure 3.10, right-hand panel). The average value of the old-age pension has exceeded the SM for pensioners since 2011 and was at 111% of this threshold in 2015, up from 56% in 2005.The disability pension was at 82% of the threshold in 2015, up from 37% in 2005, and the survivor pension benefit was at 72%, up from 19% in 2005.

**Figure 3.10. Average pension levels exceed the overall poverty line**

Adequacy of pensions relative to the overall poverty line

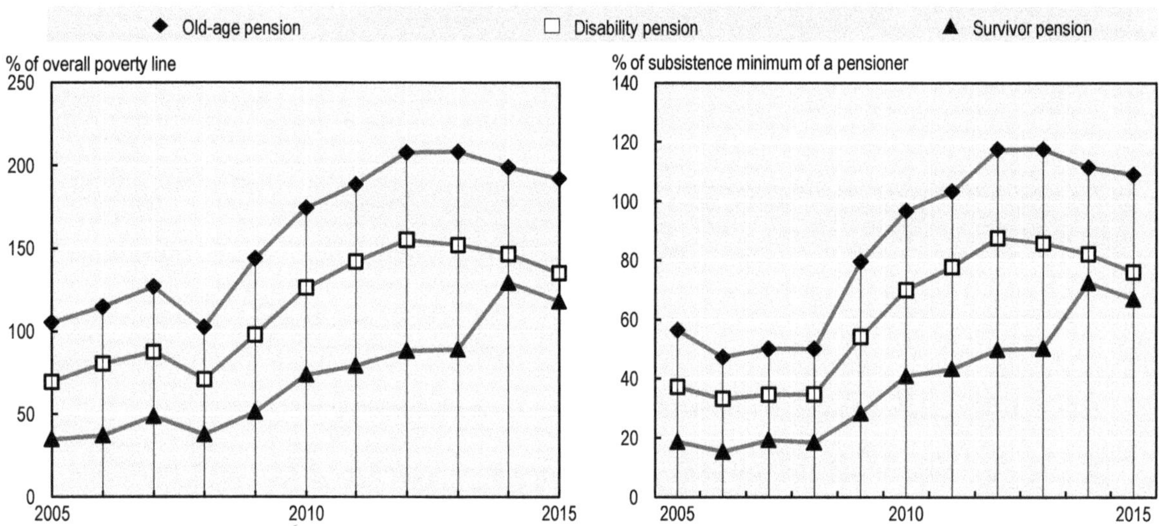


*Source*: Authors' calculations based on NSC (2015[2]), *Kyrgyz Integrated Household Survey* (database).

In the case of contributory social protection arrangements, adequacy also relates to the return workers receive on their lifetime contributions. A widely used indicator of a pension system's adequacy is the replacement rate. From an individual's perspective, this measures the value of the pension benefit as a proportion of salary (either career average or at career end). From the perspective of the system, it is calculated as the ratio of the average pension to the average wage.

The ILO (1967[9]) recommends replacement rates exceed 45% of a worker's income in retirement, a rate especially problematic given the high contribution rate: 25% of a worker's salary, divided between employee and employer. If workers consider the value of the pension benefit to be low relative to the contribution rate they might opt out of the system.

Despite the increased value of old-age pensions against the OPL, the replacement rate declined from 40.1% in 2010 to 37.9% in 2014. The aggregate decline in replacement rates likely reflects the changing composition of contributors; smaller contributions translate into lower replacement rates. However, the decline also masks adequacy dynamics among different groups of individuals, both in absolute terms and with respect to their contributions.

The maximum value of the basic pension component (which accounts for the majority of pension income for voluntary contributors) was set at 12% of the average wage or

KGS 1 500 in 2015. For workers not contributing for the full period (20 years for women and 25 years for men), the value of the basic pension is pro-rated, meaning some recipients might receive a basic pension far below the OPL and even equivalent to the MSB. Mandatory contributors, especially those at higher-income levels, will receive a low return on their contributions due to cross-subsidisation of other contributors and design features of the insured components (discussed in Chapter 2).

According to the World Bank (2014[10]), replacement rates will fall to 25% of the average contributor wage in 2035 if the second pillar component of the pension system is not reformed (the first pillar is being phased out). This implies the basic pension will comprise an ever-larger part of pension payments, increasing to 50% of the benefit paid to formal-sector workers and 95% of the benefit paid to farmers.

## *Equity*

The incidence of pension beneficiaries and benefits tends to be pro-poor, with the first two deciles accounting for more than one-quarter of benefits and beneficiaries (Figure 3.11). The distribution of benefits does not vary greatly between the third and the ninth decile but is notably higher among the first two deciles and the top decile.

**Figure 3.11. The pension system is pro-poor**

Incidence of pension beneficiaries and benefits across income distribution

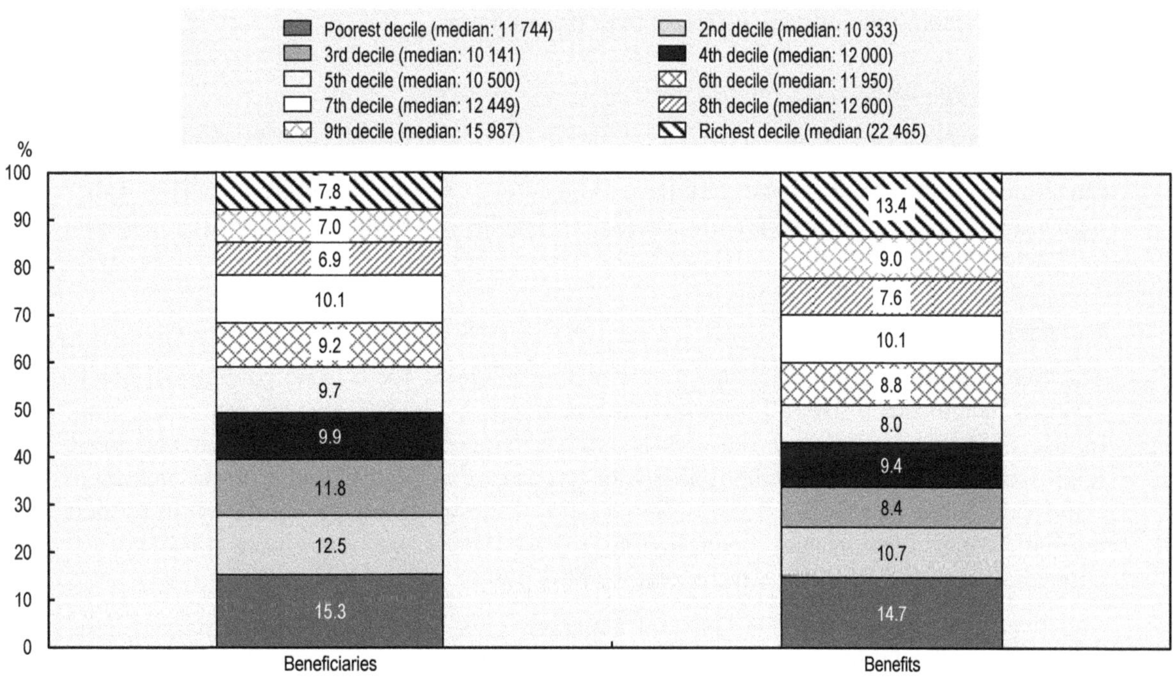


*Source*: Authors' calculations based on NSC (2015[2]), *Kyrgyz Integrated Household Survey* (database).

The distribution of benefits does not vary greatly between the third and ninth deciles but is notably higher among the first two deciles and in the top decile. This reflects the weak link between pension contributions and benefits received. In a typical pension arrangement (whether defined benefit or defined contribution), upper income deciles would receive a larger proportion of overall benefits paid annually because they contributed more in absolute terms, even though the rate of contributions might be the same for all income levels.

This is not the case in Kyrgyzstan due to the system's design. The basic pension component is quasi-contributory: the value of a contributor's benefit is determined by the duration not size of contributions, so the replacement rate declines with income. As workers' contributions to the second pillar component lose their value and the weight of the basic pension increases, the system will become more redistributive from the better-off to the worse-off, especially given the basic pension is financed almost entirely from the Republican Budget.

However, workers may respond by withdrawing from the Social Fund or under-reporting their earnings, which will exacerbate the financial strain caused by the imbalance between contributors and beneficiaries and could harm public finances more broadly, if it causes a decline in tax revenues (thus also affecting the GoK's ability to finance the basic pension component).

Equity analysis must also consider workers not covered by the contributory system. Providing an MSB benefit that is significantly lower than the minimum pension payment is perceived as a means of promoting compliance with the contributory system. However, trends discussed in Chapter 1 indicate the number of MSB beneficiaries will increase substantially in the coming years, driven by workers who worked informally or abroad their whole careers. Maintaining a tax-financed non-contributory scheme (the MSB) and a tax-financed quasi-contributory scheme (the basic pension) might not be politically sustainable or administratively efficient over the long term.

## Health coverage has increased but poses equity challenges

The level of health care coverage in Kyrgyzstan reflects a combination of the State Guaranteed Benefits Package (SGBP), Mandatory Health Insurance (MHI), other demand-side mechanisms under the Mandatory Health Insurance Fund (MHIF) umbrella and supply-side initiatives.

### *Coverage*

The SGBP forms a non-contributory universal entitlement for a basic package of health services. Under the SGBP, all primary and emergency health services are free at the point of use. However, enrolment requires at least a temporary residence permit and basic identification documents, a potential barrier to access for migrants who might lack them (Giuffrida, Jakab and Dale, 2013[11]). Some 22% of those without resident permits at their current living location had been unable to use health services when they needed assistance, versus only 12% of those who had the permit.

SGBP does not cover co-payments for inpatient care and specialised outpatient care. There are two additional levels of co-payment coverage: they are waived entirely or partly for vulnerable groups and certain medical conditions, while a lower co-payment schedule applies for those covered by the MHI. Those not covered by the exemption schemes or MHI have to pay the maximum co-payment (Table 3.4).

Co-payment exemption categories are heterogeneous, from World War II veterans to children under age 5 and the disabled. They cover 48% of the population: in 2012, around 640 000 patients benefited, with more than half of the exemptions covering care for children under age 5 and pregnant women (Giuffrida, Jakab and Dale, 2013[11]). The exemption mechanism has been found to be effective in lowering the health payment burden in exempted categories (Jamal and Jakab, 2013[12]).

According to the 2012 Demographic Health Survey (DHS), around 12% of the population does not have MHI coverage (NSC/MoH/ICF International, 2013[13]). Those not covered seem to be wealthier and younger. Age is a clear factor for women, with 81% of those aged 15-30 covered by MHI, versus 92% for those aged 30-49. For men, the difference is around five percentage points between the two age groups. Wealth is a more important determinant for men, with 96% of men in the poorest two quintiles covered by MHI, versus 86% in the richest three quintiles. This pattern of coverage points to an important factor of adverse selection whereby the younger and wealthier (thus likely healthier) opt out. Opting out is made possible for informal workers by the *de facto* voluntary nature of their enrolment in MHI (see also Giuffrida, Jakab and Dale, 2013).

Those enrolled in MHI, either through payroll contributions or a flat rate enrolment contribution of KGS 550 by informal workers and the self-employed, pay a reduced co-payment rate, while those not covered by MHI and not part of the exemption scheme pay the full co-payment rate.

**Table 3.4. Co-payment rates under the SGBP**

| Forms of co-payment | | | In-patient facilities, other than national hospitals, KGS | National hospitals, KGS |
|---|---|---|---|---|
| Co-payment for the general practice | With a referral for hospitalisation | Minimum rate | 330 | 330 |
| | | Average rate | 840 | 1 160 |
| | | Maximum rate | 2 650 | 2 980 |
| Co-payment for surgery | With a referral for hospitalisation | Minimum rate | 430 | 430 |
| | | Average rate | 1 090 | 1 510 |
| | | Maximum rate | 3 440 | 3 870 |

*Source*: Authors' calculations based on NSC (2015[2]), *Kyrgyz Integrated Household Survey* (database).

Co-payments data show the average co-payment rate for surgery in non-national hospitals closely matches the minimum wage (KGS 1 060 per month), while the maximum rate is three times the minimum wage. Even the minimum rate of KGS 430 represents 41% of the minimum wage, with levels even higher in national hospitals. The overall level of co-payments can thus be rather high and points to the limits of the financial coverage provided by the health care system, especially for catastrophic events and, in theory, for those not covered by MHI or the exemption system.

The level of health coverage is also determined by the Additional Drug Package (ADP) scheme. ADP coverage is linked to MHI enrolment, so those not covered by MHI are disadvantaged by both higher co-payments for consultations and no reimbursements for medicines. Even for those covered by ADP, coverage is limited, as the reimbursement has a ceiling of 50% of a baseline price for a generic drug, which is often exceeded by the actual price because of prescription of brand names (WHO, 2016[14]).

### *Adequacy*

The adequacy of health coverage in Kyrgyzstan can be evaluated by using the global Universal Health Coverage Outcome Monitoring Framework, which looks at service coverage and financial protection (WHO/World Bank, 2017[15]). Beside the outcome-focused indicators, the availability and quality of health services are key elements in judging how the health care system ensures de facto coverage.

### *Access to care*

SGBP entitlement does not fully translate into access to health services. Kyrgyzstan compares unfavourably to a set of regional countries for antiretroviral (ART) coverage[8] and care for children with respiratory symptoms but favourably for antenatal care and tuberculosis (TB) treatment (Figure 3.12).

**Figure 3.12. Access to care is variable**

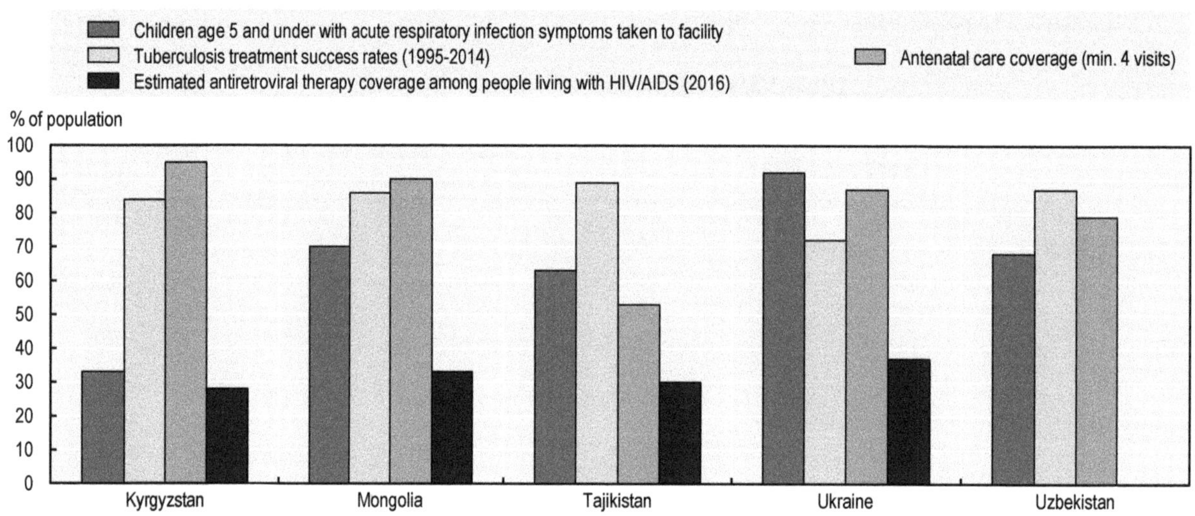


*Source*: WHO (2017), *Universal Health Care Data Portal* (database), apps.who.int/gho/cabinet/uhc.jsp.

Low ART coverage partly owes to the vertical nature of the HIV/AIDS programme, limiting SGBP's reach to cover the disease (Ancker S. and Rechel, 2015[16]). Good TB coverage is due to its integration into the SGBP (Ibraimova A., Akkazieva and Ibraimov, 2011[17]), expressly including outpatient TB drugs (van den Boom, Mkrtchyan and Nasidze, 2014[18]).

According to the 2015 KIHS, 31.8% of individuals who declared a medical need did not access any health services. The majority (88.5%) instead opted for self-treatment. Other reasons cited were the high cost of health visits (2.3%), the high cost of drugs (5.8%) or a decision to let the disease/illness run its course (2.7%). Similarly, 61.9% of those referred to a hospital (or who required inpatient treatment) but did not stay at a hospital also opted for self-treatment, 18.0% cited the expense and 6.4% let the disease run its course.

### *Financial protection*

According to a recent WHO study, out-of-pocket (OOP) health expenditure initially decreased after major health care system reforms starting in the 1990s (discussed in

Chapter 2) but has since been on the rise. OOP health spending in per capita household budgets decreased from 5.3% in 2006 to 3.5% in 2009 (WHO, 2017[19]). Between 2009 and 2014, OOP spending rose, reaching 5.2% in 2014. However, if considering only those who used health services (at least one medical contact in a year), household OOP expenditure was 22%. There is wide regional distribution, with Osh City and Bishkek having higher OOP spending and Batken having the lowest (Figure 3.13).

**Figure 3.13. Out-of-pocket health spending varies by region**

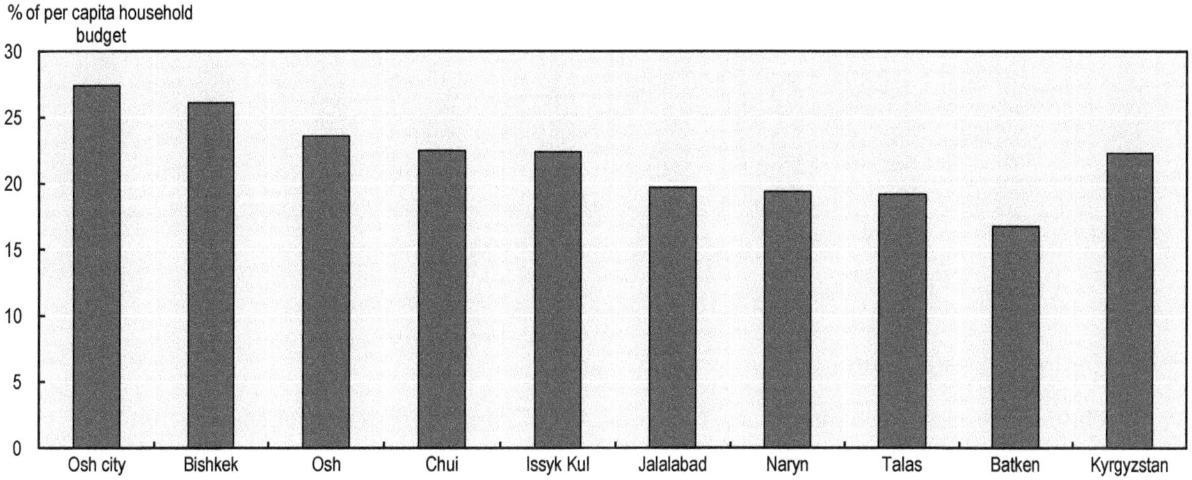


*Source*: Authors' calculations based on NSC (2015[2]), *Kyrgyz Integrated Household Survey* (database).

Individuals needing health care and having to pay OOP often resort to alternative coping mechanisms to afford treatment. The 2015 KIHS showed that 845 146 individuals used their savings to pay for health care costs, 401 665 reduced expenditure considerably as the second most common mechanism, and 151 310 relied on assistance from relatives (NSC, 2015[2]).

Health care expense coping strategies are more prevalent among upper deciles (Figure 3.14). This is expected, as those in higher deciles are also more likely to seek treatment in the first place and to use expensive private providers or seek care abroad. Lower MHI coverage among the richest could also explain their higher need for OOP and coping strategies for catastrophic health events.

**Figure 3.14. Main coping mechanisms for financing health treatment, by decile**

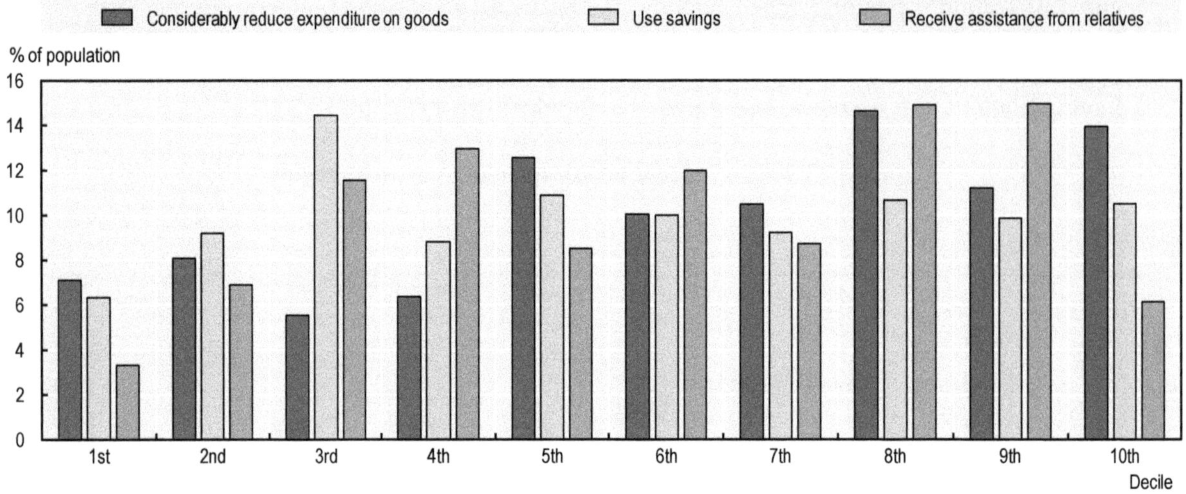


*Source*: Authors' calculations based on NSC (2015[2]), *Kyrgyz Integrated Household Survey* (database).

## *Availability and quality*

While there has been important focus on developing coverage mechanisms on the demand side, there is some question how well service delivery has matched this evolution. Important gaps in service largely relate to lack of health workers, especially in primary health care, and to their uneven regional distribution. In 2015, 60 family group practices had no doctors, and 198 had only one (Abdraimova, Abdurakhmanova and Ybykeeva, 2015[20]). Staff shortages, even in hospitals, owe partly to large numbers of doctors leaving public hospitals to join the private sector or find work abroad (Ibraimova A., Akkazieva and Ibraimov, 2011[17]). The GoK has implemented many stick and carrot policies, including mandatory posting of medical graduates and bonuses for working in rural areas, with limited effect.

Service delivery is further constrained by gaps in equipment and infrastructure. This is especially true for rayon (district) hospitals, some of which lack basic utilities, such as running water or electricity (Ibraimova A., Akkazieva and Ibraimov, 2011[17]). Moreover, medical practices, which are rarely in line with clinical guidelines, are a system-wide issue affecting quality of care.

The impacts of low health service quality on effective coverage and health outcomes can be seen through several indicators. For example, men with high blood pressure cited low quality of care as the main reason they did not seek services (Abdraimova A., Iliasova and Zurdinova, 2016[21]). Knowing maternal mortality is linked to quality of hospital obstetric care for normal and emergency delivery, the relatively high maternal mortality, coupled with the high levels of access to skilled personnel at birth, points to quality gaps in service delivery.

The Den Solook programme, aimed explicitly at increasing quality of care, has made important strides. Under the programme, the GoK has introduced improvements to facilities, purchased new equipment, and established new methods of quality assurance and of developing and implementing a new set of clinical guidelines (Ibraimova A., Akkazieva and Ibraimov, 2011[17]).

## *Equity*

Several equity challenges in health coverage relate to the design and implementation of the health care system, regarding both health insurance mechanisms and health services availability and quality.

### *Equity in service coverage*

Outpatient utilisation patterns reveal inequities in service coverage. In Kyrgyzstan, outpatient utilisation is skewed towards richer population groups, although the equity gap in utilisation has narrowed in recent years (Figure 3.15).

**Figure 3.15. Utilisation of outpatient services in the past 30 days by income quintile (2000-14)**

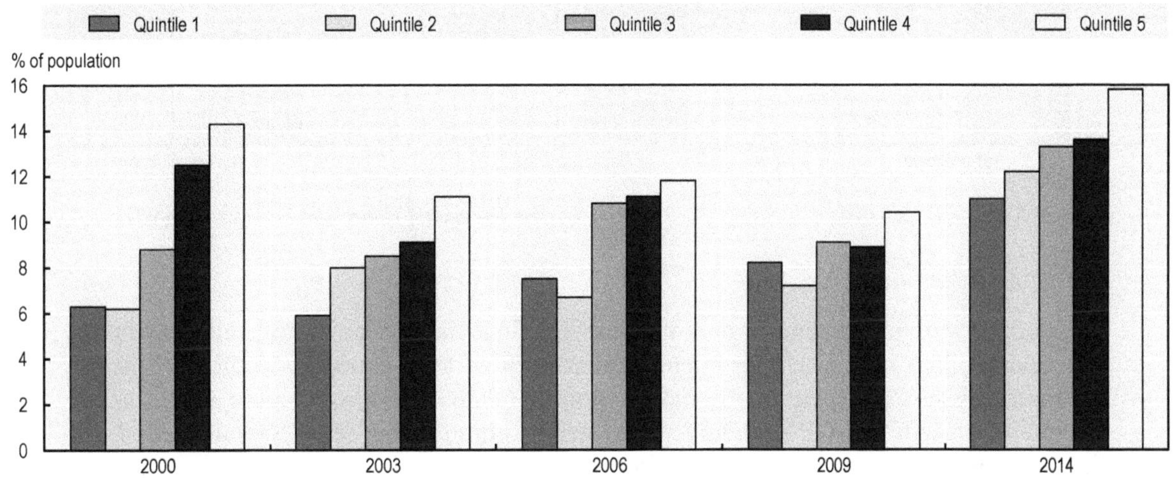


*Source*: Akkazieva, Jakab, and Temirov (2016[22]), "Long-term trends in the financial burden of health care seeking in Kyrgyzstan, 2000–2014".

Access to services inequities are also geographical. Rural residents more often face self-treatment and high visit and drug costs (Figure 3.16). Among those who reported self-treatment, 56.0% lived in rural areas. Among those who cited high drug costs as a reason to avoid services, 86.9% lived in rural areas.

**Figure 3.16. Financial barriers to health services are higher for rural residents**

Reasons for not accessing health services (2014)

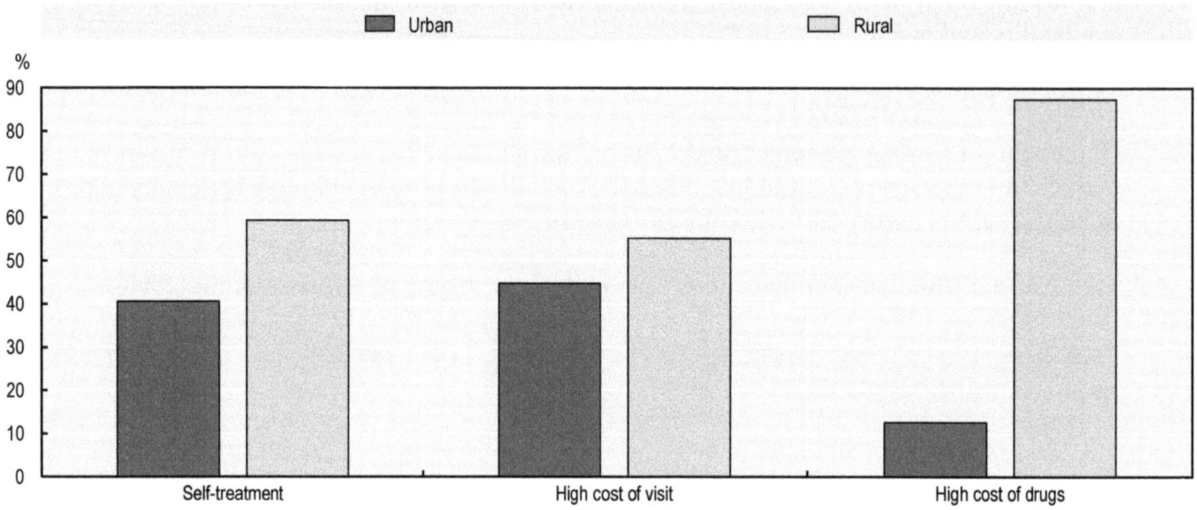


*Source*: Authors' calculations based on NSC (2014[23]), *Kyrgyz Integrated Household Survey* (database).

## *Equity in financial protection*

The poorest individuals tend to bear the heaviest financial burden from health payments. The poorest 20% of households spends about 30% of total expenditure on OOP health expenses, versus 22% spent by the richest quintile (WHO, 2016[24]) (Figure 3.17).[9] While the rate of growth in OOP spending varied across quintiles between 2009 and 2014, the financial burden increased most for the poorest quintile.

**Figure 3.17. Out-of-pocket health spending is a larger burden on the poor**

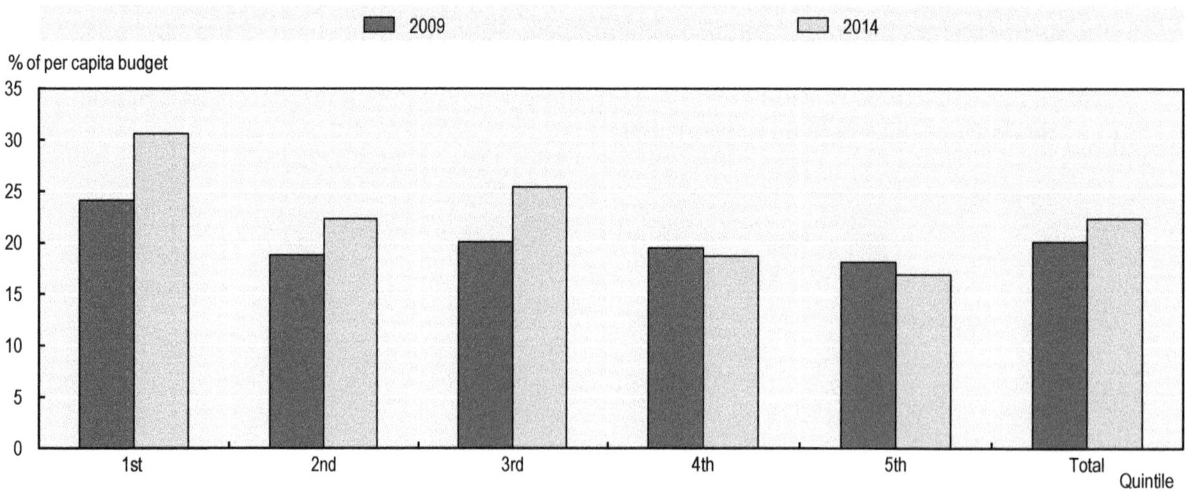


*Source*: Akkazieva, Jakab, and Temirov (2016[22]), "Long-term trends in the financial burden of health care seeking in Kyrgyzstan, 2000–2014".

Co-payment exemptions tend not to be pro-poor, targeting the poor ineffectively and benefiting the non-poor substantially. The exemptions cover less than 50% of the poorest two income quintiles and 39% of the richest quintile (Figure 3.18). Although the GoK provisions the right to further co-payment exemption for those in low-income households, this is inaccurately and inadequately implemented.[10]

**Figure 3.18. Health-care user fee exemptions are poorly targeted**

Coverage of user-fee exemptions by decile (2010)

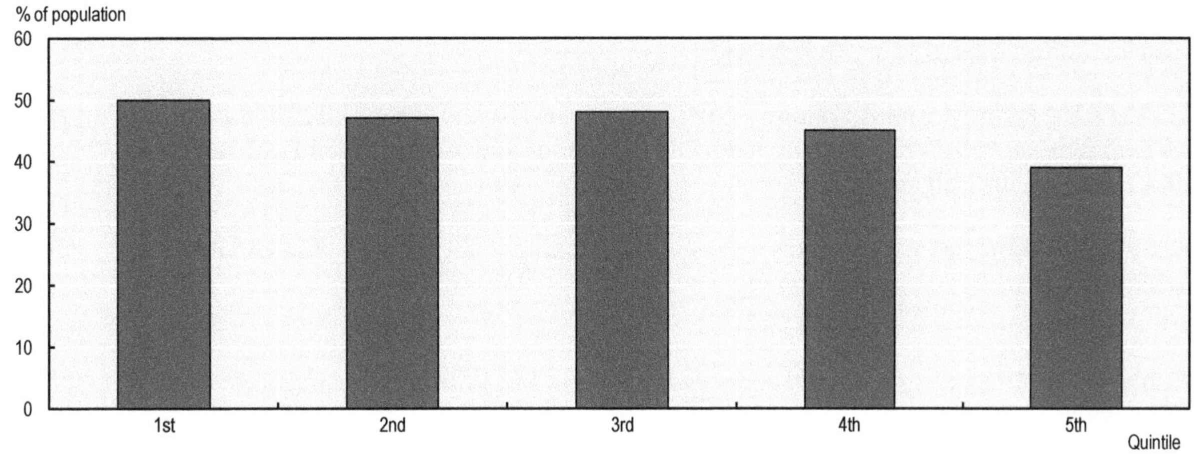


*Source*: Jamal and Jakab (2013[25]), "Targeting performance of co-payment exemptions in the State Guaranteed Benefit Package", http://hdl.handle.net/10986/13311.

## Notes

[1] Consultation with Ministry of Labour and Social Development, 2017.

[2] The government of Kyrgyzstan calculates the minimum subsistence levels for children, adults and pensioners and uses those as national benchmarks. These calculations include costing the subsistence needs of each of the groups – the cost of tailored baskets of goods and services most suitable to each of the groups.

[3] For every KGS 100 of transfers, the poverty gap reduces by KGS 60.08.

[4] For every KGS 100 of transfers, extreme poverty gap reduces by KGS 8.25.

[5] Disability is categorised Group I (total disability and requiring constant attendance), Group II (total disability with an 80% loss of mobility) or Group III (partial disability with some loss in working capacity).

[6] Previously, the guaranteed minimum consumption level (GMCL).

[7] Based on consultations with the Social Fund on 22 June 2016.

[8] There is no data for ART coverage for Uzbekistan.

[9] Including only those households with a member who has come into contact with the health care system.

[10] Article 4, paragraph 23, Government Decree No. 350 of 1-July 2011 on the SGBP.

## References

Abdraimova A., A. Iliasova and A. Zurdinova (2016), *Reasons for low health care seeking among men with hypertension in Kyrgyzstan*, Health Policy Analysis Center, Bishkek. [21]

Abdraimova, A., A. Abdurakhmanova and E. Ybykeeva (2015), *Addressing underutilized capacity for NCD care: New role for family doctors/general practitioners and nurses?*, Health Policy Analysis Center, Bishkek. [20]

Akkazieva B., Jakab M. and A. Temirov (2016), *Long-term trends in the financial burden of health care seeking in Kyrgyzstan, 2000–2014*, World Health Organization Regional Office for Europe, Copenhagen. [22]

Ancker S. and B. Rechel (2015), "HIV/AIDS policy-making in Kyrgyzstan: a stakeholder analysis", *Health Policy and Planning*, Vol. 30/1, pp. 8-18, https://dx.doi.org/10.1093/heapol/czt092. [16]

Gassmann, F. (2012), *Kyrgyz Republic: Evaluation of the Draft Strategy on Social Protection Development 2012-2014.* [28]

Gassmann, F. and L. Trindade (2016), "The effect of means-tested social transfers on labour supply: heads versus spouses-An empirical analysis of work disincentives in the Kyrgyz Republic", *UNU-MERIT Working Paper Series*, No. 2016-030, Maastricht Economic and social Research institute on Innovation and Technology (UNU-MERIT), Maastricht. [1]

Gassmann, F. and L. Trindade (2016), "The effect of means-tested social transfers on labour supply: heads versus spouses-An empirical analysis of work disincentives in the Kyrgyz Republic", *UNU-MERIT Working Paper Series*, No. 2016-030, Maastricht Economic and social Research institute on Innovation and Technology (UNU-MERIT), Maastricht. [26]

Gassmann, F. and L. Trindade (2015), *Kyrgyz Republic Analysis of Potential Work Disincentive Effects of the Monthly Benefit for Poor Families in the Kyrgyz Republic*, World Bank, Washington DC. [4]

Giuffrida, A., M. Jakab and E. Dale (2013), "The Case of the State Guaranteed Benefit Package of the Kyrgyz Republic", *UNICO Studies Series*, No. 17, World Bank, Washington DC, http://openknowledge.worldbank.org/handle/10986/13311. [11]

Ibraimova A., B. Akkazieva and A. Ibraimov (2011), *Kyrgyzstan: Health System Review*, European Observatory on Health Systems and Policies, Brussels. [17]

ILO (1967), *Convention concerning Invalidity, Old-Age and Survivors' Benefits (Entry into force: 01 Nov 1969).* [9]

IVEST (2016), "In Kyrgyzstan, for 10 years the number of disabled persons increased by 50 thousand", *Информ-Вест [Inform-West]*, http://news.ivest.kz/70601156-v-kyrgyzstane-za-10-let-kolichestvo-invalidov-uvelichilos-na-50-tys. [8]

Jamal, S. and M. Jakab (2013), *Targeting performance of co-payment exemptions in the State Guaranteed Benefit Package*, World Health Organization Regional Office for Europe, Barcelona. [12]

Jamal, S. and M. Jakab (2013), *Targeting performance of co-payment exemptions in the State Guaranteed Benefit Package*, World Health Organization Regional Office for Europe, Barcelona. [25]

NSC (2015), *Kyrgyz Integrated Household Survey*, National Statistics Committee of the Kyrgyz Republic, Bishkek. [2]

NSC (2015), *Kyrgyz Integrated Household Survey*, National Statistics Committee of the Kyrgyz Republic, Bishkek. [6]

NSC (2014), *Kyrgyz Integrated Household Survey*, National Statistics Committee of the Kyrgyz Republic, Bishkek. [23]

NSC (2014), *Kyrgyz Integrated Household Survey*, National Statistics Committee of the Kyrgyz Republic, Bishkek. [29]

NSC (2004), *Kyrgyz Integrated Household Survey*, National Statistics Committee of the Kyrgyz Republic, Bishkek. [30]

NSC/MoH/ICF International (2013), *Kyrgyz Republic Demographic and Health Survey 2012*, National Statistical Committee of the Kyrgyz Republic, Ministry of Health of the Kyrgyz Republic, and ICF International, http://dhsprogram.com/publications/publication-FR283-DHS-Final-Reports.cfm. [13]

UN DESA (2017), *World Population Prospects: The 2017 Revision*, United Nations Department of Economic and Social Affairs, New York, http://un.org/en/development/desa/population/publications. [7]

UNICEF (2014), *Analysis of the Situation of Children in Mongolia*, United Nations Children's Fund Mongolia, Ulaanbaatar. [27]

van den Boom, M., Z. Mkrtchyan and N. Nasidze (2014), *Review of tuberculosis prevention and care services in Kyrgyzstan, 30 June – 5 July 2014*, World Health Organization Regional Office for Europe, Copenhagen. [18]

WHO (2017), *Universal Health Coverage Data Portal*, World Health Organization, Geneva, http://apps.who.int/gho/cabinet/uhc.jsp. [19]

WHO (2016), *Pharmaceutical pricing and reimbursement reform in Kyrgyzstan*, World Health Organization Regional Office for Europe, Copenhagen. [14]

WHO (2016), *Pharmaceutical pricing and reimbursement reform in Kyrgyzstan*, World Health Organization Regional Office for Europe, Copenhagen. [24]

WHO/World Bank (2017), *Tracking Universal Health Coverage: 2017 Global Monitoring Report*, World Health Organization, Geneva. [15]

World Bank (2014), "Kyrgyz Republic Public Expenditure Review Policy Notes: Pensions", in *Public Expenditure Review Report No. 89007*, World Bank, Washington DC. [10]

World Bank (2014), "Kyrgyz Republic Public Expenditure Review Policy Notes: Social Assistance", in *Public Expenditure Review Report No. 89022*, World Bank, Washington DC. [3]

World Bank (2013), *Kyrgyz Republic - Poverty update, 2011*, World Bank, Washington DC, http://openknowledge.worldbank.org/handle/10986/16075. [5]

# Chapter 4. Financing social protection

*This chapter examines spending on social protection from a systemic and whole-of-government perspective. It locates social protection expenditure within the Government's overall budget and examines spending trends across the different pillars of the social protection sector, as well as across individual programmes within this sector. It also analyses the composition of government revenues and the financing of social protection in particular, identifying the increasing subsidisation of the social insurance system by the Republican Budget as a major cause for concern. It concludes with a fiscal incidence analysis showing the overall system of taxes and transfers significantly reduces inequality but its impact on poverty is less clear.*

Social protection is the largest component of public spending in Kyrgyzstan. Exceeding spending on health and education combined, social protection spending is particularly high for a country at Kyrgyzstan's income level. Within the social protection sector, spending on contributory pensions benefits dwarfs expenditure on all other programmes.

Social protection spending has grown in recent years and the modalities of financing are changing. Contributions to the Social Fund have not risen at the same pace as pension expenditure, with the result that the Social Fund is increasingly reliant on transfers from the Republican Budget to meet its obligations. The sustainability of the pension system is a concern not only for the social protection sector but also for public finances as a whole.

Strong growth in tax revenues and sustained support from donors have accommodated growth in social protection spending. However, donor support is declining now that Kyrgyzstan has attained middle-income status and the prospects for social protection to receive additional financing are low, given the proportion of expenditure already allocated to the sector and broader concerns about the country's debt level.

## Social protection dominates public spending

Public spending on social protection includes contributory programmes (financed by earmarked revenues) and non-contributory programmes (financed through general taxation) catalogued in Chapter 2.

Social protection, including both contributory and non-contributory programmes, is the largest function group in terms of public expenditure. It accounted for 28.0% of total public spending in 2015 (Figure 4.1A), more than spending on education (17.0% of total spending) and health (9.2%) combined. In 2009, social protection accounted for 21.7% of spending but this figure jumped in 2010 as a result of higher social assistance spending and has since stayed at an elevated level.

The next largest function group is economic spending (19.1% of expenditure in 2016), which had been the largest function group in 2009 (23.5%), but its allocation was reduced sharply the following year, in contrast to allocation to social protection.

**Figure 4.1. Social protection is the largest function group by spending**

Spending by function group (2005-15)

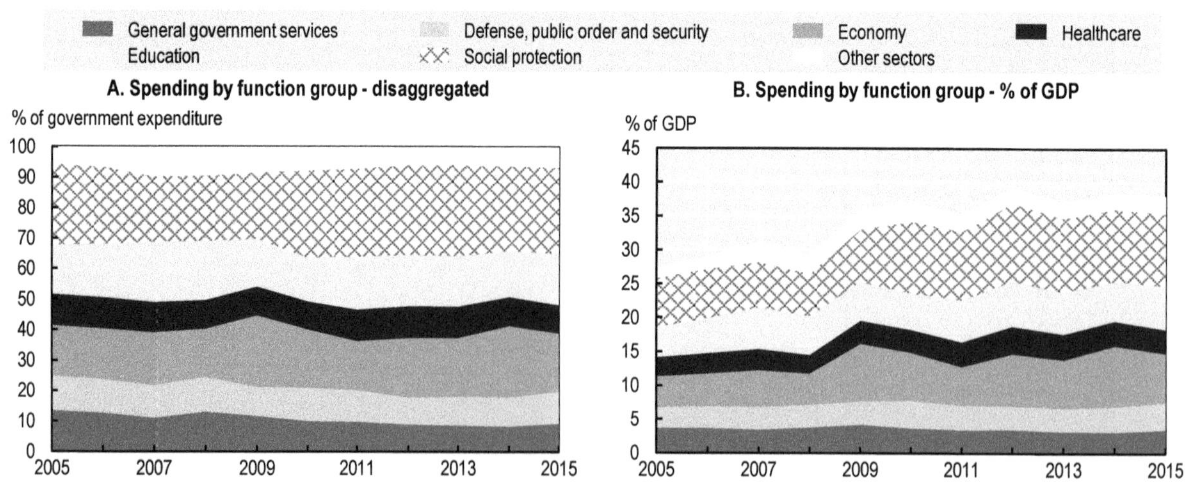


*Source*: NSC (2016a), "Government budget expenditures", available at stat.kg/en.

Social protection spending has also increased as a percentage of gross domestic product (GDP) (Figure 4.1B). In 2015, social protection spending equated to 10.7% of GDP, versus 7.8% in 2009. Over the same period, spending on the economic function group fell from 8.5% to 7.3% of GDP. In the years since 2010, functional allocations have remained relatively consistent, with only the education budget showing significant growth (rising from 5.4% to 6.5% of GDP between 2010 and 2015).

Kyrgyzstan's education spending is also high, allocating approximately 17% of spending to the sector in 2015 compared with Russia (7.3%), Uzbekistan (7.9%) and Kazakhstan (3.5%) in 2014.

In 2015, Kyrgyzstan spent between 3% and 4% of GDP on the health sector, a large proportion of which went towards outpatient and inpatient treatments (including those at primary health facilities). By comparison, Russia spent 6.2% of GDP, Uzbekistan 2.9% and Kazakhstan 2.2% in 2014.

The weight of social protection in the budget is reflected by the classification of spending. Transfers to households is the largest category of spending, accounting for 27.7% of expenditure and 10.5% of GDP in 2015 (Figure 4.2). This indicates that significant redistribution takes place through the budget, although the majority occurs between generations of workers rather than between income groups due to the preponderance of pension expenditure.

**Figure 4.2. A high level of transfers makes the fiscal framework highly redistributive**

Public expenditure by economic classification (2005-15)

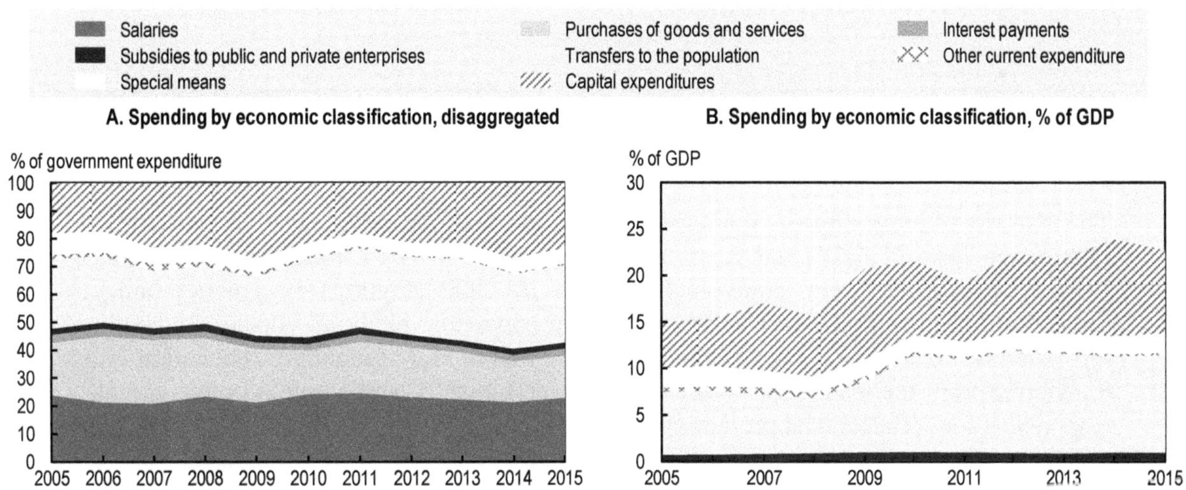


*Source*: NSC (2016[1]), "Government budget expenditures", available at stat.kg/en.

The next largest categories of spending in 2015 were capital spending (23.6%) and the public sector wage bill (22.8%), although capital spending fluctuates significantly over time. The wage bill fluctuated between 21% and 25% between 2008 and 2015, partly due to ad hoc salary increases; the GoK is currently aiming to reduce its wage bill. The goods and services budget (which in broad terms captures expenditure on the day-to-day activities of public servants) fell from 21.0% to 15.2% between 2008 and 2015.

The Ministry of Finance (MoF) calculates discretionary expenditure as total expenditure excluding debt service costs, external assistance and special means. By classifying the public wage bill and social spending as discretionary, the Government of the Kyrgyz Republic (GoK) provides significant flexibility for reallocating spending within the existing resource envelope, although the extent to which pension spending is truly discretionary is worth considering.

The share of recurrent discretionary expenditure in the state budget has been decreasing since 2013 but is expected to remain fairly constant between 2016 and 2019 (based on estimates from the Medium-Term Budgetary Framework) (Figure 4.3). Recurrent discretionary expenditure represented 64% of the Republican Budget in 2016, down from 78% in 2013.

**Figure 4.3. Discretionary spending is declining**

Discretionary spending (2013-19)

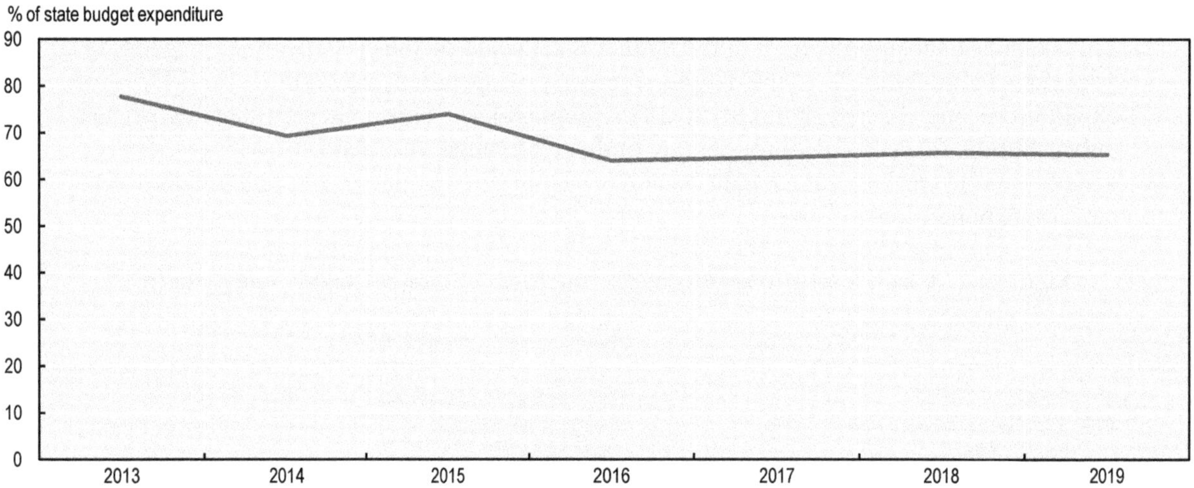


*Source*: NSC (2016[1]), "Government budget expenditures", stat.kg/en.

The majority of expenditure is managed centrally through the Republican Budget (65% of total expenditure in 2015) and the Social Fund (24%). In 2015, local budgets managed 11% of total expenditure, equivalent to 4.1% of GDP (Figure 4.4). District budgets finance utilities (such as water and heating) and education, although education spending fell sharply in 2013, when financial responsibility for secondary education was transferred from the local level to the Republican Budget. Local administrations are also responsible for certain social protection activities.

**Figure 4.4. Centralisation of education spending greatly reduced local budgets**

Local budgets expenditure (2005-15)

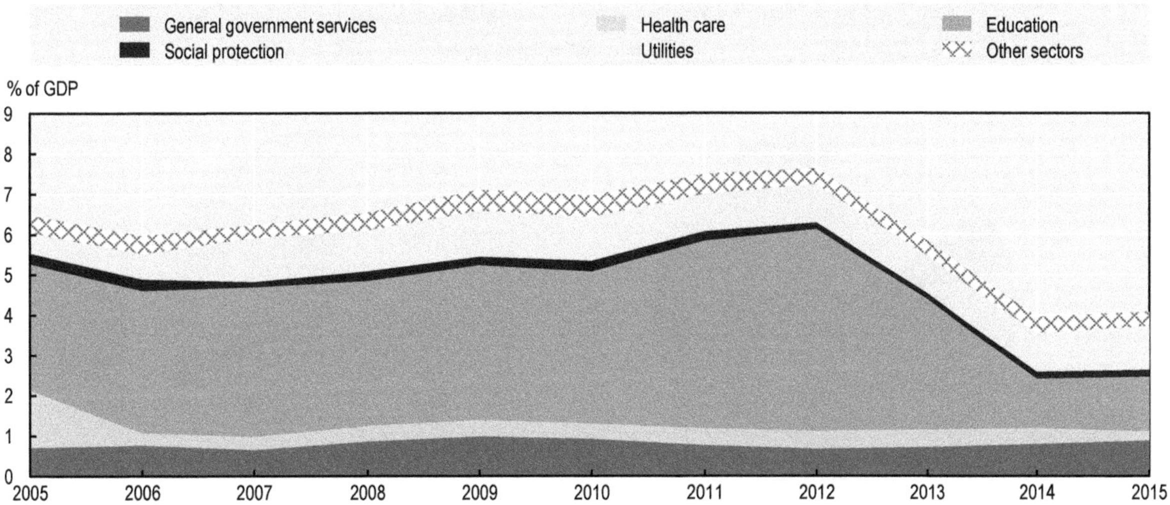


*Source*: NSC (2016[1]), "Government budget expenditures", stat.kg/en.

## *Social protection spending is dominated by pensions*

The contributory pension and health-care programmes have different financing mechanisms, while non-contributory programmes comprise two categories of spending: state benefits and compensations for privileges.

## Spending on social assistance has shifted among programmes

Expenditure on non-contributory benefits amounted to KGS 10.2 billion (Kyrgyz soms) in 2015 or 2.5% of GDP. Figure 4.5 shows this spending disaggregated by programme type. Figure 4.5A shows direct social assistance expenditure, which includes state benefits, compensations for privileges, school feeding programmes and labour market policies. Figure 4.5B shows this spending dwarfed by transfers from the Republican Budget to the Social Fund to fill funding gaps on the contributory side of the system. These transfers finance the basic pension component, military pensions and pension top-ups for other designated categories.

**Figure 4.5. Subsidies to the pension system dominate tax-financed social protection spending**

Social assistance spending including and excluding transfers to the Social Fund, 2015

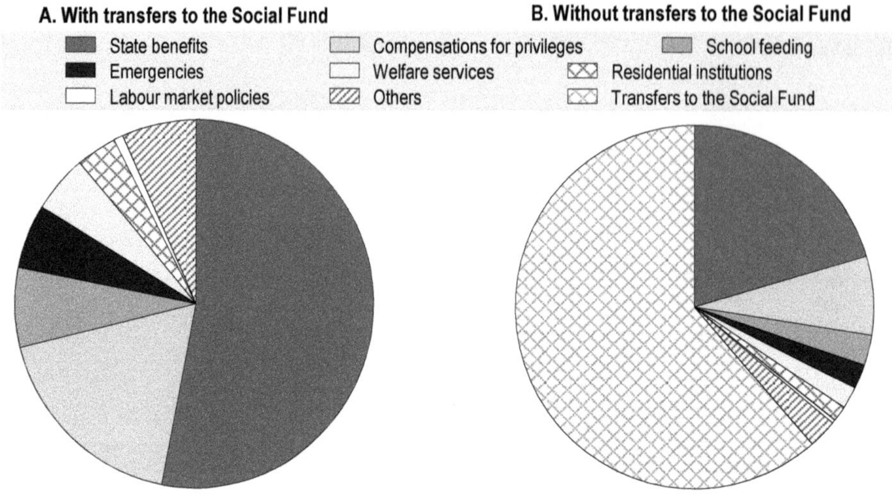


*Source*: NSC (2016[1]), "Government budget expenditures", available at stat.kg/en.

## *State benefits*

Expenditure on state benefits in 2015 amounted to KGS 5.4 billion, representing 3.5% of total government spending and nearly 1.3% of GDP (Figure 4.6). This expenditure was financed predominantly via the Republican Budget. Between 2011 and 2015, the composition of spending on state benefits changed: the Monthly Social Benefit (MSB) was the largest programme in expenditure terms between 2011 and 2014, overtaken in 2015 by the Monthly Benefit for Poor Families with children (MBPF).

**Figure 4.6. The MBPF is driving growth in social assistance spending**

Spending on state benefits and privileges, 2011-15

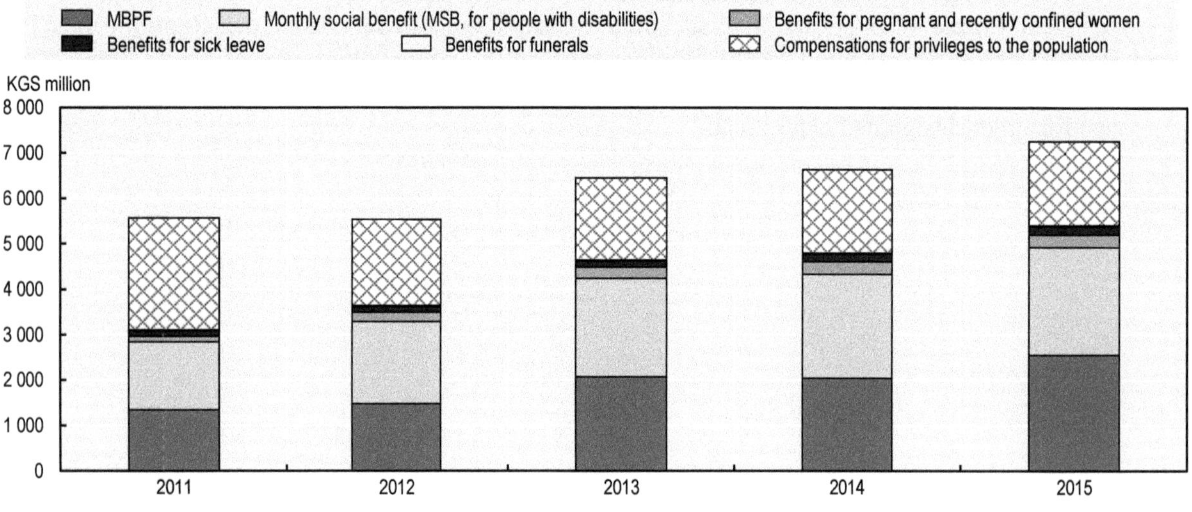


*Source*: NSC (2016[1]), "Government budget expenditures", stat.kg/en.

The MBPF accounted for 0.5-0.6% of GDP between 2011 and 2015, representing 4.1-5.6% of total social protection expenditure. Growth in the allocation to the MBPF coincided with a reduction in the number of beneficiaries. Between 2011 and 2015, spending on the MSB was between 0.5% and 0.6% of GDP and accounted for between 5.1% and 5.5% of total social protection expenditure; higher spending was driven by increases in benefits (for some categories) and higher coverage.

The three remaining types of state benefits (for pregnant women, sick leave and funerals) are much smaller, with a cumulative budget of 0.1% of GDP in 2015. Funeral benefits is the only state programme that receives funds from both the Republican Budget and local budgets, with the latter accounting for 43% of spending in 2015.

### *Compensations for privileges*

In 2011, spending on compensations for privileges was approximately 80% of the level of spending on state benefits in the same year. Since then, privileges spending has declined sharply in nominal terms, from KGS 2.5 billion to KGS 1.8 billion in 2015, falling to 34% of the level of spending on state benefits.

This decline reflects both policy choices and demographic trends. The value of compensations was frozen in 2012 in nominal terms; as a result, total spending on the compensations fell from 0.9% of GDP (2.3% of total expenditure) in 2010 to 0.4% of GDP (1.2% of total expenditure) in 2015. The decline is partly natural, as the number of surviving World War II veterans and invalids, who comprise a significant portion of recipients, declines with time.

### *Other social protection programmes*

Kyrgyzstan's social protection system also includes labour market policies, emergency assistance, social services and residential institutions. Expenditure on these programmes, which are managed by various institutions amounted to KGS 2.8 billion in 2015, a level that exceeded spending on the MBPF that year. Figure 4.7 disaggregates this spending from 2011 to 2015.

**Figure 4.7. Spending on other tax-financed social protection has declined in real terms**

Spending on other non-contributory social protection programmes, 2011-15

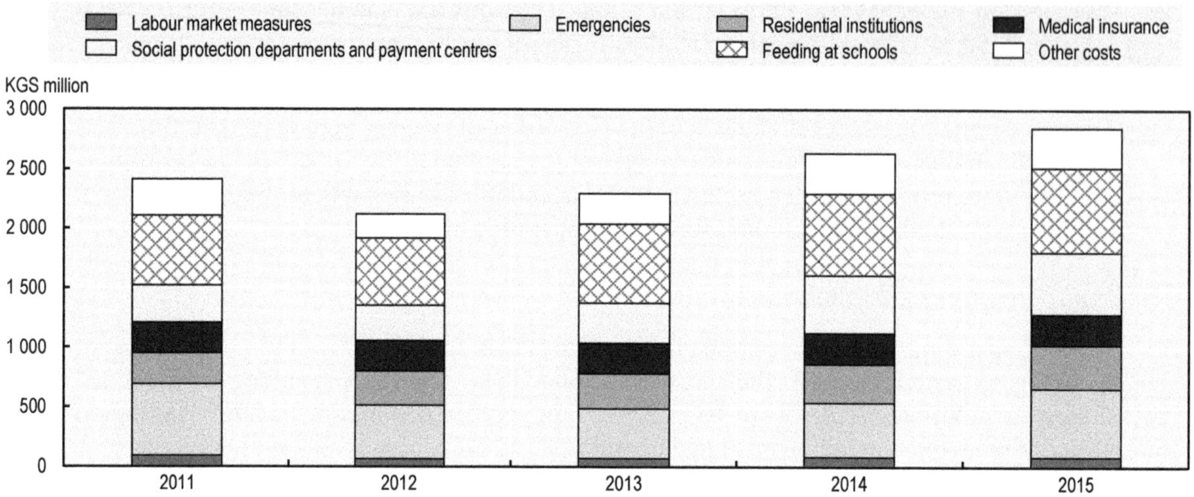


*Source*: NSC (2016[1]), "Government budget expenditures", available at stat.kg/en.

### *School feeding*

All school children in grades 1-4 are entitled to breakfast at school, funded by the Republican Budget and local budgets. In 2015, the GoK spent KGS 7 million (less than 0.2% of GDP or less than 0.5% of total expenditure). Over the last five years, spending on the programmes has been relatively stable in real terms.

### *Social protection departments and payment centres*

Rayon-level units of the MoLSD and aiyl okmotu are active in the provision of social services and the implementation of social protection policies in rayons, towns and aiyl aimaks. The resources allocated to these activities are extremely low: spending by the social protection departments of the MoLSD averaged 0.1% of GDP or 0.3% of total public expenditure from 2011 to 2015. Information on social protection spending by aiyl okmotu is not available.

### *Natural disasters*

Aid for those affected by natural disasters is provided in the form of grants and loans. Chapter 1 noted the significant increase in such emergencies in Kyrgyzstan in recent years, but it has not been matched by increasing allocations. Between 2011 and 2015, expenditure on grants and loans combined fluctuated between KGS 417 million and KGS 600 million (0.1%-0.2% of GDP) or between 0.3% and 0.4% of total expenditure. On average, loan expenditure was about five times larger than grant expenditure over this period.

### *Health spending*

The Republican Budget finances the health insurance contributions of children under age 16, pensioners and the recipients of state benefits. Between 2011 and 2015, the quantum of contributions financed by the Republican Budget was frozen in nominal terms at

KGS 295 million, leading to a 20% decrease in real terms over the period. Currently, spending on the programme is less than 0.1% of GDP.

### *Residential institutions*

Kyrgyzstan has several types of residential institutions for different vulnerable categories (discussed in Chapter 2): children under age 3 and their mothers (managed by the Ministry of Health), orphaned children and adolescents (Ministry of Education), children and adults with disabilities (MoLSD and local governments) and the elderly (MoLSD and local governments). Expenditure by the MoLSD on these institutions has increased each year in nominal terms but is below 0.1% of GDP, or 0.3% of total expenditure.

### *Labour market policies*

The levels of coverage and funding for labour market policies (unemployment benefits, public works programmes and professional training) are very low. Allocations for unemployment benefits and public works programmes declined in nominal terms between 2011 and 2015, while expenditure on professional training declined in real terms and fluctuated significantly over the period. The allocation to public works programmes was the largest of the three labour market interventions in 2015. Local administrations occasionally contribute additional financing to public works projects.

## Social insurance is increasingly reliant on transfers from the Republican Budget

The Social Fund is the central financing mechanism for social insurance in Kyrgyzstan. Its annual expenditure in 2015 was KGS 37.3 billion or 9.2% of GDP – nearly four times the level of social assistance spending. The Social Fund comprises three components: the Pension Fund (which comprises contributory and non-contributory components as well as the quasi-contributory basic pension component); the State Cumulative Pension Fund ([SCPF], the funded pillar of the pension system) and the Fund for Health Improvement of the Working People (FHIWP). The Social Fund also collects contributions on behalf of the health insurance system.

The imbalance between benefits and contributions in the Pension Fund has worsened in recent years. Although pension coverage among pensioners is close to universal, a much lower proportion of today's workforce is contributing to the Social Fund, reflecting high levels of informality and emigration. Moreover, expenditure on non-contributory military pensions is rising at a steep rate.

As a result, the Social Fund's financial position is deteriorating, and ever-higher transfers from the Republican Budget are required. This trend undermines the contributory principle of the Social Fund and jeopardises the fairness of the social protection system as a whole.

### *The Pension Fund*

Payments by the Pension Fund (comprising benefits for old age, disability and survivors) totalled KGS 31.3 billion in 2015 and accounted for 89.9% of Social Fund spending. The Pension Fund's spending grew at an average annual rate of 7.1% between 2011 and 2015 in nominal terms, primarily due to an increase in the number of beneficiaries (from 575 000 pensioners in 2010 to 634 000 in 2014). The average pension benefit also increased, from KGS 2 886 to KGS 4 710 per month, over the same period.

Increased expenditure has not been matched by increased contributions. Although Kyrgyzstan's demographics are favourable for a pay-as-you-go arrangement, high levels of emigration and informality have resulted in the ratio of contributors to pensioners declining to between 1:1 and 2:1. This situation is exacerbated by the non-contributory pensions and pension top-ups paid by the Social Fund as well as by the design of the basic pension component, which accounted for 27.4% of all pension payments in 2015; the benefit is based on the duration of contributions rather than the value.

In 2015, these supplementary pension payments were almost as expensive as basic pensions (KGS 7.7 billion vs. KGS 8.6 billion). The strongest growth is in expenditure on military pensions, which is the fastest-growing category of social protection spending.

To finance the basic and additional pension components, the Social Fund is increasingly reliant on transfers from the Republican Budget (Figure 4.8). In 2005, contributions represented 82% of the Social Fund's total revenue, while transfers amounted to 16.6%. The share of contributions dipped sharply in 2010 to 66% and has kept declining since. In 2015, contributions accounted for 57% of revenues.

**Figure 4.8. The Social Fund is increasingly reliant on transfers from the Republican Budget**

Source of revenue for the Social Fund, 2005-15

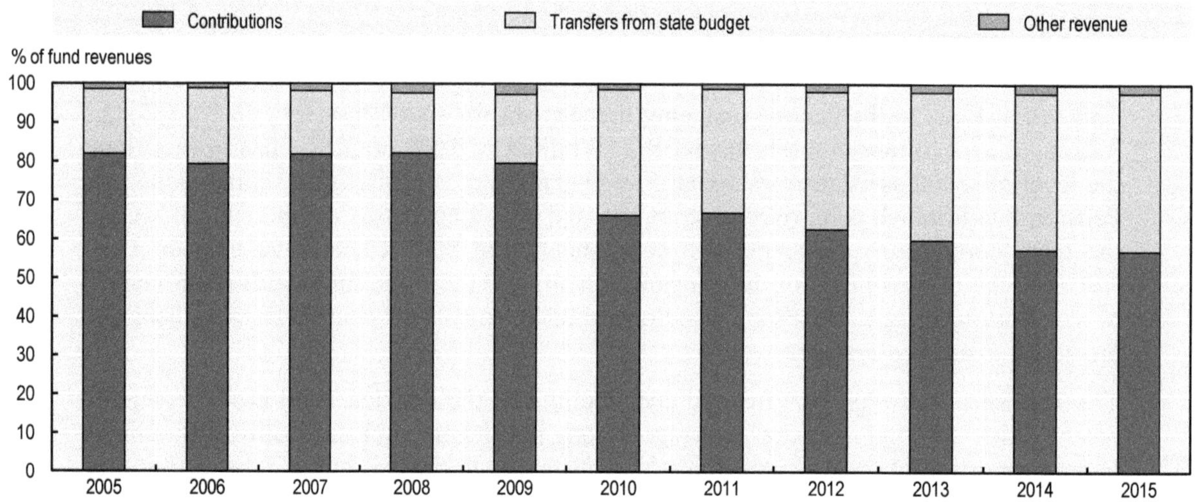


*Source*: NSC (2016[2]), "State budget revenues", stat.kg/en.

The proportion of Social Fund revenues coming from the Republican Budget are expected to continue over the medium term due to the GoK's commitment to finance 100% of basic pension expenditure via such transfers. According to the MTBF, adopted in May 2016, the Republican Budget achieved this target in 2017.

In total, transfers from the Republican Budget to Social Fund programmes amounted to KGS 16.3 billion in 2015, 60% more than was spent on social assistance. These transfers are disaggregated in Figure 4.9, which reflects the high growth in transfers needed to finance the basic pension component. Old-age pensions absorbed 53% of these transfers in 2015, up sharply from 36.4% in 2011.

**Figure 4.9. The basic pension component is a growing burden on the Republican Budget**

Transfers from the Republican Budget to the Social Fund by spending item, 2011-2015

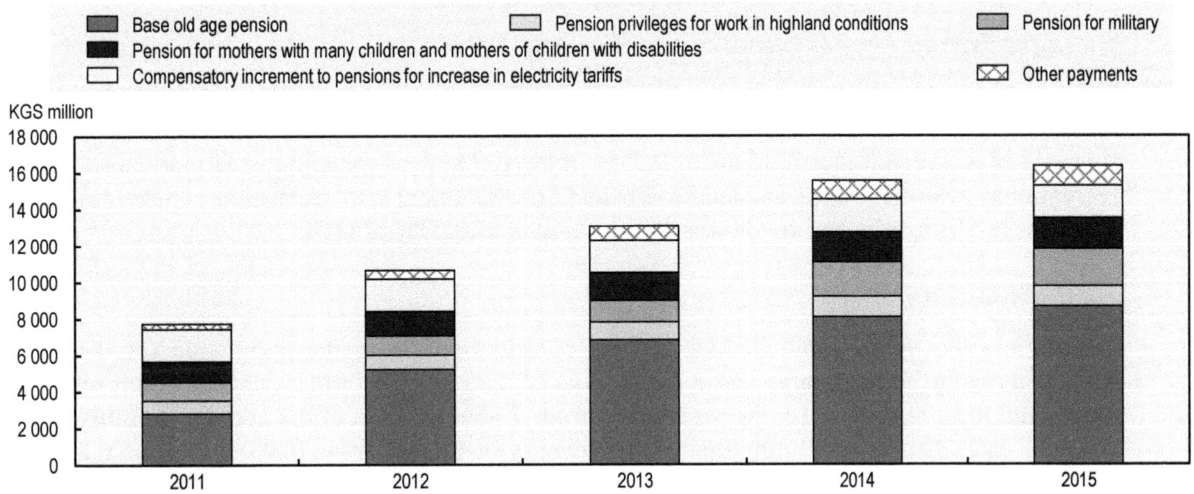


*Source*: NSC (2016[2]), "State budget revenues", stat.kg/en.

Figure 4.10 shows total expenditure on pensions by the Social Fund (including both spending financed by contributions and Republican Budget transfers). The increase in pension spending moderated after strong growth between 2011 and 2012, but military pension spending grew strongly over the period. Old age pensions accounted for 85% of total spending.

**Figure 4.10. Pension spending is growing in nominal terms**

Social Fund expenditure by spending item, 2011-15

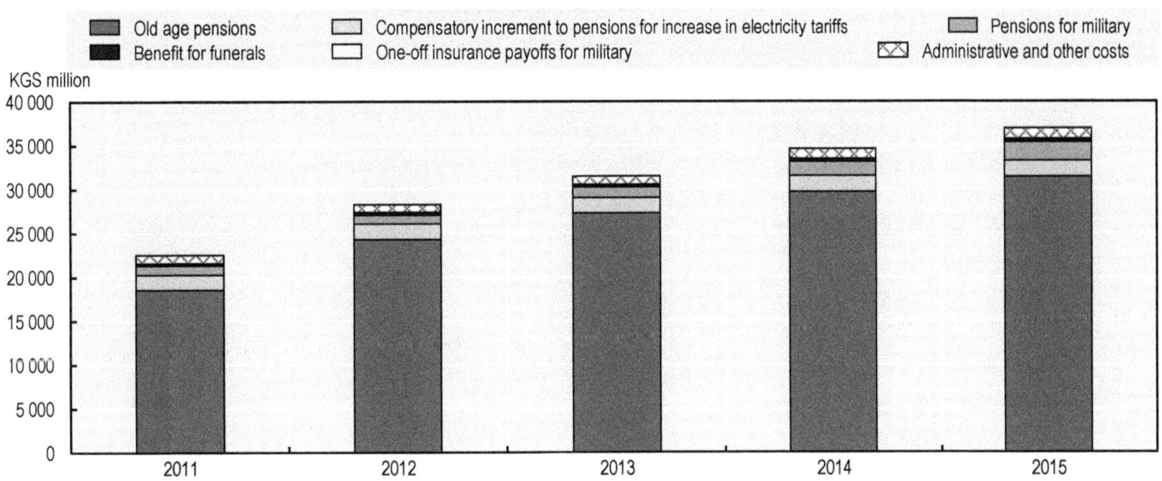


*Source*: NSC (2016[1]), "Government budget expenditures", stat.kg/en.

## *State Cumulative Pension Fund*

Established in 2010, the SCPF is a fully funded component of the Social Fund. It receives contributions worth 2% of payroll from male workers born after 1964 and female workers born after 1969. Older workers are excluded from contributing, as they will not make sufficient contributions before retiring to generate a meaningful income when they do. SCPF expenditure is presently very low at just 0.3% of Pension Fund expenditure, but it had accumulated assets worth KGS 8.2 billion by the end of 2015.

### *Fund for Health Improvement of the Working People*

The Social Fund collects contributions for the FHIWP, a small contributory arrangement managed by the Federation of Trade Unions of the Kyrgyz Republic. The FHIWP is financed by employer contributions of 0.25% of payroll and its spending is earmarked for recreational activities, such as sanatorium and spa treatment and recreation centres for children. In 2015, spending by the FHIWP amounted to 0.05% of GDP.

### *Health spending*

In addition, the Social Fund budget collects contributions from the population for the MHI at a rate of 2% of salaries, paid by employers. The rate for farmers depends on how much land they own: in 2016, the rate ranged from 0.05% to 0.3% of the average monthly wage in each district. For individual entrepreneurs, it ranged from 0.3% to 1% of the average monthly wage. Other informal workers can also enrol in the MHI with a flat rate contribution of KGS 550. As with the Pension Fund, health insurance also has a non-contributory element as the SGBP covers everyone for primary care with no co-payments; the funding for this is largely provided by transfers from the government budget (see Table 4.1).

The MHIF manages its funds through a single pooling system, which consolidates the financial resources for health care from government budgets (Republican Budget and Bishkek's local budget) and mandatory contributions, as well as from co-payments from the population. Table 4.1 presents the budget for 2015.

**Table 4.1. The MHIF relies largely on budget transfers to provide primary care services**

Single Payer Systems Budget (2015)

| Revenue | Million KGS |
|---|---|
| Transfers from the Republican Budget and Bishkek's Local Budget | 8 551.9 |
| Transfers from the Social Fund (contributions to FCMI + transfers from the Republican Budget for children, pensioners, and social benefit recipients) | 1 855.7 |
| Patients' Co-payments | 389.2 |
| Special Means | 580.4 |
| Total | 11 377.2 |
| | |
| Expenditure | |
| In-patient services | 6 682.4 |
| Tuberculosis hospitals | 683.4 |
| Out-patient services | 3 020.8 |
| Dental care | 341.3 |
| Ambulance/Emergency aid | 423.3 |
| Medicines | 22.0 |
| Total | 11 377.2 |

*Source*: Authors' calculations based on data of the Treasury Department of the MoF, Social Fund.

## Social insurance is crowding out other social protection spending

Figure 4.11 shows total spending on social protection between 2011 and 2015 as a proportion of GDP (right-hand panel) and in KGS in real 2015 prices (left-hand panel). Social protection spending increased by an average of 5.7% per year over this period in real terms but fluctuated as a proportion of GDP.

Spending on old-age pensions accounted for 78% of the increase in social protection spending between 2011 and 2015, while pensions for the military accounted for 7.9% of the increase and the MBPF for 8.4% of the rise. Military pensions were the fastest-growing spending item in the social protection budget, increasing by 13.3% per year on average in real terms between 2011 and 2015, while the MBPF averaged 11.3% growth in spending per year and old-age pensions 8.0%.

Overall, old-age pensions accounted for 68.4% of social protection spending in 2015, up from 62.8% in 2011, while military pensions rose from 3.6% to 4.7% and the MBPF from 4.5% to 5.6%. The MSB increased only slightly (from 5.1% of social protection spending to 5.2%) while compensations for privileges declined sharply, from 8.3% to 4.0%, and the electricity subsidy for elderly pensioners fell from 5.8% to 4.0% of social protection spending.

**Figure 4.11. Old-age pensions dominate social protection spending**

Total social protection expenditure (2011-15)

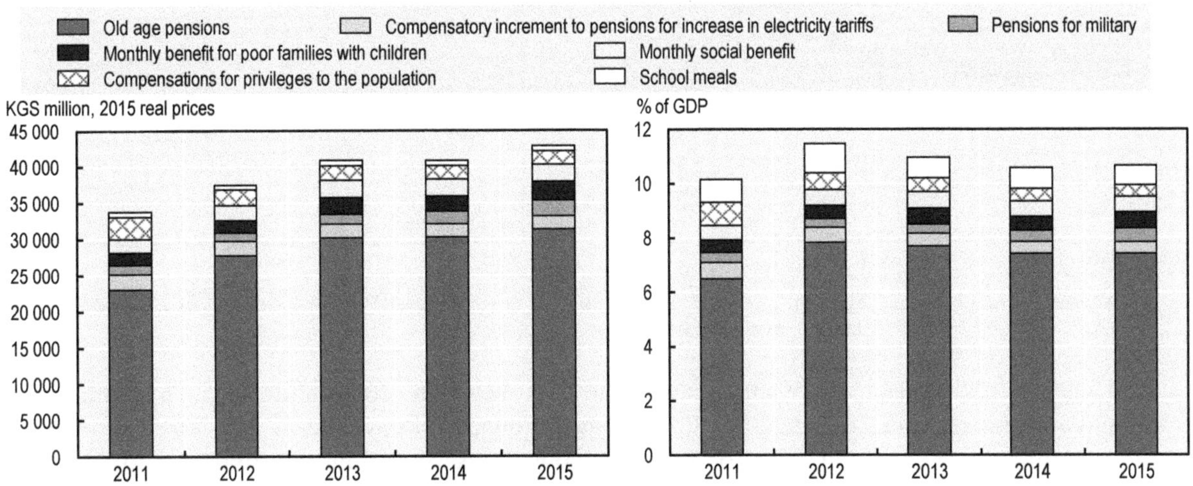


*Source*: NSC (2016[1]), "Government budget expenditures", stat.kg/en.

Social protection spending fluctuated as a proportion of GDP over 2011-15. Social protection spending accounted for 10.7% of GDP in 2015, up from 10.2% in 2011 but below a peak of 11.5% in 2012 (a year in which GDP contracted). Social protection spending was 11.0% of GDP in 2013.

As the number of elderly increases, pension spending (both old-age and military) will continue to crowd out other components of social protection expenditure. The decrease in spending on compensations for privileges created fiscal space for an increase in MBPF expenditure between 2011 and 2015. However, spending on pensions will reduce or even eliminate the scope for further growth in social assistance spending because pension payments represent entitlements (meaning there is relatively little scope for discretion in adjusting benefit levels) and because pensioners are a highly influential group politically.

## Government revenues are high but Kyrgyzstan relies heavily on foreign support

Growth in government revenues has accommodated increases in social protection spending. Figure 4.12A shows the long-term increase in general government revenues, which comprise tax revenues, contributions to the Social Fund, non-tax revenues, capital revenues and foreign grants. Between 2005 and 2015, revenues more than doubled in real terms and increased from 24.7% to 34.9% of GDP. Kyrgyzstan's revenues have grown significantly relative to the benchmark countries (Georgia, Mongolia, Russian Federation, Tajikistan and Uzbekistan); in 2015, Kyrgyzstan generated the highest amount of revenues as a proportion of GDP (Figure 4.12B).

**Figure 4.12. Public revenues are growing strongly and lead the region**

Kyrgyzstan's general government revenues, 2005-15

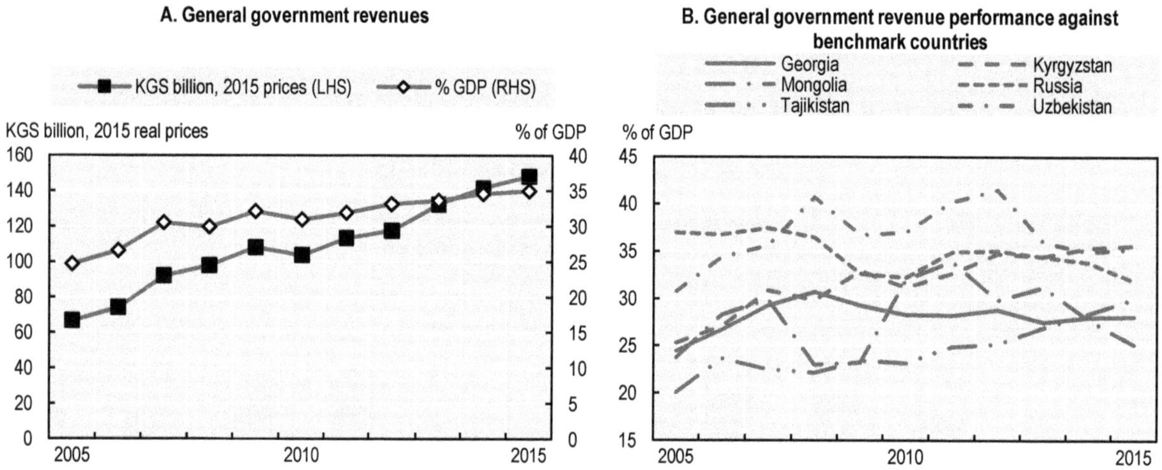


*Source*: NSC (2016[2]), "State budget revenues", available at stat.kg/en; IMF (2016[3]), *World Economic Outlook, October 2016* (database), available at imf.org/external/datamapper/datasets/WEO.

Kyrgyzstan's revenue buoyancy exceeded 1.00 between 2005 and 2015, meaning government revenues outpaced GDP. Estimates indicate a buoyancy of 1.62 for general government revenue and 1.44 for total tax collections (including contributions to the Social Fund). However, these high buoyancy rates may not extend into the future. Between 2005 and 2015, the economy witnessed a revenue catch-up from a very low level (typical for periods of economic transition) to the current revenue as a share of GDP. This current level is high by international standards, given the level of per capita income.

As Figure 4.13 shows, the increase in general government revenue has been driven by growth in all three major components: tax collections (including contributions to the Social Fund); non-tax and capital revenue; and official transfers/foreign grants. Although tax collections account for the majority of revenues, their share fell from 81.0% in 2005 to 69.9% in 2015.

Tax collections peaked in 2012 at 25.5% of GDP, falling to 24.4% of GDP in 2015. By contrast, non-tax revenues have grown strongly in recent years: from 5.6% of GDP in

2013 to 8.1% in 2015. Rents from mineral (gold) deposits have substantially boosted non-tax revenue growth; in 2015, the GoK auctioned mining rights for the country's second-largest gold deposit, Jerui.

**Figure 4.13. Contribution of taxes to total revenue is declining**

Dynamics of state budget revenue components, % of GDP (2005-15)

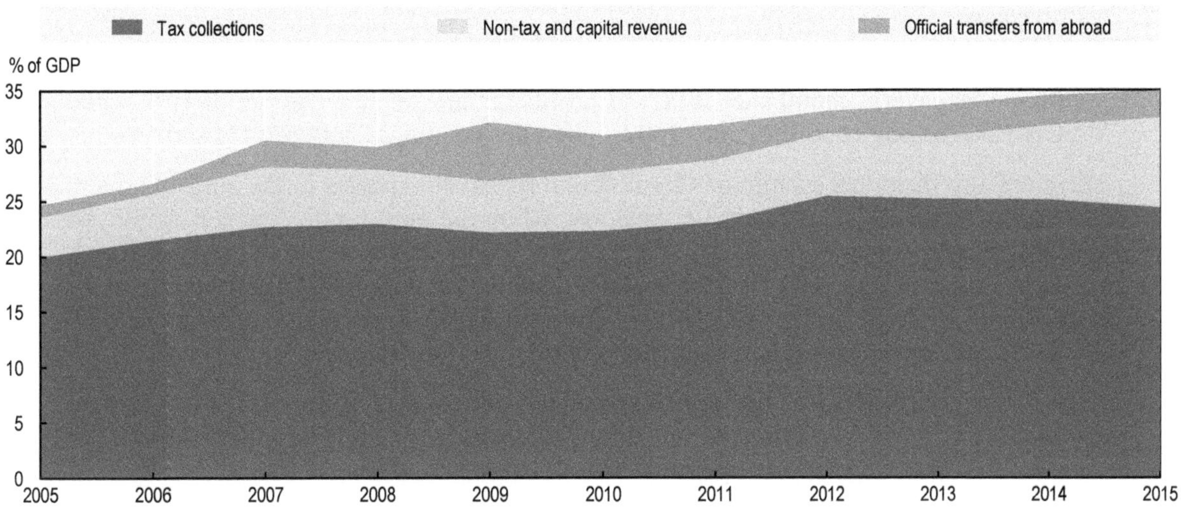


*Source*: NSC (2016[2]), "State budget revenues", stat.kg/en.

Indirect taxes provide 70% of Kyrgyzstan's tax revenues. Value-added tax (VAT) on imports contributed 28.4% of tax revenues in 2015, while VAT on domestic production accounted for 10.8% of revenues (Figure 4.14). A sales tax provides 10.7% of tax revenues and excises contributed 9.3%. International trade taxes accounted for 11.4% of total taxes.

**Figure 4.14. Indirect taxes account for the majority of tax revenues**

Structure of tax revenues, 2005-15

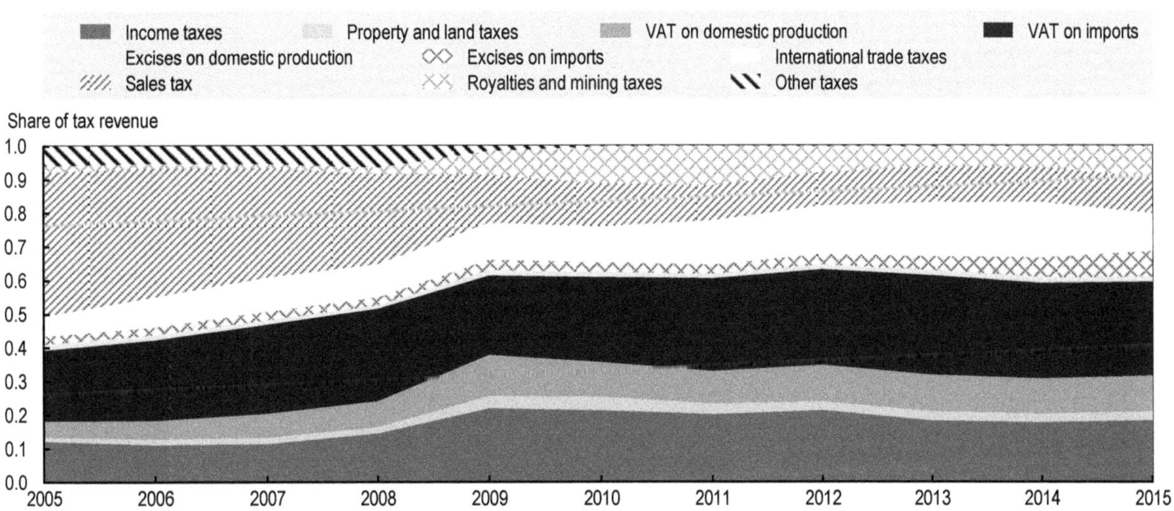


*Source*: NSC (2016[2]), "State budget revenues", stat.kg/en.

Direct taxes on income provided 18.8% of total tax revenues in 2015. These include a flat-rate 10% personal income tax (PIT) for individuals (mostly workers in formal, non-agricultural enterprises), a profits tax for large formal legal entities and a simplified taxation regime for small and medium-sized enterprises (SMEs) and those employed in the informal economy. Taxation of the mining industry includes a separate income tax for the country's largest enterprise, Kumtor gold mine, as well as bonuses and royalties for other mineral deposits. In 2015, taxation of mining activities yielded nearly 9.8% of total tax revenues.

The statutory rates for many taxes are currently set very low, with the objective of improving taxpayers' compliance. PIT and profits tax are set at a flat rate of 10% while VAT is 12% (having been 20% until 2009). The sales tax ranges between 1% and 5%.

There are also many tax exemptions for different types of taxpayers or tax bases. Farmers are exempt from all taxes except the land tax, while the only tax for the self-employed and SMEs in the informal economy – the patent – is a lump sum set at a low level, which varies by sector. These rates stand in marked contrast to the required contribution to the Social Fund by legal entities (27.25% of payroll), which is very high by international standards and deters many enterprises from entering the formal economy.

Kyrgyzstan has a two-tier budget system: the upper tier consists of the Republican Budget and the Social Fund. The lower tier combines the budgets of all local governments. The sources of revenues for local budgets are:

- Local taxes – mostly land and property taxes – and non-tax revenues assigned to this level of government;
- Shared taxes (income tax, sales tax and royalties); and
- Transfers from the Republican Budget – categorical, equalising grants and mutual settlements.

In practice, only Bishkek has independent budget revenue sources. All other local governments rely heavily on transfers from the Republican Budget. The size of transfers from the Republican Budget has fallen sharply in recent years following the elimination of categorical grants; in 2014-15 these transfers amounted to 0.5-0.6% of GDP, compared with 4.5-4.6% of GDP in 2011-12.

### *Foreign assistance*

Official transfers from abroad (Official Development Assistance [ODA], considered part of non-tax revenue) and foreign borrowing together meet a substantial part of GoKR financing needs (Figure 4.15). Since 2009, foreign aid has exceeded 16% of total general government expenditure, reaching 20% of government resources in some years, indicating a high degree of aid dependency (Figure 4.16). Having recently attained middle-income status, Kyrgyzstan's access to grants and lending on highly concessional terms will be significantly reduced.

**Figure 4.15. Official Development Assistance is declining**

ODA by sector, 2007-15

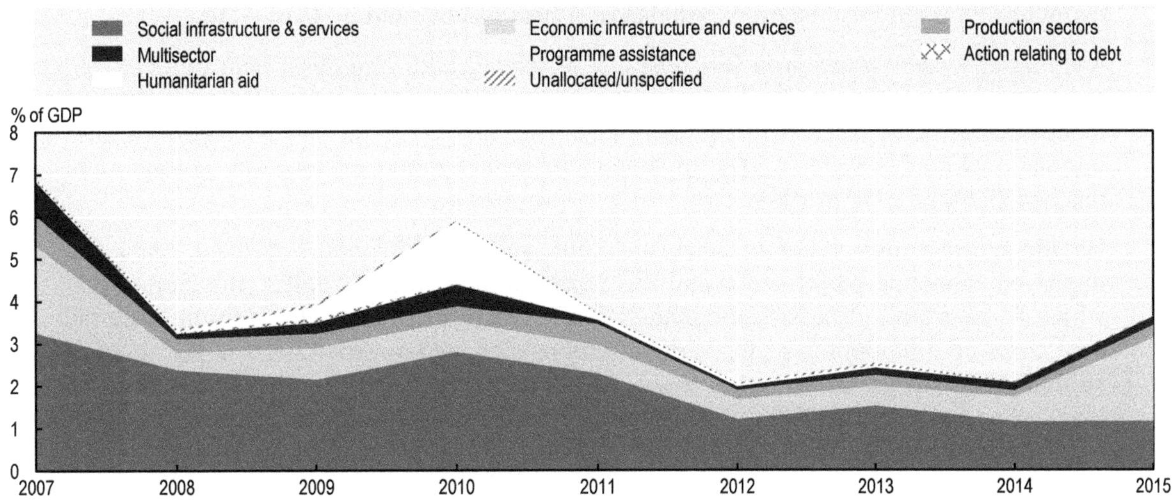


*Note:* Includes only ODA from member countries of the Development Assistance Committee.
*Source*: OECD (2016[4]), *OECD.Stat* (database), data.oecd.org (accessed June 2017)

**Figure 4.16. Foreign aid finances a sizeable proportion of public spending**

Percentage of foreign aid in general government expenditure, 2005-15

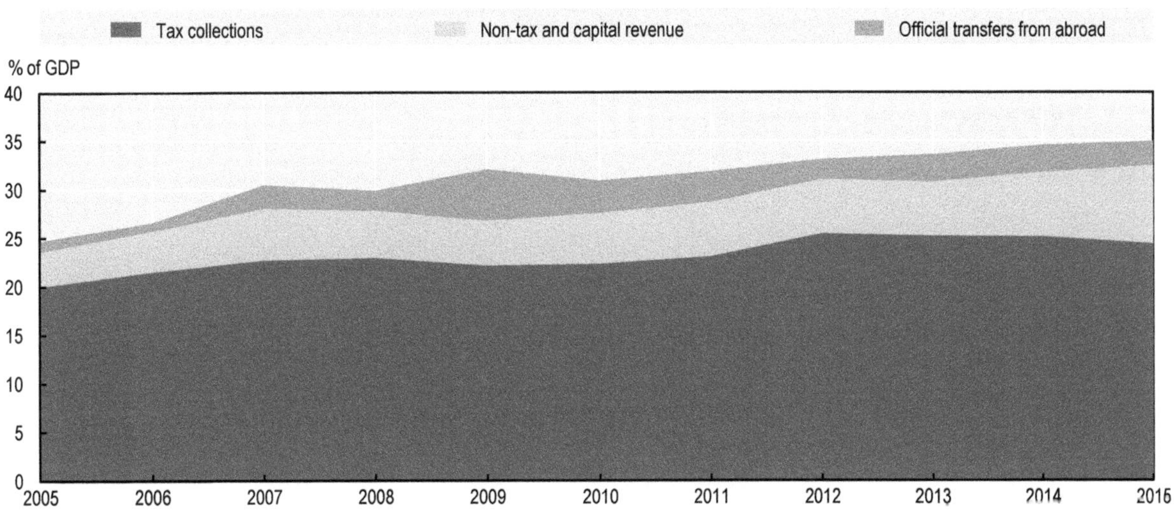


*Source*: NSC (2016[1]), "Government budget expenditures", stat.kg/en.

Kyrgyzstan's ability to mobilise resources through domestic borrowing is limited, and it can only borrow externally on concessional terms. Programmes implemented by the International Monetary Fund (IMF) almost uninterruptedly since 1993 do not allow for any borrowing on non-concessional terms on the basis that Kyrgyzstan could not afford to service commercial debt. However, there are positive signs in this regard; in December 2015, Kyrgyzstan received credit ratings (for the first time in the country's history) of B and B2 from S&P and Moody's, respectively. These speculative grades are associated with high interest rates, should the GoK issue sovereign bonds.

External financial support has created a benign fiscal environment. Debt service costs are relatively low and interest payments constitute a small share of general government expenditure, equivalent to 0.8-1.0% of GDP. For the last three years, the GoK has maintained a small positive primary balance of between 0% and 0.7% of GDP.

Kyrgyzstan's debt situation is less positive, reflecting both long-term debt burdens and short-term macroeconomic dynamics. Despite having no debt when it gained independence, Kyrgyzstan's foreign debt level rose quickly in the 1990s, in part because international donors were so keen to support its rapid economic transition. Foreign debt reached 134% of GDP in 1999.

Having received debt relief in 2001 and 2005, the debt situation improved, thanks to improved economic performance and the depreciation of the US dollar (the currency in which Kyrgyzstan's debt is denominated) against many currencies. In addition, after the debt crisis of 2005-06, many donor organisations switched to providing a larger share of aid in the form of grants instead of loans. As a result, foreign debt continued increasing in USD terms but fell dramatically in relative terms to just above 40% of GDP in 2012, before rising again (Figure 4.17A).

In 2014, the GoK introduced a ceiling of 60% of GDP for the total level of foreign debt. Recently, the GoK resumed larger foreign borrowing, mostly from the Government of China on International Development Association (IDA)-comparable terms. As a result, its foreign debt accumulation rose to 64.5% of GDP in 2015, exceeding the 60% ceiling.

**Figure 4.17. Kyrgyzstan has breached its debt limit**

Kyrgyzstan debt

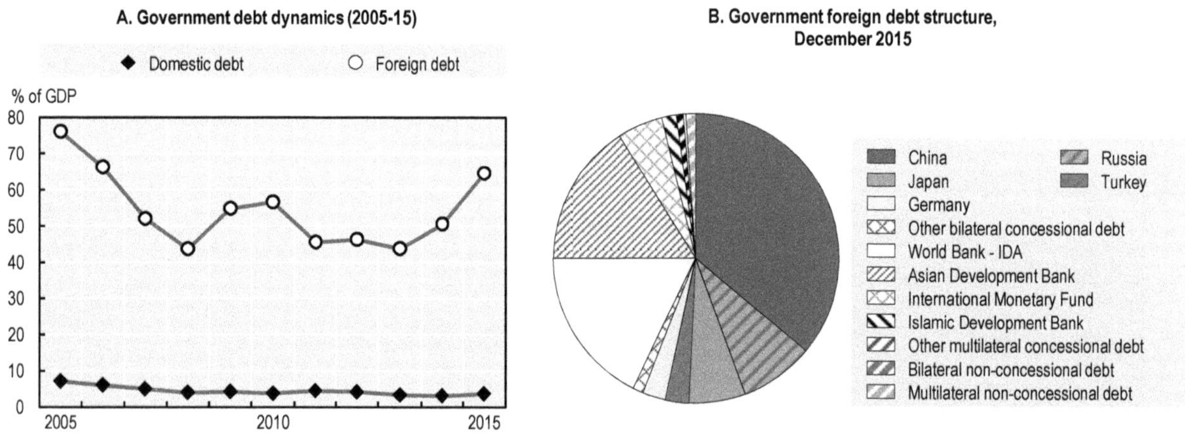


*Source*: Ministry of Finance/NSC.

Analysis of the foreign debt structure (Figure 4.17B) illustrates that 98.6% of total debt is concessional. The main sources of this debt are China, World Bank IDA and the Asian Development Bank. Other major lenders include Russia, Japan and the IMF. These six lenders account for almost 90% of the total government foreign debt of Kyrgyzstan. The long-term reliance on the IMF weighs upon the GoK's capacity to determine its own policy agenda, including with respect to social protection policy (see Chapter 5).

Debt Sustainability Analysis (DSA) carried out in 2017 concluded that Kyrgyzstan's external public and publicly guaranteed debt will remain at a moderate risk of debt distress and recommended immediate action to contain it. Currency depreciation, a slowdown in GDP growth and a deterioration of the fiscal balance represent the greatest risks to debt sustainability. The DSA recognises remittances to be a key source of financing and expects these to increase in the coming years.

## The fiscal framework reduces inequality but has little impact on poverty

To understand the impact of social protection on poverty and inequality, it is necessary to analyse not only who receives social protection benefits but also who pays the taxes that finance them. By calculating the distribution of taxes and transfers across the income distribution, it is possible to identify both the distributional impact of the fiscal system and its overall impact on poverty.

This section uses data from the 2015 Kyrgyz Integrated Household Survey (KIHS) to identify this "net social protection" effect by examining the impact of direct, indirect and trade taxes, as well as contributions to the Social Fund[1]. It distinguishes between formal and informal workers for the calculation of personal income taxes and applies differential contribution rates for the Social Fund. The analysis then compares the incidence of taxation to the distribution of the four largest social protection programmes: pensions, the MBPF, the MSB and privileges.

Taxes paid by the population are relatively high; even among the poorest decile tax payments equate to more than one-quarter of expenditure (Figure 4.18), reflecting the preponderance of indirect taxes among government revenue instruments. There is little difference in the effective tax rates for much of the population; it is only for the ninth and tenth consumption deciles that the tax rate increases significantly. This might reflect that participation in the formal economy (and thus the payment of PIT) is skewed towards those at the upper end of the distribution: 67% of those working in the formal sector belong to the top five consumption deciles.

The total taxes paid by each decile vary significantly more than the tax rate (Figure 4.18). In 2015, the top consumption decile faced a tax bill that was just less than the total taxes paid by the bottom four deciles combined.

**Figure 4.18. The tax system is only progressive at upper income levels**

Tax rates at different income deciles and total taxes paid, USD million (2015)

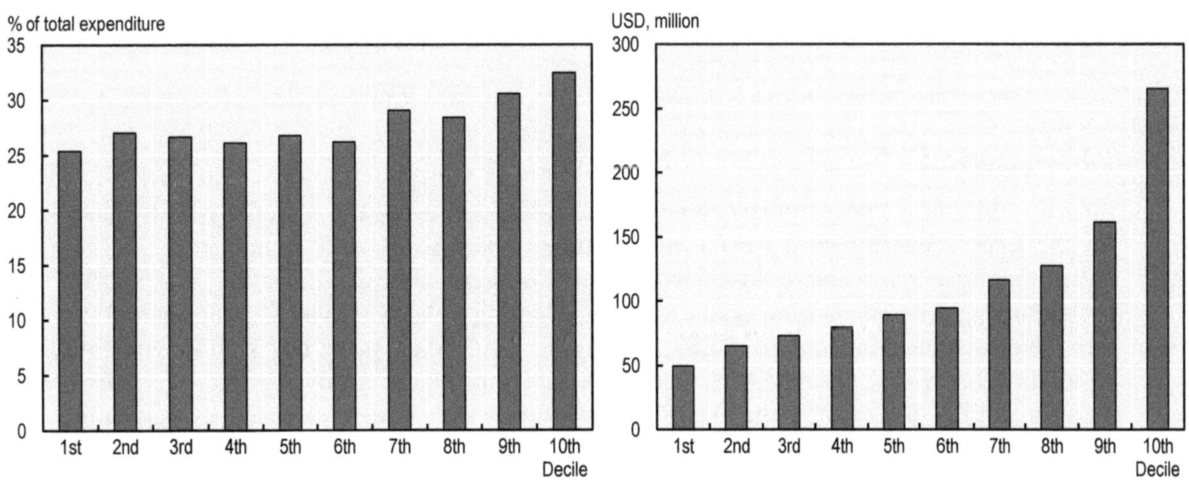


*Source*: Authors' calculations based on the NSC (2015[5]), *Kyrgyz Integrated Household Survey* (database).

To understand the overall effect of the fiscal system, a counterfactual analysis was carried out by modelling scenarios whereby taxes and social protection benefits are eliminated from individuals' consumption. The microsimulations start from a baseline that reflects taxes paid and social protection benefits received. Counterfactual 1 reports household consumption in the absence of social protection benefits. Counterfactual 2 shows household consumption in the absence of tax payments (but with social protection benefits included). Counterfactual 3 shows an individual's market income (their income before they pay taxes or receive social protection benefits).

Figure 4.19A shows the distributive impact of the fiscal system. The Gini coefficient increases from 0.19 under the Baseline scenario to 0.26 in Counterfactual 1, demonstrating the progressive nature of social protection transfers. At 0.22, Gini inequality under Counterfactual 2 is also higher than under the baseline, indicating that the tax system is progressive as well. As is to be expected given these results, inequality is significantly higher under Counterfactual 3 (which excludes taxes and transfers) than the Baseline measure. The difference between the Baseline and Counterfactual 3 is 6.4 percentage points.

**Figure 4.19. The fiscal system reduces inequality but slightly increases poverty**

Poverty and inequality under different scenarios

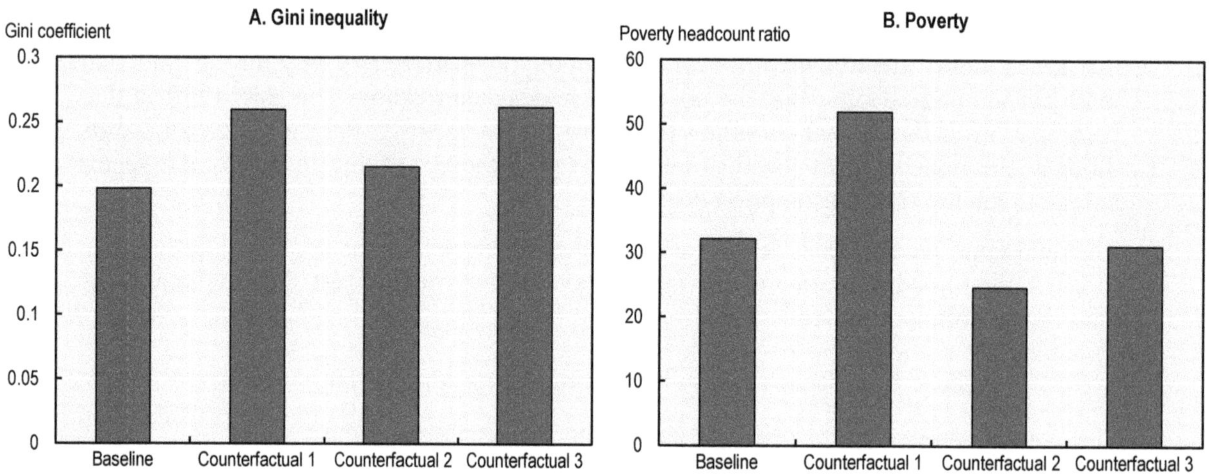


*Note*: Counterfactual 1 = no transfers; counterfactual 2 = no taxes; counterfactual 3 = neither transfers nor taxes.

*Source*: Authors' calculations based on NSC (2015[5]), *Kyrgyz Integrated Household Survey* (database).

### *Poverty impact*

Figure 4.19B shows poverty headcount ratios, calculated using the national poverty line for the same scenarios used for the distributional analysis. Poverty jumps from 32.1% under the Baseline scenario to 51.9% under Counterfactual 1, indicating that social protection benefits play an important role in mitigating poverty. Under Counterfactual 2, the poverty rate decreases to 24.6%, implying that taxes push about 7.5% of the population below the poverty line. Counterfactual 3 produces a poverty rate of 31.0%. This is slightly lower than the baseline and shows the burden of taxes exceeds the monetary benefits poor individuals receive.

However, neither the distributive nor the poverty analysis includes in-kind transfers, such as public spending on education or health. According to the World Bank, education spending in 2011 was slightly regressive while spending on health in 2009 was slightly pro-poor (World Bank, 2014[6]). However, it is not clear what the overall effect would have been in 2015 given the policies implemented since this analysis was conducted.

Another important point to bear in mind is that taxes and transfers will vary along the lifecycle, thanks in part to the preponderance of pay-as-you-go pensions in social protection spending. The fiscal system might be more advantageous for the elderly than the working-age population (especially as pension payments are not taxed), such that the most significant redistribution is horizontal (between groups of individuals at a similar income level) rather than vertical (between groups at different income levels).

Such a finding would be consistent with the results of fiscal incidence analysis in Russia (López-Calva et al., 2017[7]). In the case of Russia, whose social protection system is also dominated by pensions spending, working-age individuals (including both those with and without children) are net payers to the fiscal system while pensioners are net beneficiaries, meaning they get more out of the system than they put in.

## Social Fund imbalances constrain increases in social protection spending

This report identifies three major reforms as necessary for the establishment of a functioning social protection system: partial universalisation of state benefits, a scaling-up of social services and a substantial increase in the provision of labour-market programmes. It is important to note that the need to increase allocations to state benefits and social services does not allow for an either/or approach: investing in the local social workforce is essential for achieving value-for-money from spending on state benefits, whether these are increased or not.

The analysis in this Chapter indicates these major reforms would have to be phased in very gradually due to overall fiscal constraints and because of imbalances in the Social Fund. Fiscal transfers to the Social Fund were 160% larger than spending on social assistance and labour-market programmes in 2015. These transfers will need to keep increasing as the Social Fund's contribution base shrinks and the elderly population grows. The imbalance between contributions and expenditure is likely to worsen, requiring one or more of the following policy responses:

- an increase in the contribution rate to the Social Fund
- lower benefits for current and future pensioners
- larger transfers from the Republican Budget to the Social Fund.

None of these represent a long-term solution. Increasing the already high contribution rate is likely to disincentivise enterprises from operating or employing in the formal sector, risking further reduction in contributions and lower tax receipts overall. Lowering benefits will have significant welfare consequences, given the average replacement rate has already fallen below the ILO minimum. Higher transfers from the Republican Budget, the current approach, will crowd out other social protection spending.

The GoK's potential to increase revenues to finance higher social protection spending is limited. Its revenues are high relative to those of its neighbours but foreign grants and concessional lending are falling away thanks to the country's graduation to middle-income status. Maintaining public spending at its current level will thus be a challenge and might put pressure on the poor, since the GoK currently relies primarily on indirect taxes. Shifting the tax mix towards taxes on income could make the tax system more progressive, but this approach risks incentivising informality in the same way as higher social security contributions would.

The high proportion of spending already allocated to social protection creates the possibility for reprioritisation of resources within the sector. However, to fully exploit this potential would require shifting resources between programmes managed by the Social Fund and those managed by the MoLSD. This would be made more straightforward if the non-contributory and quasi-contributory pensions managed by the Social Fund (but financed by the Republican Budget) were moved to the MoLSD.

Bringing these programmes under the budget of the MoLSD would make the system more transparent by distinguishing between different sources of financing for the different programmes. This in turn would promote the overall sustainability of social protection provision and make it easier to understand and optimise its distributive impact. It would also an important step in rebalancing social protection from being primarily a set of contributory arrangements to a system that achieves an appropriate balance between contributory and non-contributory programmes according to the needs of the population and the structure of the labour force. However, as will be discussed in Chapter 5, such a reform would be highly contentious politically.

Another means of increasing per capita expenditure on social protection lies in growing the overall economy, thereby increasing the quantum of resources available for redistribution. An important overarching question, therefore, is whether higher expenditure on social protection would improve growth in the long-term. To answer this question, a detailed understanding of the impact of social protection through robust monitoring and evaluation is of great importance, as will be discussed in Chapter 5. Even if additional resources were made available, social protection must compete with other government priorities and expenditures, including health, education and (unsustainable) electricity subsidies.

## Notes

[1] This methodology is based on that employed by the Commitment to Equity (CEQ) initiative, which has to date been completed in 39 countries. The methodology is described in the CEQ Handbook, Edition June 2017 (CEQ, 2017[8]).

## References


Nora Lustig (ed.) (2017), *Commitment to Equity Handbook: Estimating the Impact of Fiscal Policy on Inequality and Poverty*, Brookings Institution Press and Commitment to Equity (CEQ) Institute, New Orleans. [8]

IMF (2016), *World Economic Outlook*, http://imf.org/external/datamapper/datasets/WEO (accessed on 01 April 2017). [3]

López-Calva, L. et al. (2017), "Who Benefits from Fiscal Redistribution in the Russian Federation?", in Inchauste, Gabriela, A. (ed.), *The Distributional Impact of Taxes and Transfers: Evidence From Eight Developing Countries*, World Bank, Washington DC. [7]

NSC (2016), *Government budget expenditures*, Finance statistics webpage, Bishkek, http://stat.kg/en. [1]

NSC (2016), *State budget revenues*, National Statistics Committee of the Kyrgyz Republic, Bishkek, http://stat.kg/en. [2]

NSC (2015), *Kyrgyz Integrated Household Survey*, National Statistics Committee of the Kyrgyz Republic, Bishkek. [5]

OECD (2016), *OECD.Stat*, OECD Publishing, http://data.oecd.org (accessed on 01 June 2017). [4]

World Bank (2014), "Kyrgyz Republic Public Expenditure Review Policy Notes: Education", in *Public Expenditure Review Report No. 88978*, World Bank, Washington DC. [6]

# Chapter 5. Building a social protection system

*This chapter outlines a vision for a social protection system in Kyrgyzstan. It considers systematisation along a number of dimensions, including institutional, financial and programme-level, as well as the existence of an information architecture underpinning this system. The breadth of social protection programmes and high expenditure levels provide great potential for gains through systematisation but to fully capitalise on these requires rebalancing between different pillars of social protection provision and an increase in expenditure. Such reforms would complete the transition of the social protection provision from its Soviet legacy but the political economy of these measures would be highly challenging.*

The provision of social protection in Kyrgyzstan is unsustainable in its current form, both financially and politically. Coverage is far higher for the elderly population than for any other group and spending on pensions dwarfs expenditure on all other social protection programmes combined. The GoK should integrate reforms to rebalance provision within the broader framework of its commitment to establish a social protection system.

This chapter examines the potential for systematisation of Kyrgyzstan with a particular focus on how to establish an appropriate combination of programmes, resources and beneficiaries. Systematisation is achieved along a number of dimensions. From a citizen's perspective, systematisation means being able to access appropriate social protection instruments at different stages of the lifecycle and in response to different risks or shocks. From an administrative perspective, it means having information systems that can link beneficiaries to the right programme at the right time and keep track of individuals throughout the lifecycle.

A systemic approach to social protection is also required at an institutional level, not only among government departments and agencies working in the sector but also across government as a whole. This enables social protection to feed into developmental processes at the local, regional and national levels. Last, a systemic approach to financing the social protection sector is required to ensure programmes are allocated adequate and sustainable levels of funding that are proportionate to their impact and importance.

## The MoLSD's structure should be optimised for a systemic approach

The MoLSD has responsibility for establishing a social protection system in Kyrgyzstan. However, the structure of the central Ministry is not well aligned to a systemic approach, in part because the Ministry's composition and mandate have changed on numerous occasions since independence, generating frequent changes that have created instability and made it difficult to align the institutional architecture with its functions.

A Ministry of Labour and Social Protection was established in 1992. Since then, the status of the institution has changed. In 2009, for example, the Ministry of Labour was a stand-alone institution while the Social Protection component was downgraded to government agency. In 2015, the Ministry of Labour, Migration and Youth with the Ministry of Social Development were amalgamated to form the MoLSD, with the Minister of Social Development placed in charge of the combined portfolio.

As highlighted by functional analysis of the Ministry of Social Development carried out by USAID in 2014, these changes have strained critical systems related to information technology, human resource management, financial management and monitoring and evaluation (USAID, 2014[1]). At the same time, instability has reduced the extent to which the MoLSD's structure matches the policies it is mandated to implement. The challenge is particularly acute for the labour portfolio, reducing the capacity to generate synergies with the social protection portfolio that can realise the promotive potential of social protection.

The merger of the Labour and Social Development portfolios is relatively common internationally. However, the structure of the MoLSD consists of a labour department and an employment department rather than units aligned to specific active labour market policies that are able to stimulate the labour market participation of vulnerable groups. (Figure 5.1). Specialised units co-ordinating and devising policies for public employment services, public works programmes, vocational training and microcredits should be considered. The work of these units should be able to call on strong analytical capacity within the Ministry regarding current trends in the labour market, in particular changes in the skills that employers are demanding.

Moreover, the current strategy for labour and employment was designed for implementation by the Ministry for Labour, Migration and Youth rather than the MoLSD. This misalignment is likely to undermine the likelihood of its effective implementation, especially if institutional links to the State Migration Service and the State Agency for Youth Affairs are weakened as a result of the break-up of the former Ministry.

**Figure 5.1. The MoLSD's structure reinforces fragmentation**

Organigram of the Ministry of Labour and Social Development (MoLSD)

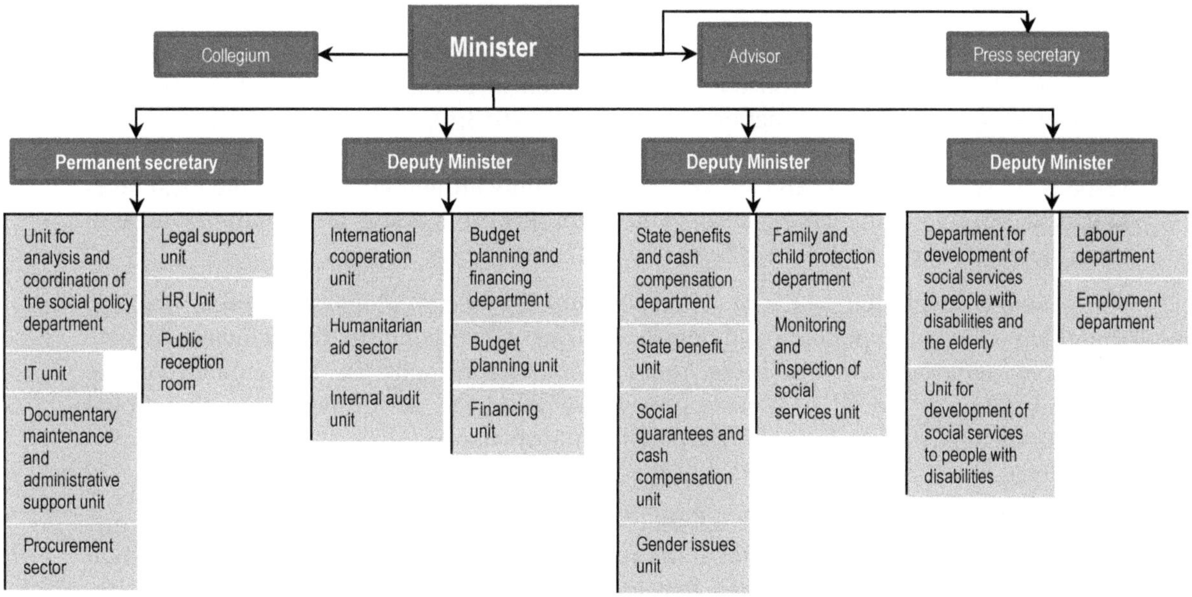


*Note*: The numbers within each box designate the number of officials assigned to the aforementioned function or unit.
*Source:* MoLSD (2016[2]), Order Number 2 of 01 Nov. 2016, Kyrgyzstan.

The structure of the social protection components of the MoLSD better reflects the social protection strategies for 2012-14 and 2015-17, with specific units for the three vulnerable groups prioritised in the latter (families in difficult life situations, people with disabilities and the elderly). However, the structure is not well aligned to a systemic approach. Social protection policy making is divided across two divisions, each headed by a different deputy minister. One division contains units responsible for programmes (state benefits and compensations) and financing, while the other division is structured according to vulnerable groups. Given that there is a strong link between the design of different programmes and the groups they are meant to serve, this separation is not intuitive.

Meanwhile, the specific unit in the Ministry responsible for co-ordination of social protection policies is not overseen by a Deputy Minister but by the Permanent Secretary. It thus risks being excluded from the core policy-making activities and appears to perform an administrative function, alongside units responsible for human resources, legal services and information technology. A co-ordination unit located above the Deputy Ministers that reported directly to the Minister would be better placed to oversee co-ordination and thus the development of a social protection strategy. The unit for policy co-ordination should also be expanded to cover labour and employment.

The new social protection strategy (2018-22) is an opportunity to bring the social protection and labour portfolios closer together. It would be optimal if the structure of the MoLSD were reconfigured to maximise the potential for this to occur.

Looking further ahead, this report proposes that non-contributory arrangements currently managed by the Social Fund be brought under the MoLSD. For this to happen, specific capacity would be required within the Ministry and its structure would need to change accordingly. This is likely to be extremely complex from an administrative perspective; such a transition should be planned and implemented over a long timeframe with careful attention paid to retaining the highly skilled staff of the Social Fund.

## Stronger capacity at local level is critical to enhance provision of social protection

Social protection provision is decentralised, with the majority of MoLSD staff employed at rayon level: before the Ministry's amalgamation in 2016, some 70% of the MoLSD workforce operated at a sub-national level (GoK, 2013[3]). However, responsibility for delivery of services is fragmented between the aiyl okmotu and the MoLSD staff with responsibility for a specific aiyl aimak. The uncertainty around provision at the local level makes it hard for national policies to gain traction at a local level and has created confusion around the MoLSD's role.

At a central level, the Ministry is responsible for social protection policy making, designing strategies, policies and legislation that correspond to the demands of the executive authority. At the same time, it is also responsible for monitoring the implementation of social protection policy, analysing the performance of sub-national social protection staff and developing policies in response to information that is generated at the local level.

The inter-governmental structure of the MoLSD conforms to a clear systemic logic. Policies are made at the central level but implemented at the local level in collaboration with local government on the basis that local-level workers will inform the centre how well these policies are responding to the needs of individuals, households and communities. Staff at rayon level were initially intended to provide oversight, monitoring and co-ordination of local-level staff and social protection activities.

In practice, the weak capacity of the social workers employed by the aiyl okmotu undermines the effectiveness of social protection policy and requires rayon-level staff to play a more active role at a local level. Not only is local government unable to provide social services at a community level but it also struggles to support the implementation of national policies, in particular the identification of households eligible for state benefits. At the same time, households identified as poor and vulnerable are excluded from the benefits to which they might be eligible and do not receive other forms of social support to promote inclusion and well-being.

Filling this gap in the social protection system will not be straightforward. For the MoLSD to take full responsibility for the provision of social services would require changes not only to the legislation governing social protection but also to the Constitution and budget laws to formally shift responsibility for the provision of social services to the MoLSD. Such a radical change might have significant political costs.

Whichever model is chosen for strengthening local services will also require a major change of focus within the Ministry from an emphasis on payment of social protection benefits to the holistic provision of social protection, including services. The addition of a specific unit for social services to the structure of the MoLSD would be an important first step in this direction.

Such a reform would also require a significantly higher allocation to the MoLSD's activities at a local level, both to fund the salaries of social workers and give them the resources to fulfil their functions. It would thus raise the Ministry's salary costs in a context where the GoK is seeking to reduce the public sector wage bill. New financial arrangements that bring together the MoLSD and non-state actors are likely to be essential for providing the resources required.

It is important to note that investment in the local social workforce is likely to enhance the MoLSD's overall operations. In particular, it would improve the GoK's capacity to target benefits at the intended beneficiaries, thereby generating efficiency gains in spending on state benefits. Even with this additional capacity, however, there remains an overwhelming case for simplifying the application process and eligibility assessments for potential MBPF beneficiaries.

A stronger social workforce would also facilitate the co-ordination of social protection policy with other aspects of public policy at the local government level, such as health and education services. Coherence of early childhood services (including benefits) should be considered as a high-priority subsystem within the broader social protection system given the high rates of child poverty and long-term benefits of a healthier, better educated workforce in terms of Kyrgyzstan's future productivity. Such an approach also has great potential to reduce demand for residential institutions.

### Stronger mechanisms are needed for collaboration across the social protection sector

In 2016, the MoLSD was made responsible for co-ordinating social protection policy, replacing a council chaired by the Deputy Prime Minister on social affairs that combined representatives from all relevant agencies as well as civil society. However, the MoLSD's weak influence on social insurance policy, which remains the mandate of the Social Fund, is a fundamental limitation on the development of a social protection system from an institutional, policy, financial, information and citizen perspective.

There is not a clear mechanism for discussions between the MoLSD and the Social Fund and it not apparent that the Social Fund takes the MoLSD into consideration when designing policy. This is not to say that the Social Fund is not cognizant of the challenges it confronts. However, there does not exist a formal process for addressing these challenges that includes the MoLSD; without this, it will not be possible to formulate a systemic policy response.

As discussed elsewhere in this report, non-contributory schemes represent a growing burden on the Social Fund. Moving these programmes to the MoLSD would restore the contributory and non-contributory arrangements and ensure that the required reforms to the pension system take into account non-contributory and contributory arrangements (as well as the labour-market implications of different reform options).

The GoK should consider establishing a task team headed by the Vice Prime Minister to examine long-term reform options for retirement arrangements. As well as the Social Fund and MoLSD, the task team should include the Ministry of Health, the MHIF (which is part of the contributory system), the Ministry of Finance, the State Tax Service as well as the Tri-Partite Commission of government, trade unions and workers and civil society organisations.

**Figure 5.2. Responsibility for social protection rests with MoLSD and the Social Fund**

Co-ordination of all activities in the social sector

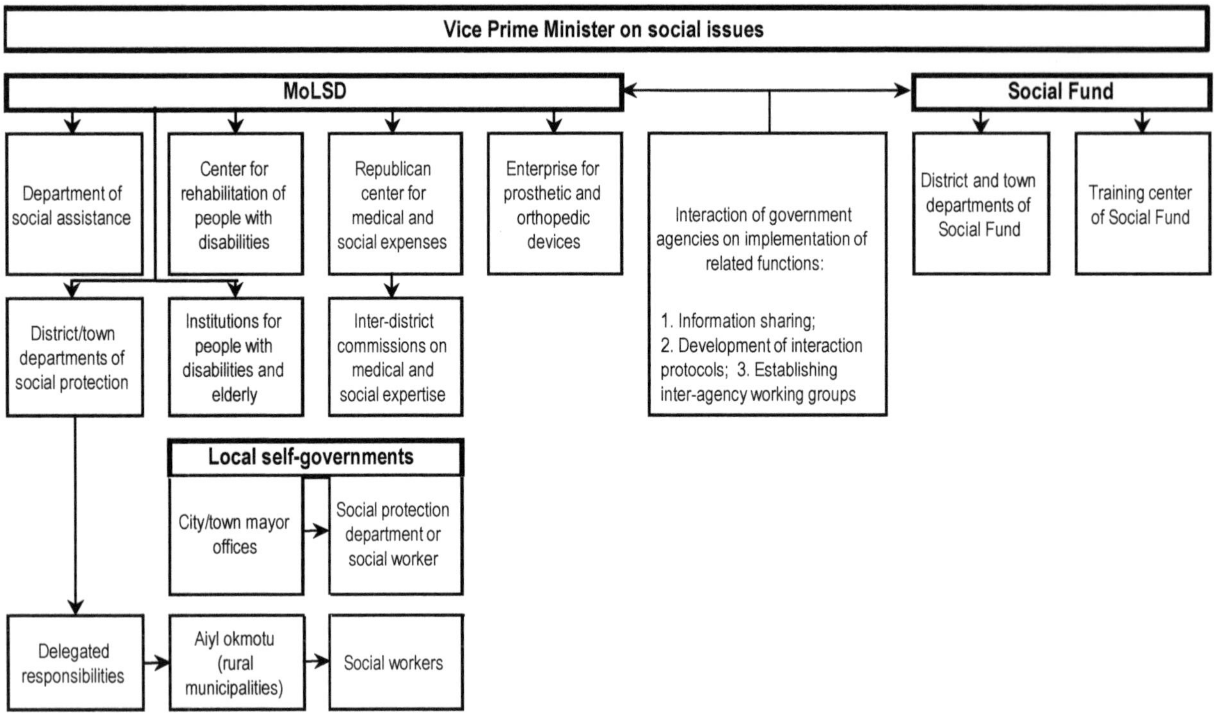


*Note*: Model protocol of interaction between government agencies of executive branch.
*Source*: GoK (2013[4]), Government's Decree No. 404 from 9 July 2013, Kyrgyzstan.

Responsibility for co-ordination of social protection with other areas of social policy falls under the Vice Prime Minister on social issues (Figure 5.2). An example of productive collaboration across the social sector is in the provision of health care, where vulnerable groups are exempt from co-payments for various services and thus partly protected from the impoverishing impact of out-of-pocket health expenditure. However, challenges with the identification of vulnerable households undermine this mechanism.

With the mandatory health insurance scheme and the SGBP providing financial protection against health care payments, formal sector workers and many vulnerable individuals are at least partly covered. However, the resources available to this arrangement are limited: of the 27.25% contribution by formal sector workers, only 2% goes towards the health insurance. The resultant financial constraints mean that insurance beneficiaries receive support with small health-care expenses but not with larger and more substantive outlays, leaving households vulnerable to major health shocks.

At the same time, the expansion of the exemption of co-payments through the SGBP to cover children under age 5, pensioners older than 70 years and pregnant women in 2004 led to a surge in hospitalisations, increasing demand for hospital services. By subsidising health care costs, the social protection interventions in health care substantially increase the financial and institutional load on the health care sector, without resourcing the rising burden.

The shortfall of human resources to manage the demands, inefficient manual management systems, financial unsustainability and a lack of preventive health initiatives are four key supply-side constraints to Kyrgyzstan's health sector. An important step would be the completion of the Unified Health Information System, which will improve the procurement and management of health care services.

Meanwhile, fragmentation of responsibility for residential institutions is an impediment to the government's optimisation strategy (discussed in Chapter 2). Although different ministries involved in this sector are responsible for different types of institution – such as those for infants, children or people with disabilities – the MoLSD should be empowered to oversee all such institutions to ensure policy coherence and implement the required information systems as well as monitoring and evaluation. The MoLSD's capacity to monitor private institutions should also be enhanced to ensure they provide an appropriate level of care and abide by the same standards and protocols as public institutions.

## A universal grant for infants will have multiple benefits

Current discussions regarding reform options for the MBPF recognise the drawbacks inherent both to a universal benefit and to poverty-targeting. A hybrid option comprising universal benefits for newborns and infants and poverty-targeted benefits for older children is emerging as a means of balancing affordability with impact on child poverty, but this should be complemented by other interventions under a systemic approach to maximise its impact.

Cost concerns render a hybrid option more feasible than a universal approach. However, this should be combined with reforms to the administration of the MBPF to overcome the targeting challenges identified previously. As mentioned above, strengthening the capacity of local-level social workers and simplifying the process for assessing eligibility are essential, so too are steps to raise the means test threshold to a higher level. Proposals to increase from 30% to 100% the proportion of beneficiary households visited by the MoLSD to verify their eligibility might reduce errors of inclusion but will not address errors of exclusion.

This report recommends initially establishing a universal benefit up to a child's second birthday as a means of ensuring all children receive some support during the first two years of their lives. This is not only a crucial period in a child's physical and cognitive development, but it is also a time when children require the most attention, meaning it is difficult for parents to combine care with paid work.

Within five years of implementation, eligibility should be increased to age three, at which point children can be enrolled in pre-school institutions. It is critical that coverage of pre-school institutions, particularly in rural areas, be expanded to ensure this transition for children takes place, both for children who are eligible for the MBPF and for those who are not. The cost of this higher eligibility age will be partly offset by a decrease in the number of children being born over this period, which will reduce demand for the newborn and infant benefits.

The advantages of an infant benefit extend beyond the immediate welfare of beneficiary children. Enrolling children on an information system for state benefits at an early age allows for the early identification of vulnerable children. It would also mean that every individual born after a certain date would be included on such a system, thereby providing social protection planners with detailed knowledge of future populations and removing some of the administrative hurdles associated with, for example, internal migration.

## The basic contributory pension should evolve into a universal social pension

The MoLSD's mandate to design policy for the social protection sector as a whole entitles it to determine the policies of the Social Fund, which is responsible for developing and implementing policies for social insurance, paying benefits and collecting pension contributions. In reality, co-ordination between the two institutions is limited and the Social Fund continues to take the lead in social insurance policy.

This lack of co-ordination between MoLSD and the Social Fund constrain the potential for the systematisation of social assistance and social insurance. This is a major concern in a context where the number of people contributing to the Social Fund (and thus covered by social insurance) is gradually declining and coverage of social assistance is also being reduced, meaning the population as a whole is much less protected, both today and looking ahead. The financial imbalances of the system also require remedying action.

In Kyrgyzstan, as in many countries, programmes exist that cover the same eventuality but with different financing mechanisms (contributory and non-contributory) reflecting individuals' income level. This is the case with pensions and the MSB, with both systems providing benefits to people with disabilities or the elderly. Challenges arise when the value of the benefits paid by the contributory system approaches the level of the non-contributory benefit, which is only accessible by individuals with no contribution records. This is likely to disincentivise individuals from contributing, undermining the social insurance principle and threatening the system's sustainability.

This phenomenon is apparent in Kyrgyzstan. Although the value of the social pension component of the MSB is low (and declining in real terms), it is still worth more than the pensions received at retirement for some individuals whose contribution period did not attain the threshold required to receive the full value of the basic pension. The same applies for individuals with incomplete contribution histories who have suffered a disability.

The declining tendency for workers to contribute to the Social Fund (in full or at all) and the reduced value of contributory pensions will reinforce each other; the resulting erosion of the system's sustainability will be compounded by growth in the elderly population. As individuals opt out of the Social Fund, demand for the MSB will increase. The recent increase in the age of eligibility for the MSB above the statutory retirement age for the contributory system (65 against 63 years for men and 60 against 58 years for women) will have little long-term impact on this pressure but has created an inconsistency in the public provision for old age that impedes coherence across contributory and non-contributory pensions.

At an institutional level, the distinction between the contributory and non-contributory arrangements is becoming increasingly blurred. As discussed in Chapter 4, the quasi-contributory basic pension component is now entirely funded by the Republican Budget, in common with non-contributory pensions for the military and other pensions and pension top-ups or increments.

The sharp increase in spending on military pensions is an issue for public finances as a whole rather than just the Social Fund, and a reform of this arrangement is a priority. Bringing expenditure on military pensions under control is likely to require a combination of higher retirement ages and the introduction of contributions for those eligible for military pensions. It would be very difficult to institute such changes for existing members of the military (and other agencies eligible for military pensions), which heightens the imperative of establishing these rules for new staff at the earliest opportunity.

Aside from military pensions, it might be optimal to bring the tax-financed instruments under the administration of the MoLSD, including the basic pension component. If this were to happen, it would be increasingly difficult to justify maintaining the old age and disability components of the MSB and the basic pension component as different systems given that they are each financed from the state budget and there is no link between the value of an individual's contributions and the benefit they receive from the basic pension component. Replacing the relevant aspects of the MSB and the basic pension component with a universal social pension would greatly simplify the system, make it fairer and easier to manage financially.

A costing exercise of such a reform is beyond the scope of this paper but the World Bank Public Expenditure Review on pensions (2014[5]) calculates that replacing the current basic pension and the MSB with a universal pension available in the event of disability or at age 65 will be significantly less costly than the current system, especially if the grant is indexed against prices rather than wages. However, it also states that this reform would require parametric change to the insurance components.

So far, there has been resistance to such a reform, on the basis that it would undermine the contributory principle. Existing pensioners might also object, on the grounds that their successors will benefit from the new system for free while they had to contribute over their lifetimes. According to the Kyrgyz Republic Pension System Development Concept Paper, the Government is also considering reforms to target the basic pension component towards individuals with low pension pay-outs. However, this raises equity issues along the income distribution.

It is unrealistic to expect a rapid reform to the pension system given political economy dynamics and the present lack of capacity within the MoLSD to expand its role into this domain. However, a reform of some kind appears to be inevitable and the sooner this is planned the easier it will be to transition gradually to a new system. As discussed earlier, pension reform should be an inclusive process that reflects social insurance's role within a broader social protection system, which it is MoLSD's responsibility to co-ordinate.

## Expand public works programmes for promotive social protection

The low coverage, low financing and minimal impact of active labour market policies are major constraints on the promotive impact of social protection and restricts its ability to break the inter-generational transmission of poverty. The MoLSD should consider scaling up public works programmes as the most direct means of supporting individuals excluded from the labour market. Local government should be at the forefront of identifying appropriate projects but central government would need to be far more involved in the sector.

As identified in Chapter 2, public works programmes are the largest active labour-market policy in terms of coverage. However, they only cover a very small proportion of the unemployed population, in part due to restrictive eligibility criteria. Women are almost entirely excluded. Moreover, there is no national strategy for public works programmes, and little monitoring or evaluation. As a result, public works programmes have very little impact on poor or vulnerable groups.

Relatively simple measures could be adopted to improve this situation. The first step would be to catalogue and analyse the projects that are currently being implemented to understand the current provision of public works programmes. The next would be to design a national strategy for public works programmes that establishes an appropriate balance between the three principal objectives of such interventions: the income support they provide to participants, the training and experience that participants receive and the assets (physical or otherwise) they generate.

In the context of Kyrgyzstan's broader social protection provision, it is arguable that the second objective is the most important of these (though the first and third should not be overlooked). The emphasis on enhancing the skills of workers means that the programmes should contain a training component and the work should be aligned to the needs of the local labour market. Preferential access (perhaps through quotas) might be established for groups at highest risk of being out of work, particularly women, youth and people with disabilities. The time commitment should balance the need to acquire skills with that of looking for other work; participants might be expected to stay on a project for a number of months but only work two days a week during this period.

To maximise the acquisition of productive skills, public works projects should involve skilled and/or semi-skilled activities. Projects should not be limited to infrastructure development (though this might be very useful in rural areas). Social and environmental projects have become an integral component of South Africa's Expanded Public Works Programme, for example (Philip, 2013[6]).

Projects should not only serve the skills requirements of participants but also the needs of local communities. Aiyl okmotu could play a role in the selection of participants and the design of projects so that they are of benefit to the broader community. This improves the likelihood that any assets or initiatives generated by the public works project will be maintained once the scheme ends. It would also give aiyl okmotu an important stake in social protection policy in a situation where provision of social services were to become more centralised or involves more non-state actors.

## Systematisation can leverage ongoing improvements in the information infrastructure

An important aspect of systematisation is that individuals should have access to social protection programmes appropriate for their circumstances across the lifecycle. To achieve this requires not only that these programmes be in place but also that social protection provision be underpinned by one or more information systems that automatically link individuals to the programmes they need.

Registration for social assistance follows an on-demand approach in Kyrgyzstan. To access benefits, potentially eligible households must complete an application with supporting documents to prove their eligibility to the social protection department. Upon receipt, local-level social workers verify eligibility, which involves substantial time, resources and expertise given the complex income indicators and the remote locations where many potential beneficiaries reside.

The on-demand system requires that individuals know whether they are eligible for a specific programme and can provide the required supporting documents – factors that cannot be taken for granted, especially in very remote areas. The lengthy eligibility assessment also raises the potential for corruption in the application process.

Since 2000, aiyl okmotus have been responsible for monitoring household incomes in their villages, working with the MoLSD to assess eligibility for state benefits and maintaining the SPPF. The GoK has used this SPPF as a management information system with the objective of improving targeting and monitoring and informing planning.

Despite broad coverage, the manual processing and analysis of the SPPF data has created information distortions that have had an adverse impact on targeting effectiveness and generated misleading information for policy making. In response, the government has been developing a Corporate Information System for Social Assistance (CISSA) over a number of years. This is intended to automate all business processes related to acceptance, processing, assignment/rejection and payment of benefits that fall under the responsibility of MoLSD and its departments.

At the time of writing, CISSA includes beneficiaries of the MBPF and other state benefits, the MSB, the Supplementary Monthly Social Benefit and Veterans of the Second World War. It also contains individual modules for specific vulnerable groups, such as people with disabilities (including medical examination data), children or elderly individuals in residential institutions run by MoLSD and recipients of compensations for privileges. It also includes a humanitarian aid database.

CISSA has the potential to revolutionise social protection provision in Kyrgyzstan. It could significantly improve efficiency, accuracy and transparency of data collection, decision-making and policy implementation through automation of these processes. It can also keep track of internal migrants as they move location, allowing for the swift transfer of entitlement from one place to the next. Because the state benefits system is demand-based, the CISSA will contain information on both potential and actual social protection, enhancing its capacity to respond to short-term shocks or evolve to longer-term trends.

However, there are challenges with CISSA that need to be addressed to ensure its viability and sustainability. For instance, there are problems with its operability: the system is reported to be very slow, in part because of the slow internet connections in parts of the country and in part because of the size of the documents that must be uploaded. Reducing the number of documents to be uploaded might ease this problem, though it will be harder to fix if the challenge relates to the country's IT infrastructure. While these issues are being addressed, the paper-based SPPF remains operational, leading to duplication of effort and gaps or inconsistencies in data collection.

The MoLSD's capacity to maintain CISSA is also a cause for concern. At present, the system is supported with the assistance of the World Bank. To take over responsibility, the MoLSD will need to ensure that capacity exists at both the national and the district level to maintain its operation. The MoLSD's IT unit has shrunk over time and it struggles to attract highly skilled IT professionals due to a disparity between public-sector salaries and wages for equivalent work in the private sector.

Another important step in the development of CISSA is to link it to other official databases, thereby creating a single registry for the social protection system that can also be linked to other administrative data sources. In the social protection sector, CISSA should be linked to the Social Fund (especially if pension arrangements become a combination of a universal social pension and the contributory schemes) and the MHIF, each of which operate their own database. It should also be connected to a new database for residential institutions, which is at an advanced stage of development.

It is also envisaged that CISSA will be linked to the State Registration Service (SRS), which gathers a range of administrative data on births, deaths, real estate and vehicle ownership. Since August 2016, the SRS has been responsible for issuing Personal Identification Numbers (PIN) to newborn children. This number was previously issued by the Social Fund upon an individual joining the formal labour force for the purpose of tax and social security deductions as well as accessing health care. Linking CISSA to the PIN system would theoretically ensure that individuals are registered with social protection system at the earliest opportunity.

The SRS has also made considerable progress in developing an electronic unified population register; only individuals included on this register were allowed to vote in the presidential election in 2017. Coverage of the new register is not yet universal, with some individuals unwilling or unable to go through biometric registration. Nonetheless, when complete and integrated with the other databases, the new electronic register will provide information on the entire population and will thus be a major asset for social protection provision and planning. The SRS is presently rolling out information kiosks nationwide to facilitate the registration of marriages, births and deaths as well as applications for ID cards or passports.

The next step is to enhance monitoring and evaluation of social protection. This is an important component of the Programme for the Transition of the Kyrgyz Republic to Sustainable Development 2013-2017, which emphasises the importance of performance management, the implementation of monitoring systems and the evaluation of policies and programmes across government. The programme proposes a mixed-methods approach with a "formative" evaluation in 2016 and a "summative" evaluation in 2017. The results of this evaluation will inform reforms that improve the policies and aim to maximise impact for target groups. The guidelines indicate an M&E plan as well as a staff training plan for those involved in implementation and M&E.

The results of this plan for the social protection sector are not yet available. As a result, analysis of the impact of different programmes (as discussed in Chapter 3) is largely reliant on the KIHS, the national household survey. The KIHS is a valuable tool for social protection analysis, containing specific questions about whether households benefit from different social protection programmes (MBPF, MSB, compensations for privileges and pensions). It is a partial panel survey, which means it is able to follow certain individuals or households over time.

At the same time, however, it is difficult to reconcile the KIHS to administrative data. Part of the complication lies in the proxy means test applied to test eligibility for the MBPF, which is difficult to pick up through household surveys. The varying level of the MBPF benefit (until its standardisation in 2015) and the fact that households might have been eligible for more than one child-related benefit are also likely to have complicated reporting on benefit receipt.

An important aspect of the CISSA will be the extent to which its data serves as a basis for analysis within the MoLSD. This in turn depends on two factors: the usability of the database for analysis and the demand for data within the Ministry. On this second point, the development of analytical capacity within the Ministry has not been a priority owing to the fact that the SPPF has been difficult to analyse. Once the CISSA is fully rolled out, this analytical capacity is essential. At the same time, it would be a rich source of information for external researchers, provided the data could be anonymised.

## Social protection reforms must overcome political economy challenges

The political economy around social protection in Kyrgyzstan makes the substantial reforms envisaged in this report problematic. Despite the limited impact of social assistance on poverty and the financing shortfalls for social services and labour market policies in particular, it will be difficult to increase the social protection budget overall both due to a lack of popular support and because of external pressures. Reprioritisation between programmes is possible but this will create losers as well as winners; recent experience shows that those who lose out will let their discontent be known.

The ongoing discussions around reform to the state benefits are a useful case study. The MoLSD's plan to universalise the MBPF was opposed by the IMF and World Bank, which considered the reform to be unaffordable given fiscal constraints. The IMF places an emphasis on improving the efficiency of social assistance spending through improved targeting and cautions against the universalisation of the MBPF on the grounds that it might "give disincentives for women to participate in the labour force" (IMF, 2018[7]), a concern that does not appear to have a strong empirical basis.

The reform also experienced opposition within Kyrgyzstan. Upon learning that they would be worse-off under the universal system (Bengard, 2017[8]), a small number of MBPF beneficiaries in Naryn region took to the streets in protest at the reform and went on hunger strike in December 2017 (Podolskaya, 2017[9]). The MoLSD postponed implementation of the reform shortly afterwards. An interim state benefit system will be in place for 2018 while the MoLSD redrafts the reforms (with input from the World Bank) and consults with parliament.

It is not clear whether external or domestic influences played a greater role in persuading the MoLSD to reconsider the reform. However, it is apparent that there was not strong support from other constituencies in the GoK or elsewhere for universalisation of the MBPF. Part of the reason might be that social assistance is a less established component of the social protection system. It might also reflect the fact that the main beneficiaries of such a reform would be individuals who are of working age (such as those identified as the largest poor cluster within the LCA in Chapter 1) and who thus are perceived as being responsible for supporting themselves financially.

The relative lack of prominence of social assistance in the discourse around social protection is likely to be a major impediment to a reform of the pension system that introduces a social pension in place of the current basic pension component. Despite diminishing coverage among the working-age population, social insurance remains an important public institution, founded on the principle that individuals earn an income in retirement through their contributions.

However, the contributory principle is already being substantially weakened, not only by the substantial transfers to the pension system (and the health system) but also by the diminishing replacement rates provided by pensions (and strains on the quality of health coverage). A reform of the basic pension component would be a critical step in institutionalising the transition from the Soviet system to a social protection system appropriate for a modern-day market economy.

Such a reform will not be easy. Pensioners represent a very strong (and large) constituency who are quick to mobilise in response to problems with pension payments or perceived threats to the value of their pensions. This is one factor behind the regular (and relatively generous) indexing of pension payments to wage growth in the economy. It is likely that a reform that aligned the basic contributory pension with the social pension for elderly individuals would be received with great suspicion, both by today's pensioners and by individuals who have contributed to the Social Fund but not yet retired.

However, the Social Fund's long-term solvency issues and the inevitable decline in the value of pensions make reform essential. Whatever approach the GoK adopts, it will be important to consult broadly on the proposed reforms, reassure existing pensioners that the value of their entitlements will not be affected and explain that reform is intended to safeguard the contributory system rather than dismantle it. An information campaign regarding the state of the pension system would be an important means of sensitising the population as a whole.

Another significant challenge with changing the design of the bottom pillar relates to the strength of the institutions involved. The Social Fund has emerged much stronger politically than the MoLSD over the past 25 years, not least thanks to the power that pensioners wield. The MoLSD is also more vulnerable than the Social Fund to the demands of the electoral cycle, having to implement policies on behalf of the executive which might be motivated by political rather than technical considerations.

The MoLSD is likely to receive support from the World Bank and IMF in the case of pension reform. The World Bank was instrumental in retaining the basic pension component as part of the 1997 reforms (Andrews et al., 2006[10]) and recently advocated for the creation of a demogrant (World Bank, 2014[5]). Whether the World Bank would (publicly) support a transfer of the non-contributory programmes from the Social Fund to the MoLSD is not clear. It remains lukewarm on the FFDC component, which at 2% will not generate very high benefits for contributors.

The other large-scale reform involves the establishment of legislation governing the provision of social services, including the minimum level of social service provision that should be guaranteed by the state. This process might lead to important changes in how responsibility for provision of social services is apportioned between local government and the MoLSD, which in turn would require changes to the Kyrgyzstan's political, administrative and financial structures.

While the scale of the crisis confronting social services might justify fundamental reform, greater centralisation of social protection provision risks reducing the participation of local government in the sector and thus the system's capacity to understand local needs and vulnerabilities. At a larger scale, centralisation risks undermining the building of the Kyrgyz state. For generations during USSR rule, decision-making was highly centralised outside its borders. Establishing and supporting the development of local government structures is a key component of Kyrgyzstan's emergence as a representative democracy (Gjørven, 2013[11]); great care should be taken when undertaking reforms that might weaken or subvert this process.

## References

Andrews, E. et al. (2006), *Pension reform and the development of pension systems : an evaluation of World Bank assistance*, World Bank, Washington DC, http://documents.worldbank.org/curated/en/629861468166150111/Pension-reform-and-the-development-of-pension-systems-an-evaluation-of-World-Bank-assistance. [10]

Bengard, A. (2017), "Naryn residents protest against new law on state benefits", *24.kg news agency*, http://24.kg/english/70909. [8]

Gjørven, G. (2013), *Decentralisation and Participatory Development in Kyrgyzstan: The Dual Role of Continued and Reconfigured Institutions*, European and American Studies Faculty of Humanities, University of Oslo. [11]

GoK (2013), *Government Decree No. 404 of 9 July 2013.* [4]

GoK (2013), *National Sustainable Development Strategy, 2013-17*, http://donors.kg/images/NSSD-final-version-eng-Feb4.doc. [3]

IMF (2018), *Kyrgyz Republic: Fourth and Fifth Reviews under the Three-Year Arrangements under the Extended Credit Facility, and Request for Modification of Performance Criteria-Press Release; Staff Report*, International Monetary Fund, Washington DC. [7]

MoLSD (2016), *Order Number 2 of 01 Nov. 2016.* [2]

Philip, K. (2013), "The transformative potential of public employment programmes", *Occasional Paper Series No.1/2013*, Graduate School of Development Policy and Practice, University of Cape Town. [6]

Podolskaya, D. (2017), "Women in Naryn go on hunger strike demanding to repeal benefits law", *24.kg*, http://24.kg/english/71475. [9]

USAID (2014), *USAID/Kyrgyz Republic: Country Development Cooperation Strategy, FY 2015 - FY 2019*, U.S. Agency for International Development, Washington, DC, https://www.usaid.gov/sites/default/files/documents/1861/CDCS%20Kyrgyz%20Republic%20Public%20Version%20Final%209-2014.pdf. [1]

World Bank (2014), "Kyrgyz Republic Public Expenditure Review Policy Notes: Pensions", in *Public Expenditure Review Report No. 89007*, World Bank, Washington DC. [5]

# ORGANISATION FOR ECONOMIC CO-OPERATION AND DEVELOPMENT

The OECD is a unique forum where governments work together to address the economic, social and environmental challenges of globalisation. The OECD is also at the forefront of efforts to understand and to help governments respond to new developments and concerns, such as corporate governance, the information economy and the challenges of an ageing population. The Organisation provides a setting where governments can compare policy experiences, seek answers to common problems, identify good practice and work to co-ordinate domestic and international policies.

The OECD member countries are: Australia, Austria, Belgium, Canada, Chile, the Czech Republic, Denmark, Estonia, Finland, France, Germany, Greece, Hungary, Iceland, Ireland, Israel, Italy, Japan, Korea, Latvia, Luxembourg, Mexico, the Netherlands, New Zealand, Norway, Poland, Portugal, the Slovak Republic, Slovenia, Spain, Sweden, Switzerland, Turkey, the United Kingdom and the United States. The European Union takes part in the work of the OECD.

OECD Publishing disseminates widely the results of the Organisation's statistics gathering and research on economic, social and environmental issues, as well as the conventions, guidelines and standards agreed by its members.

# OECD DEVELOPMENT CENTRE

The OECD Development Centre was established in 1962 as an independent platform for knowledge sharing and policy dialogue between OECD member countries and developing economies, allowing these countries to interact on an equal footing. Today, 27 OECD countries and 25 non-OECD countries are members of the Centre. The Centre draws attention to emerging systemic issues likely to have an impact on global development and more specific development challenges faced by today's developing and emerging economies. It uses evidence-based analysis and strategic partnerships to help countries formulate innovative policy solutions to the global challenges of development.

For more information on the Centre, please see *www.oecd.org/dev*.

OECD PUBLISHING, 2, rue André-Pascal, 75775 PARIS CEDEX 16
(41 2017 28 1 P) ISBN 978-92-64-30226-6 – 2018

www.ingramcontent.com/pod-product-compliance
Ingram Content Group UK Ltd.
Pitfield, Milton Keynes, MK11 3LW, UK
UKHW051503290926
15471UKWH00008B/1380

9 789264 302266